Born to Prophesy is not just a b
cate, and help prophets and prop
ministry of the prophet and mii
new prophetic voice called to up,
cially into the things of the Spirit. *Born to Prophesy* is a must read for those
who desire to be a voice used of God to minister to others.

—Dr. Bill Hamon
Bishop, Christian International Apostolic Network (CIAN)
Founder, Christian International Ministries Network (CIMN)
Author of *The Day of The Saints, Prophets and
Personal Prophecy* and ten other major books

Hakeem Collins has written a powerful masterpiece for a prophetic generation! He reveals the importance of developing a prophetic culture through
proper relationships and training. His book, *Born to Prophesy*, is a great tool
to equip you to fulfill the call of God on your life.

You will be stirred by the Holy Spirit as you read this amazing book.
You will be sharpened with prophetic accuracy and zeal. I encourage every
believer to read and apply the principles found in this book!

—Barbara Wentroble
President, International Breakthrough Ministries (IBM)
President, Business Owners for Christ International
Author of *Prophetic intercession; Praying with Authority;
Rise to Your Destiny, Woman of God; Removing the Veil of
Deception;* and *Fighting for Your Prophetic Promises*

Honor is what love looks like! One year ago I met Hakeem in a conference
where I was the guest speaker. A friend encouraged me to receive from this
young man. During the fifteen minutes I was with Hakeem I encountered
a *prophet* and experienced God's voice speaking through him. The creative
power of the word, kissed by the Spirit, gave me a fresh upgrade.

Born to Prophesy is a prophetic book written by a *prophet* to restore a
culture where we listen and speak, see, and do. This book is for you!

—Leif Hetland
President, Global Mission Awareness
Author of *Seeing Through Heaven's Eyes*

Born to Prophesy is a powerful book that is a necessary read and will
become a classic read in the hands of future generations. This book is a
revolutionary instrument that has the ability to sharpen seasoned prophets,
to shape emerging prophetic voices, and to summons prophetic generations.
However, this book is not written just for prophets but for *all* whom God

wants to speak through. There are a plethora of books out there written on the prophetic gift and the ministry of the prophet, but I strongly recommend this genre of work because it simply captures the genesis and heartbeat of the prophetic at work in a believer's life when activated.

This book will encourage, educate, upgrade, cultivate, and inspire you, the believer, [if you] have ever coveted or desired to prophesy according to 1 Corinthians 14:39 and those who passionately want to become a relevant prophetic voice for their generation. After applying the principles in this book you will know that God has formed *you* in your mother's womb to be the type of unique voice He wants heard in the earth. As you read through each chapter, you will began to feel the heartbeat of God's voice in you waiting to be awakened, and *you* will begin to see the ultrasound of your prophetic nature, identity, personality, and purpose taking shape and becoming clearer.

Hakeem is not only a new, cutting-edge, radical apostolic and prophetic voice called to nations, but he so happens to be my *twin* brother with whom I had the incredible opportunity to share the same prophetic and natural womb. We are commonly known as "The Twin Prophets" or "Sons of Thunder" as we travel as a prophetic team. In this book, Hakeem shares much of his personal journey in God raising His voice in him to be a prophet and understanding God's developmental process as a youth to learn, hear, obey, and speak the word of the Lord as one destined to prophesy while transforming and changing his world at the same time. *Born to Prophesy* was written skillfully with revelatory knowledge to expound, restore, and disclose hidden truth in the prophetic that will help you discover and comprehend God's prophetic womb in you to prophesy!

—Naim Collins
President, Naim Collins Ministries Worldwide,
Fan the Flames Global Ministries
Wilmington, Delaware

Born to Prophesy is a book that will take you through the journey of the call of Jeremiah and Hakeem Collins, a prophet of God. Hakeem overcame fatherlessness, was raised in a drug-infested violent housing project, and was teased by his classmates for his mumbling speech, as he lacked self-confidence. Yet at twelve years old he pursued God on a three-day fast from all food and water, and he literally heard the voice of God!

Hakeem Collins attends our church at Destiny Christian Church. He travels as a *prophet* and speaks at our regional prophetic conferences as well. Hakeem and his twin brother, Naim, have a reputation for releasing powerful, precise prophetic words. It is my joy to see him fulfill his call by writing this book to help you to fulfill yours.

—DALE AND LUANNE MAST
SENIOR PASTORS, DESTINY CHRISTIAN CHURCH
AUTHOR OF *GOD, I FEEL LIKE CINDERELLA*

This book, *Born to Prophesy,* is a book that speaks volumes to the global glory of the saints. It is not just another prophetic book but a book for our generation and a foundation for generations to come. Hakeem Collins' book brings to heart the importance of the voice of the Lord as well as (in His corporate grace) becoming His voice to others in these epochal times.

It reveals significantly that we are *born to prophesy,* reminding us of the Book of Jeremiah chapter one how the Lord spoke to Jeremiah that before he was born God knew him, sanctified him, and ordained Jeremiah as a prophet over nations and kingdoms. *Born to Prophesy* will bless you immeasurably as you draw closer to God and His eternal purpose and plan for your own life.

—DR. TIM AND THERESA EARLY
APOSTLES AND FOUNDERS,
THE FOUNDATION OF THE APOSTLES AND
PROPHETS INTERNATIONAL (FAP)
RUSTON, LOUISIANA

In every generation, there is a call for a prophetic voice to rise up with a clarion call that draws the body of Christ back to the fundamental principles provided by the Holy Spirit to unlock the depth of potential and greatness that awaits us. *Born to Prophesy* is a guiding light that leads us back to the depth of the prophetic power that lies within every believer to speak something that radically shifts their lives and ultimately changes their generation. Prophet Hakeem is a voice crying in the wilderness to prepare this generation for the revival of supernatural kingdom power that has long been prophesied! I fully endorse the powerful message contained in this book. I recommend it to every person who is ready to step into the next dimension in their lives! The captivating words written on these pages will enhance, develop, and cultivate every reader to do what they were born to do, prophesy!

—DR. MARIO MAXWELL
PROPHET AND PRESIDENT, MARIO MAXWELL INTERNATIONAL MINISTRIES
SENIOR PASTOR AND FOUNDER, NEW DIVINE
DESTINY CHRISTIAN CENTER
EDMOND, OKLAHOMA

What a moving story of Hakeem's journey to realize the prophetic calling on his life! His call out of darkness was from a very young and tender age, and nothing would give him comfort until he realized the innate desire to preach the gospel of Jesus Christ. This story describes his own walk out of disobedience to pursue the high calling of the Lord. Hakeem Collins is an encourager of the brethren. He desires to stir up the gifts in the church and activate *dormant* believers. There are gold nuggets to be found in Hakeem's *Born to Prophesy*.

—KENNETH MCDONALD
PRESIDENT, PROPHETIC-MINISTRY.COM

"Their lifestyle represented the God they believed, valued and obeyed"—a quote from Hakeem Collins' book *Born to Prophesy*. Indeed, this is Hakeem's life, and his book reflects just that. The teachings on Jeremiah, Isaiah, Moses, and other prophets gives true insight as to the definition, clarification, and understanding of what a prophet is and is not as well as the ministry gift of prophecy. *Born to Prophesy* will be one that we will always have in supply on our bookshelf to share with others as they come into awareness that indeed the office of the prophet and the gift of prophecy is for today! We consider him one of our best gifts from the Lord when He brought Hakeem into our lives, and we are now privileged to call him friend!

—DALE AND BARBARA WORKS
DALE AND BARBARA WORKS MINISTRIES
LANCASTER, PENNSYLVANIA

For thousands of years Israel's prophet spoke of the coming Messiah. John the Baptist declared that his mission was to prepare the way for the coming of the Lord. In this season of great change in the earth we must be a people who use the keys G-d has given us to prepare a pathway into unchartered waters. In his book *Born to Prophesy*, Hakeem Collins speaks of the necessary purpose of prophets and prophecy and their role in the earth today. This is also an invitation to G-d's greatest desire, intimacy with His people. Those who know their G-d shall be strong and do exploits and speak words that release a dimension in the earth that has never been seen! This book has been written toward that end.

—ABNER SUAREZ
FOUNDER AND PRESIDENT, FOR SUCH A TIME AS THIS, INC.

HAKEEM COLLINS

BORN TO PROPHESY

CREATION
HOUSE

Born to Prophesy by Hakeem Collins
Published by Creation House
A Charisma Media Company
600 Rinehart Road
Lake Mary, Florida 32746
www.charismamedia.com

Design Director: Bill Johnson
Cover design by Nathan Morgan

Visit the author's website: www.hakeemcollinsministries.com

Library of Congress Cataloging-in-Publication Data: 2013941266
International Standard Book Number: 978-1-62136-404-7
E-book International Standard Book Number: 978-1-62136-405-4

While the author has made every effort to provide accurate telephone numbers and Internet addresses at the time of publication, neither the publisher nor the author assumes any responsibility for errors or for changes that occur after publication.

First edition

13 14 15 16 17 — 9 8 7 6 5 4 3 2 1
Printed in Canada

DEDICATION

With a heart to give honor to whom honor is due, I dedicate this book to the thousands of prophetic trailblazers who have gone before me to pave the way for something new and innovative.

There is an emerging prophetic and apostolic generation rising to the forefront with tremendous prophetic calling, gifting, and anointing. With those unique people, God dedicated them unto Himself and has released them into the world to bring radical change. These are the prophets and prophetic people who will be the ones that will turn the world upside down. Ready or not, here come the world changers!

I would also like to dedicate this book to every leader who has sacrificed by putting their lives on the line to restore present truth about the role, function, operation, and biblical truth about modern-day prophets, apostles, prophecy, and the fivefold ministry gifts.

This book has been written for the sole purpose with *you*, the reader, in mind as a prophetic people and race. It is my desire that each of you who has invested in this book will be stirred up to bring perpetual breakthroughs and societal transformation through the word of the Lord.

Finally, I dedicate this book to every future apostle, prophet, pastor, evangelist, teacher, and prophetic leader who will come into present truth for their generation. This book is written for you, your children, and your children's children to prophesy as God's voice in the earth. Also, to my future wife and unborn children, you will carry on what I have imparted.

CONTENTS

PREFACE

WHAT YOU HOLD in your hand is a book that has been conceived from the mind of God, revealed through several prophetic voices, and communicated to me in the form of a prophecy. As I have undertaken writing this book, I had to reflect on the many personal trials and tribulations that got me to this point of putting to pen and paper what I have encountered, experienced, learned, and discovered through twenty years in the prophetic ministry. Through my prophetic journey, I have come to the realization that there will always be a hunger and thirst for more of God, the supernatural, His presence, voice, and desire to speak as His spiritual representatives in the earth.

The purpose of me writing this book was to answer and correct many unspoken questions and teachings by cessationist Pentecostal believers and teachers who had a limited understanding, revelation, paradigm, and belief systems on the restoration of modern-day apostles, prophets, and prophecy in the church. (See Ephesians 4:11–13.) Furthermore, burning in my heart was God's leading to write on the prophetic function in born-again and Spirit-filled believers. Generally speaking, God revealed this to me through a holy discontentment and dissatisfaction of how the prophetic ministry, prophecy, and prophets were misrepresented today in the church and world. It was my decision to bring clarity, understanding, and simplicity to the misunderstood gift of prophecy. I see countless tongues-speaking believers lack the faith required to prophesy what's on God's heart and mind.

Most charismatic Christian believers and leaders throughout their walk with the Lord have trouble at times hearing the voice of God, question whether prophecy is still a valid gift in today's world, and struggle with believing that through the Holy Spirit, God wants to speak through them. As a result, they are likely to experience discouragement, fear, intimidation, doubt, frustration, and low self-esteem.

The primary emphasis of this book is to draw the church's attention to God's perspective on modern-day prophets, prophecy, and the supernatural gifts of the Holy Spirit and to help each individual determine his or her God-given birthright, assignment, and purpose as a Spirit-filled, born-again believer. At this same time, this book offers practical, instructional, and comprehensive teaching to those who are born, called, and desire to prophesy according to 1 Corinthians 14:1 and speak as God's ambassadorial voice in the earth with power, authority, faith, love, boldness, and confidence in Christ.

Born to Prophesy: God's Voice Speaking Through You shows believers how innovative, comprehensive, narrative, instructive teachings about communicating God's original plan and purpose through the supernatural gift of prophecy and the prophetic ministry brings revolutionary change, transformation, healing, breakthrough, prosperity, confirmation, edification, encouragement, comfort, revival, and liberty. In this inspiring book the reader will discover and understand through foundational biblical teaching and present truth the role, function, and purpose of modern-day prophets, prophecy, and prophetic ministry that is desperately needed in the world and church today. This book is preferred for the mature believer but will also attract the attention of the new believer who may be interested in the prophetic ministry or who has a prophetic anointing on their life. These readers will discover the eternal purposes of God and understand the purpose of being born of the Spirit to prophesy as His mouthpiece in the earth. In addition, this guidebook can be used as a study tool for small groups, teachers, prophets, or pastors wishing to teach and encourage others to come up higher in their calling regardless of who they are in Christ or the gifting and callings upon their lives. It will also help believers understand how the gift of prophecy, when operated correctly, can birth perpetual movements of the Spirit and transform whole cities, nations, territories, and present and future generations.

Born to Prophesy: God's Voice Speaking Through You has been written to upgrade those who have been taught cessationist teaching, which denies the continuation of contemporary apostles after the death of the apostles, including Paul. They believe that the charismatic gifts ceased in the first century and were replaced by the Holy

Canon of the New Testament Scriptures. This type of theological doctrine has caused many believers also to deny present-day apostles and prophets and the full restoration of these ministry offices in the church today. Moreover, I wanted this book to be an exhaustive study of the gift of prophecy's function and operation in a believer's life and to give practical, foundational teaching that every born-again, Spirit-filled believer can pursue to prophesy and embrace a prophetic culture. It is not God's desire that a believer pursue solely prophecies but to pursue, covet, or desire to prophesy according to 1 Corinthians 14:1.

Born to Prophesy: God's Voice Speaking Through You shines light on the gift of prophecy and the fact that God's still speaks today and desires to speak through the believer. Moreover, this book is unique in that it differentiates itself from other books written on the prophetic topic of the residential gift of prophecy because it's not only a book but becomes a spiritual one-on-one coach, point of reference, mentor, and resource center while inspiring, encouraging, activating, motivating, challenging, and equipping the reader to arise as God's unique voice in the earth. I have completed this book through countless times of fasting and praying, hours of research, studying, meditation, frustration, and tears, as well as with much encouragement from pioneering fathers in the prophetic and apostolic, such as Prophet Bob Jones, Apostle John Eckhardt, Dr. Bill Hamon, C. Peter Wagner, and others who have inspired me to continue to write and be a father and reproducer of reproducers to my generation. I truly honor them all.

The reader will finish the book empowered with the necessary tools, insight, education and understanding of how to discover and identify their own prophetic calling, identity, potential, Holy Spirit–given supernatural gifts, and God's eternal purpose. This book is relevant and will meet the reader's need and hunger, which will ignite their faith, zeal, strength, and boldness to operate in the prophetic ministry. It's a simple read, and it's not an exhaustive, in-depth study of the office a prophet but an overview of the gift of prophecy and those desiring to prophesy. This book will help the reader in fulfilling their God-given, God-born desire, call, and dream. As the secular market has Harry Potter books, the occult, and New Age, which are popular, this book has the prophetic advantage and edge to be a launching pad for those who are just starting out in the prophetic. I pray that as you read this book you are challenged, inspired, educated, and encouraged to step out in faith and prophesy with power, boldness, and love in Christ for future generations. I take the reader through my personal prophetic journey to help him or her fulfill his own.

INTRODUCTION

Living a Prophetic Lifestyle

WHEN WE THINK about prophets, what comes to mind? Typically, people may think that prophets are some weird, strange, spooky, mystical, and mysterious individuals from another planet who have been alienated from the world scene and show up suddenly like a super hero to save the world. Or they may see them as some bald-headed, hunchbacked, Igor-looking men with a word of doom, gloom, and judgment. There are some people who may believe that prophets are loners or lone rangers hidden in the obscurity of a cave or on a rock cliff until the time of release to speak a "thus saith the Lord." They walk around as the only "voice" in the wilderness, like John the Baptist, eating wild honey, locusts, and wearing irritating apparel made out of camel's hair. Also there are those who believe that prophets operate on the same level as psychics. Regardless of the many unusual and misunderstood perceptions of prophets, we must understand this ministry gift is nothing more than ordinary people speaking extraordinary words from the Lord. There are true prophets of the living God, and there are also false prophets of other gods or deities.

Furthermore, when we think about prophecy, what comes to mind? People may equate prophecy with prophets, psychics, or some famous fifteenth-century French occultist seer from France called Nostradamus. His real name was Michel de Nostradame, and his predications of the end of the world and other future events became world acclaimed; however, his prophecies were based solely on judicial astrology. Some people may think that prophecy is imminent events that will soon happen, whether it's personal, corporate, or geographical.

Ignorance can make the prophetic spooky, mystical, mysterious, and insane. But the prophetic nature and function is simply the mind, counsel, and heart of God expressed and communicated to His people, present and future. There's nothing demonic about the prophetic nature of the Spirit of God, but there are those who are false prophets, who are demonic and operate in charismatic witchcraft, which is idolatry and sin. We must understand that prophets and prophecy are God's idea and concept and not man's. We should not reject His voice through anointed prophets and prophetic people. I believe that every born-again believer who is filled with the Spirit can learn to hear the voice of God, speak the voice of God, and become the voice of the Lord in the earth.

The biblical term *prophecy* as it relates to prophets has been limited to only prophets or a chosen few of the Old Testament, but God desires that every Holy Spirit–filled believer, through regeneration of the Spirit, possess an innate gift to prophesy as His mouthpiece. Biblically, we are admonished to be zealous of spiritual gifts and excel in the edification of the church. (See 1 Corinthians 14:12.) The prophetic is a ministry of construction not destruction. Prophecy has three main operations: biblically, foundationally, and functionally, which is edification, exhortation and comfort. This should be the prophetic DNA of any believer desiring to function in the prophetic realm. God still speaks today and will raise up a people who will declare His mind, will, and eternal purpose in the Earth.

> For Moses said, "The Lord your God will raise up for you a prophet like me from among your own people; you must listen to everything he tells you."
>
> —Acts 3:22

Moses declared to the people prophetically that God was going to raise up a prophet like himself among His people and put His words in his mouth (Deut. 18:18). Jesus was that prophet that God was going to raise up. Jesus was the greater Moses, and He would be the one who would deliver His people and bring salvation, deliverance, healing, restoration and reconciliation. He would be the one that would fulfill what was written and spoken out of the mouth of His holy prophets.

God will raise up in every generation holy men and women who have been anointed by the Spirit to speak as anointed oracles of the Lord. They will have the unction by the Holy Spirit to prophesy words that bring salvation, transformation, restoration, liberty, healing, deliverance, breakthroughs, and jubilee.

There are people who believe that they have to feel Holy Ghost goose bumps, get knocked on the floor, or receive a sovereign visitation from Gabriel, the messenger angel of the Lord, to prophesy. We should not make prophecy or speaking words of edification, exhortation, and comfort as difficult as it already may seem. It doesn't take any of that type of affect to prophesy, but through the Holy Spirit by faith we should open up our mouth and encourage those who we relate to by prophesying in the love of Christ. I have heard people who lack faith say, "I only speak if there is an unction," but we must understand that when we received the infilling of the Holy Spirit, the Holy Spirit is the anointed Holy Spirit sent by the Father; if a believer possesses the Holy Spirit, then we can by faith speak holy, anointed words to build up the body of Christ both individually and corporately. It takes faith, not intellect or a natural feeling.

God wants to develop and establish a prophetic culture and lifestyle in the believer. A prophetic culture is simply the behaviors, values, paradigms, beliefs, worldviews, and ways of life of an obedient believer or child of God. We are a covenant people and His new covenant church. We are a people who know our God and will do great exploits. That being said, we must be prophetic by nature. New covenant believers have been birthed and transferred from the kingdom of darkness into the kingdom of light (Col. 1:13). We are a people of revelation, relationship, and covenant with our King.

The words of our King are resident in the believer. We have been birthed out of prophecies or prophetic prayers; there was a need for you to be born in the time that you were born. God spoke you into being, not by accident but on purpose. You are a prophecy fulfilled because God said, "Let it be," and you came forth out of your father and mother; so, you are a personal prophecy that was fulfilled for your generation. God's word does not return unto Him void, but accomplishes what He sent it out to do (Isa. 55:11).

A person's belief system is what changes their culture. In other words, people are what they believe. We must live a prophetic lifestyle that is pleasing to the Lord. What am I saying? As new covenant believers we are a people who know our God intimately, knowing His voice and leading. We speak what He says and do what we see the Father doing (John 5:19). Jesus said, "I am the good shepherd; I know my sheep and my sheep know me" (John 10:14).

Relationships are a key to moving in the spirit of prophecy, which is connected to a prophetic lifestyle or culture. Anyone who desires to prophesy should find a prophet or company of prophets, whether it's a prophetic church, schools of the prophets, or a leadership prophetic team to train, help, and equip them to become prophetic in nature. There is a saying, "Birds of a feather flock together," or, said another way, "You are the company you keep." As covenant keepers, we should aim to have in our circle of activity and influence prophets and prophetic people who understand the role, function, operation, and integrity of this ministry.

In Samuel 10:10, there is an example of Saul the king coming in contact with the prophetic spirit via a band of minstrel prophets. In that instance the Spirit of the Lord, which is a prophetic spirit, came on Saul, and he prophesied like the prophets. The same spirit of prophecy by the Lord came upon Jahaziel in the midst of an assembly, and he prophesied also in 2 Chronicles 20:12–17. The point I am making is that just about anyone can prophesy! When there is a prophetic atmosphere or environment that has been established by the believer through fasting, praying, extreme worship, praise, and unity, the heavens will open, and God's presence will drop in a place and on His people; they will prophesy by the Spirit. I call it heavenly or glory prophecy. We should be passionately hungry for prophetic manna and bread from heaven. Jesus was called the Bread of Life (John 6:35). The prophetic is heavenly bread that brings life.

A prophetic lifestyle is a culture that believes in the supernatural, modern-day prophets, prophecy, apostles, and the gifts of the Spirit. If one does not believe in the modern-day prophetic ministry, then how can one function prophetically by the Holy Spirit today? We must receive these ministry gifts of apostles and prophets, which are vital for the health and growth of the church, because they are the foundational building gifts set in the church (Eph. 2:20).

The prophetic also can deal with damage control in a local church as well. The prophet's ministry is described by the Hebrew word *shamar*. In his book *God Still Speaks*, Apostle John Eckhardt defines the word *shamar* as, "to hedge about (as with thorns), to guard, to protect, to watch, and to keep. The word *shamar* is first used in Scripture in Genesis 2:15, where Adam is told to keep (*shamar*) the garden. It is also mentioned in Genesis 4:9, where Cain asks God if he is his brother's keeper (*shamar*)."[1]

The prophetic should be governed just as the prophet's ministry governs in the church. In the New Testament church of Corinth, they were very gifted but lacked the apostolic government to bring balance to the gifts that were at work in this local assembly. God wants His people and the local church to establish a prophetic culture, identity, and DNA. In every local church or assembly the voice of the Lord should be heard. Churches, ministries and organizations that do not embrace the prophetic ministry, prophecy, and prophets are denying the governmental voice and direction of the Lord.

The Bible says, "In the last days, God says, I will pour out my Spirit on all people. Your sons and daughters will prophesy, your young men will see visions, your old men will dream dreams" (Acts 2:17). The outpouring of the Spirit of God was not limited to and did not cease in the first century or at the end of the Old Covenant age, but God will continue to bring change and pour out His prophetic Spirit on those who desire to shift and be conduits of His prophetic glory. God passionately desires to continue to raise up prophetic people and a prophetic generation that will herald His voice to the nations of the world.

The gift of prophecy is one of the gifts of the Holy Spirit, and it is given to those whom God chooses to give it to. It is not based on merit or on earning it, but it is based on the grace of God. However, Scripture gives us some indication that if we earnestly desire and ask for this gift, He might very well give it to us (1 Cor. 14:1). God wants us to be prophetic by nature and live a prophetic lifestyle, meaning to walk in prophetic integrity, honor, and dignity. We should not be people of words only but of demonstration. The gift of prophecy is a

---

1   John Eckhardt, *God Still Speaks* (Lake Mary, FL: Charisma House, 2009), 68. See also Blue Letter Bible, s.v. "shamar," http://www.blueletterbible.org/search/lexiconc.cfm?Criteria=watch&st=any (accessed July 10, 2013).

gift, and God wants the gift to be respected, honored, received, and used for His glory and purpose.

The prophetic culture is a culture that is characterized by a particular social group or organization, and it can be defined as a way of daily activity of a group of people that is governed by their own behaviors, beliefs systems, core values, and symbols that they may embrace as their own without realizing it. I am reminded of someone that isn't from New York City who suddenly decides they want to move there, but they have an accent from the southern city of Atlanta. After this person migrates to New York City from Atlanta, Georgia, and lives there for several years, when that person comes back home, people will begin to hear a difference in that person's speech or accent. What I am saying is when this person who has an Atlanta accent moves to New York City, their accent changes even if they don't realize it. The person will adapt to the environment that they live in, or the culture. Most New Yorkers are fast-paced people, while southerners are more laid back and hospitable. This person became a part of the culture of New York City without noticing it themselves, while others can see that their speech, dialect, and accent altered to more of a New Yorker than that of a down-south city of Atlanta accent.

The prophetic culture can only happen when we shift our attitudes, beliefs, values, understanding of the prophetic gift and by faith live in that realm of the supernatural that allows us to speak for God. Every culture has different paradigms and belief systems. One belief system or worldview will affect how one does things and lives. Traditional or religious cultures and lifestyles have been accepted and adopted over many centuries; there are ways, belief systems, rituals, teachings of men, or doctrines that have been passed down generationally. Sadly, people easily accept and embrace these without further personal research and study of the Word of God to find out the truth and the answer to why people do what they do and believe what they believe.

The prophetic is nothing new or should not be misunderstood when its function and emphasis is so heavily outlined throughout the Bible. The Bible is a prophetic book written by inspired, holy men who were prophets and apostles of the old and new covenant. If these men and women of old were prophetic by nature and lifestyle, then we as new covenant people should follow the same patterns of those who heard the voice of God, spoke His words, witnessed His supernatural acts, and became His voice to their generation. God wants to speak through you and use your unique voice to share His heart to His people.

The nation of Israel, God's chosen people, was a unique people and a set-apart race that had their own type of culture. Their lifestyle represented the God they believed, valued, and obeyed. They were distinct from other pagan cultures, which were considered foreigners. God's people were a special race and a chosen culture that reflected a special God, who was the only true and living God. As we are in times of restoration, there were many movements of old that brought dramatic changes, and present, restored truth became prevalent. The prophetic is not a secret but a restored truth. Many cessationist teachers remove contemporary prophets and apostles after the death of the original twelve apostles of the Lamb, including Paul. These teachers are just modern-day Sadducees who do not believe in the supernatural or the gifts of the Holy Spirit. In the twenty-first century there are modern-day Sadducees who do not believe in the supernatural, miracles, gifts of the Spirit, prophecy, etc. I see why they were "sad you see" (Sadd-u-cee). The apostolic in the new covenant came to bring culture change to the way traditional leadership was doing things during the first century. They were living a religious lifestyle that was a culture of tradition, legalism, and pride. Unfortunately, the nation of Israel embraced many of the traditions of the Mosaic Law, which was bonded by circumcision (Acts 15).

The Jerusalem Council wanted to bring the Gentile people under the Law of Moses by having them be circumcised, but the Gentiles were Gentiles and not natural Jews. They were not required to become Jews. God was changing their religious culture because their culture was not God's intended culture of freedom, liberty, and of His eternal kingdom, which is spiritual, not earthly, carnal, and of this world.

In the twenty-first century church there is still change that needs to be done. God's is raising up not just a few men and women called prophets to release His mind and heart, but He is raising up companies of prophets and prophetic people. The culture of the church is changing as apostles and prophets are taking their stance and position governmentally to bring reformation.

> Ye also, as lively stones, are built up a spiritual house, an holy priesthood, to offer up spiritual sacrifices, acceptable to God by Jesus Christ.
>
> —1 PETER 2:5, KJV

God's people are a spiritual house made up of spiritual people. That being said, it is our position in God to be a prophetic people and live a prophetic lifestyle. If we are built up as a spiritual house, then the prophetic is a building gift, or rather, the only gift out of nine gifts of the Spirit that brings edification. There is present-day truth that we should seek to understand and seek to know regarding God's perception on modern-day prophets, prophecy, and prophetic ministry. We must shift from the old wineskin, the model and structure of things of the past, and embark on the new wineskin that is for today.

There were several strategic restoration reformation movements in the past five hundred years, such as the Protestant Reformation, Charismatic movement, Pentecostal movement, Word of Faith movement, Evangelical and Prophetic movements, Apostolic New Reformation movement, Saints movement, and others that brought tremendous change to the church culture. Throughout those decades many people, even if they were stuck in denominationalism, embraced these restored truths. As covenant believers we do not have to be stuck in these restored truths but can manifest them and walk in present truth. The prophetic is for everyone, not just a few anointed vessels that God has called out from the womb as prophets, but God can use anyone to prophesy like the prophets. Everyone is not called to be a prophet, but everyone can communicate for God, which I call a prophetic culture.

In 1 Samuel 19:24, we read that in Ramah the presence of God was resident to such a degree that it impacted Saul during his paranoid, schizophrenic and double-minded behavior. Even while he was seeking to murder David, the Spirit of the Lord was mighty such that the spirit of prophecy came on Saul, and he prophesied naked all day and all night. The prophetic can change a lunatic king into a prophesying machine. The prophetic spirit changed the attitude and culture of a jealous, bipolar, and rebellious king. Prophets resident in a local church can develop a prophetic culture and impart a prophetic dimension into that assembly that will raise the water level for others to swim in and launch out in the prophetic river. My heart, focus, and emphasis in this book are to help train, develop, equip, educate, encourage, and challenge believers to live and embrace a prophetic lifestyle and culture. It's my desire that you will develop and establish a prophetic culture wherever you may go and whatever you may do in God, whether it's through worship, prophetic teams, pioneering, prayer, fasting, worship, deliverance, helps, teaching, preaching, singing, dancing, writing, arts, music, impartation, ordaining, commissioning, laying on of hands, or fathering.

The Holy Spirit is a prophetic spirit, and God will always raise up a prophetic generation (Num. 11:29; Acts 2:14–18). When the prophetic culture is established, men, women, boys, girls, young, old, "servants and handmaidens" will prophesy in their generation. The unction to function is provided by faith to speak as oracles of God biblically. God will not force anyone to speak what's on His heart and mind. God will use the faith of those among His people who want to speak for Him. We should not make prophesying complicated and confusing when it was not intended to be. This book will bring clarity and disclose many scriptural truths about this powerful building gift.

Could you imagine if everyone you came into contact with prophesied and communicated effectively God's intentions for your life? We would not see many disconnected and disenfranchised people in the body of Christ and world.

Did you know that something will never happen in your life without the prophetic word of the Lord and prayer? This ministry is something that God instituted and desires to facilitate with the help of ministering angels in order to bring your personal prophecies to pass. In Psalm 103:20 (KJV) it says, "Bless the LORD, ye his angels that excel in strength, that do his commandments, hearkening unto the *voice* of his word" (emphasis added). Notice that angels hearken— listen and act upon—the voice of God's Word. We know that the Bible is God's Word. Angels don't hearken just to God's Word, but rather they hearken to the voice of His Word. In other words, angels act on God's Word that we speak out of our mouths. They listen to us speaking God's Word or prophesying the word of the Lord. And when we speak God's Word, angels are released to perform it in our lives. In other words, when the prophetic word of God is released, ministering angels are simultaneously released to carry out His eternal purpose in our lives.

Your words are assigned to your life, just as angels are as well. (See Exodus 23:20, 22.) The Word of the Lord says that an angel hearkens unto the voice of the Lord. When God's uses anointed prophets and prophetic people to prophesy into your situation, life is created, and portals, gates, and doorways are opened for you. God wants to use your voice to reach nations. The Bible says in Psalm 19:3 (KJV), "There is no speech or language where their voice is not heard." Verse 4 continues, "Their voice goes out into all the earth, their words to the ends of the world." You were born to prophesy and communicate to the earth His original intent and purpose. God desires that every nationality, culture, and believer around the world will speak prophetically and will be heard throughout the Earth regardless of what language he or she speaks. One of the only times that unbelievers will know your Lord and King is that His divine voice is trumpeted through yours. When there is a prophetic culture, atmosphere, climate, and environment created and established, the heavens will open, the Earth will shake, and heaven will come down.

It is intense when we as Spirit-filled believers prophesy and minister through prophetic worship. The heavens will drop at the presence of the Lord. What am I saying? The Old Testament Hebrew word for prophesy is *nataph*, meaning "to ooze, distill gradually, by implication to fall in drops, figuratively to speak by inspiration, prophecy, and discourse." The Hebrew word is translated, "drop," (see Judg. 5:4; Ezek. 21:2; Amos 7:16), and "prophesy" (see Mic. 2:6, 11).[2] The dew of heaven is released when anointed prophets, prophetic worship leaders, and people begin to release God's words through prophetic utterance. The presence of the Lord will fall in that place like rain.

---

2   Kevin J. Conner, *The Church in the New Testament* (Portland, OR: City Bible Publishing, 1982), 154. See also Blue Letter Bible, s.v. "nataph" http://www.blueletterbible.org/search/lexiconc.cfm?Criteria=prophesy&st=any (accessed July 10, 2013).

I have been in places where there has been strong prophetic inspi-
rational release and radical worship, and I literally felt raindrops in
those meetings. God's tangible glory and presence came down. God
wants to come down and live with us.

The Bible says that God inhabits the praises of His people (Ps. 22:3).
When we live a prophetic lifestyle, these acts of God will not just be
visitations of His presence but will be holy habitations. God wants to
live among His people and speak through them with signs, wonders,
and miracles accompanying His word. When believers and prophets
prophesy, the word of the Lord will drop on an individual or a place
like rain, or the Lord will come in a dark cloud bringing showers of
blessings or even judgments on a nation that has turned from Him.

The Hebrew word for "prophecy" is the word *naba*, which means
"to prophesy, speak (or sing) by inspiration (in prediction or simple
discourse), and prophesy under the influence of divine spirit, in the
ecstatic state." This Hebrew word is translated *prophesy* (see 1 Sam.
10, 11; Jer. 2:8, 26:11; Ezek. 37:7; Joel 2:28; Amos 3:8), and also to make
oneself a prophet (see Jer. 29:26–27).[3] *Naba* in a sense is like a water
fountain that springs up, bubbling up, flowing forth, gushing out
or pouring down. The same word *naba* as in prophecy is another
Hebrew word *nabiy,* which is the word for "prophet," which means
"an inspired man."

The feminine form is *nabiyah,* or "prophetess," which is an
inspired woman, a prophet's wife, or poetess.[4] There are many theological debates about whether women should be called *prophet* rather
than *prophetess*, but a prophetess is a biblical term used to describe a
female prophet, just as there was the term, title, or word *shepherdess*
in the Old Testament. Rachel, the wife of Jacob and mother of Joseph,
was a shepherdess of her father's flock. She displays this principle.
The inspiration to prophesy can drop like rain (*nataph*) and bubble
up from inside one's belly (*naba*). We must not get it confused in
regard to the function of *nataph* coming down and *naba* bubbling
up. It is the same Holy Spirit initiating both functions, and the out-

---

3   Conner, 154. See also Blue Letter Bible, s.v. "naba"
http://www.blueletterbible.org/search/lexiconc.cfm?Criteria=prophesy&st=any
(accessed July 10, 2013).
4   Eckhardt, *God Still Speaks*, 10.

come is similar when God speaks them forth in an anointed man or woman.

As you read this book, it is my heartfelt desire to see a generation come into the prophetic anointing and that as you pursue love and earnestly desire spiritual gifts, one being to prophesy, you will come away with the confidence, boldness, authority, and power to prophesy like never before. I pray that this book will release the necessary impartation and activation to cause you to fulfill your prophetic destiny. Whether you are a seasoned prophet, emerging prophet, apostle, teacher, pastor, or leader in any area of society, Gods wants to develop a prophetic culture in your life. God wants to establish a prophetic culture in the DNA of your church as a pastor or an apostle of a new church plant, ministry, or work. God desires that you live a prophetic lifestyle such that as men see you they will see you as a living epistle read by men. Before you were born, God had a plan for your life and for your generation. Will you be the voice of God that He will use to change the culture and world that you live in? The time is now; this is what you have been born to do!

Chapter One

BEFORE YOU WERE BORN

Before I formed you in the womb I knew you, before you were
born I set you apart; I appointed you as a prophet to the nations.
—JEREMIAH 1:5

IN THE FIRST chapter of Jeremiah, God began to engage in a personal, one-on-one dialogue with the young Jeremiah, who had a prophetic call on his life to be a prophet of God.

The Lord began to share with him His foreknowledge of Jeremiah's call before Jeremiah was ever conceived in his mother's womb. The Lord also revealed to Jeremiah his prophetic identity in just a few statements, that God Himself had appointed him as a prophet to the nations.

Any prophet or prophetic leader can understand and bear witness with this passage of Scripture. It is a personal prophecy given by God to His chosen vessel, whom the Lord just commissioned. The Father also begins to tell Jeremiah that before He formed him, He knew him personally. This is a very interesting statement because it outlines that God was the one who created him and used the womb of his very own mother to be the vehicle to conceive him from. Before Jeremiah was birthed in the natural realm he was originally conceived out of the spiritual womb of God, which was His mind. Jeremiah was being birthed forth through a divine thought, desire, and concept of the Lord.

The Father preplanned and predestined to deliver Jeremiah in the earth long before Jeremiah was ever thought of by his natural parents. With that desire of God came Jeremiah's calling to prophetic duty. This big conversation that God had with Jeremiah was like a father telling his son about the beginning of his son's life. God's intention to conceive Jeremiah reminds me of married couples desiring and making necessary plans to have a baby of their own. They begin to use wisdom in the planning process of bringing a new life into the world.

When a husband and wife receive the news from their family physician that they are pregnant, the first thing the couple starts thinking in anticipation about their new arrival is what the gender of their child will be, the time their child will actually be born, and possible girl and boy names. Using that as an illustration, we must understand that God already knew and determined Jeremiah's name, gender, birth date, and his prophetic career. The Lord knows *you* by name and *your* destiny, which is attached to *your* purpose. The uniqueness of Jeremiah's calling is that the calling is associated with the meaning of his own name and the prophetic function that the calling applies to. Jeremiah's name in Hebrew means "May Yahweh lift up high, thrust or establish."[5] So, that being said, God was going to lift him up, thrust him, and establish him as a prophet in this high calling of the Lord.

The prophetic takes on the same function as the meaning of Jeremiah's name, meaning in Hebrew, "Yah is high."[6] In other words Jeremiah had a high calling from God. Whatever calling *you* have from the Lord is a high calling in His eyes. Jeremiah's name also took on the characteristic of what the prophetic does when it comes to a person. The prophetic comes to build up, to establish, encourage, and to exhort.

Prophecy is divinely inspired and an anointed utterance; it is a supernatural proclamation in a known language. It is the manifestation of the Spirit of God—not as a heightened natural ability]—and it may be possessed and operated by all who have the infilling of the Holy Spirit. (See 1 Corinthians 14:31.) Intellect, faith, and will are operative in this gift, but its exercise is not intellectually based. It is calling forth words from the Spirit of God. The gift of prophecy operates when there is high worship and praying (1 Sam. 10:5–6), when

---

5   *Holman Illustrated Bible Dictionary* (Nashville, TN: Holman Bible Publishers, 2003), 882. See also Blue Letter Bible, s.v. "ruwm" < http:// www.blueletterbible. org/lang/lexicon/Lexicon.cfm?Strongs=H7311&t=KJV > (accessed July 10, 2013).
6   Blue Letter Bible, s.v. "Yahh" < http:// www.blueletterbible.org/lang/lexicon/ Lexicon.cfm?Strongs=H3050&t=KJV > (accessed June 3, 2013).

other prophets are present (1 Sam. 10:9–10), and through the laying on of hands by ministers of the gospel (Acts 19:1–6).

PROPHECY WILL FIND YOU

Have you ever been in a place where you needed to hear the word of the Lord, and then suddenly the word of the Lord came to you? Or perhaps you were studying something and then revelation knowledge came to you, which brought the answers to your questions or problems. Have you ever been somewhere and a prophetic word came from a pastor, leader, prophet, or someone who just came with a confirming word that you had been waiting on? Yes, we all have in one way or another had a word of the Lord come to us. It may have been through reading the Bible in our devotional time or praying or just simply being in church hearing something that caused your spirit to bear witness.

The word of the Lord came to Jeremiah personally, and it came from God Himself and not from any other source. There is nothing like receiving a direct prophecy from the Father! The prophetic word of the Lord had Jeremiah in mind. Prophecy is the inspired mind of God communicated toward an individual that He has called and chosen.

God was the very source of Jeremiah's purpose, and he did not have any choice over his own calling, purpose, and destiny but only needed to embrace and walk in that which he was called to. The call of a prophet was predetermined and preordained by God before Jeremiah's conception and neither determined nor ordained after he was birthed. The Scripture uses this manner of speech to declare that God appointed his ministering vessels to their holy offices before they were born and not after, as in Isaiah 49:1 and Galatians 1:15.

The Lord called and set apart Isaiah as well to this office from his very birth. The emphasis here is laid on the fact that he was called and not on the particular time period when it was done. The concept is that the prophet Isaiah did not presumptuously assume his office or position, nor did he enter into it without being appointed by the Lord Himself. He had been designated and selected to the position of a prophet even before he was ever born. The Scripture does not state that Isaiah chose to run for the prophetic office like a person running for presidency or some other public office, nor was he appointed and voted to the office by human government but by the spiritual government of God, thereby being selected by the sovereign Lord only.

In the Book of Isaiah the Prophet Isaiah identifies the one who had called him and announced the calling with certainty and assurance. Isaiah was announcing his prophetic birth certificate. A person does not have any choice of selecting who their own parents are to be and when or where and how they will be conceived. Emphasis was given to these holy men of God that were chosen by the Lord to do something great for Him in their generation, and the prophetic work was at the forefront of what God was requiring out of them. These men were prophets of God but were born to prophesy.

The focus and implication here is, What is God calling *you* to do for *your* generation, and do *you* know what *you* have been born to do?

Regardless of what area of society a person may be called to impact and change for kingdom purposes, we must understand that the prophetic element is important to present and introduce to future generations that are unborn. There is power in the word of the Lord. Through the prophetic anointing and intercessory prayers, a believer can veto demonic legislations, laws, and policies.

We can overthrow existing satanic governments and thrones that are established illegally, and we can tear down and close demonic altars and portals that are opened over whole regions, territories, and nations, like Jeremiah and Elijah did. I believe in God-inspired prophecies because future generations are birthed through what we speak. The prophetic culture and way should be incorporated in the life of every believer. This particular gift should not be foreign to believers, just as the supernatural power of God through the Holy Spirit shouldn't be foreign. Throughout the history of the Bible we see the very acts of God demonstrated through holy men of God.

We see countless scriptures on the prophetic, prophets, schools of the prophetic, seers, false prophets, prophecy, prophetic declaration, proclamations, warnings, judgments, fulfillments, and the raw power of God manifested. Sadly, in Christianity most people are more concerned about rapturing out of here instead of prophesying, advancing, and expanding the culture of the kingdom and releasing people into their divine destiny, calling, and purpose. Prophecy and the supernatural power of God were not just for those who went before us like Jeremiah and Isaiah. We have access to the same God as then; He is the same God now and He will be the same God forevermore.

GOD'S WORD IN YOUR MOUTH

GOD STILL WORKS miracles, and God still speaks prophetically! Just know that God is going to use your anointed lips as a vessel to speak and demonstrate His inspired words and acts through. God put His words in Jeremiah's mouth, and He will put His words in yours if you yield to His voice. You were born to change the world. Jeremiah was called to change nations and kingdoms with the word of the Lord.

Moreover, we can see that along with God forming Jeremiah, the Lord also begins to shape, predestine, and fashion His divine blueprint and foundation in Jeremiah's life. God always creates the plan, purpose, assignment, and destiny of a man before He ever creates the actual person. Simply, our overall destiny is preordained and predetermined before we ever come into existence in this world. God has already preset, arranged, and ordered our steps. Like Jeremiah, many of us today need to come into that divine revelation of the prophetic call and anointing upon our life.

Jeremiah was born into a priestly family. He was the son of Hilkiah from the village of Anathoth. The Book of Jeremiah says that Jeremiah was called by God to prophesy the destruction of Jerusalem that would occur by invaders from the north. This was because Israel had been unfaithful to the laws of God and the covenant that they forsook by worshiping and serving the Baals and foreign gods. The people of Israel had even gone as far as building high altars to Baal and other foreign deities in order to sacrifice their very own children in fire as offerings unto Baal. This nation had deviated so far from the Lord God that they had actually breached the covenant, causing God to withdraw His divine blessing, favor, and protection. Jeremiah was instructed by the Lord to proclaim, preach, publish, and prophesy that the nation of Israel would be faced with famine, desolation, and be plundered by foreigners, who would exile them to a foreign land and territory.

Furthermore, Jeremiah's prophetic ministry was very active from the thirteenth year of Josiah, King of Judah, (626 BC) until sometime after the fall of Jerusalem and the destruction of Solomon's Temple in 587 BC.[7] During this period spanned the reigns and regimes of five kings and kingdoms of Judah: Josiah, Jehoahaz, Jehoiakim, Jehoichin, and Zedekiah. The Lord called Jeremiah to prophetic service in about 626 BC at a very young age, about one year after Josiah, King of Judah, had turned and reformed the nation toward repentance from the widespread idolatrous practices of his forefathers.

Ultimately, Josiah's reformation would not be enough to preserve Judah and Jerusalem from destruction because of the sins of Manasseh, Josiah's grandfather, which had gone too far. Such was the lust and perversion of the nation for false gods that after Josiah's death the nation would immediately return to the foreign gods of the surrounding nations. Jeremiah was appointed to prophetically address the rebellion and sin of the people, proclaiming the coming judgments and consequences of their apostasy and idolatrous ways.

NEVER TOO YOUNG OR OLD

In contrast to Isaiah the prophet, who eagerly and zealously embraced his prophetic call, and similar to Moses who was less than ambitious, Jeremiah resisted the prophetic call by complaining and murmuring that he was only a child and did not know how to speak due to his age. In other words, Jeremiah was basically telling the Lord that he was too inexperienced to prophesy the word of the Lord to an unrepentant nation and that he was too young to speak.

God countered Jeremiah's self-assessments and excuses of his inability to perform successfully and maturely in the prophetic office as young man with the fact that Jeremiah was not called and appointed by God because of chronological age and inexperience in the prophetic, but rather because he was created and born to stand in the office of an ambassadorial national prophet from his mother's

---

7   Tremper Longman III, *Jeremiah, Lamentations* (Peabody, MA: Hendrickson Publishers, 2008), 6. See also Adele Berlin and Marc Zvi Brettler, *The Jewish Study Bible* (New York: Oxford University Press, 2004), 917.

womb. To complain to the Creator that you are unable to do something that He designed and birthed you to do is an insult to the Lord. The Lord wired Jeremiah with the necessary tools to carry out this heavy assignment.

However, the Lord insisted that Jeremiah go and declare as commanded, and He touched Jeremiah's mouth and put His words in it. God told Jeremiah to get ready for work! The character traits and practices Jeremiah was to acquire in order to be prepared are specified in Jeremiah chapter 1, which included not being fearful of men, standing flatfooted to speak, speaking as commanded, and going where he was sent by the Lord.

Other prophetic disciplines that contributed to the training of the young prophet and confirmation of his message are described as not turning to the people or compromising, not giving in to marriage and fathering children, not going to weddings or funerals, not feasting, and not keeping the company of fornicators and adulterers. What a miserable and boring life Jeremiah must have had. It seems like he could not do anything, as it was the grace of God on his life that he was born to endure and live a separated life unto the Lord.

THE PROPHETIC NATURE

Inherently, the nature of a prophet can be misunderstood to the point that prophets may feel like their lives are in total isolation, obscurity, and hiding. The reason for this is that the prophet is "in the womb" in which their call has been appointed for a set time and they are separated unto God. This place is where they are covered, concealed, and unknown until the time of their coming out as a prophet. All of this is the plan and strategy of the Lord outlined before Jeremiah was born. One thing that I have learned growing in the prophetic ministry is that God will train and cultivate one's character and polish their personality before He uses them.

The Lord takes prophetic people and prophets through intense boot camp to shape, humble, father, nourish, discipline, and deliver them from their own will, desires, ambitions, and agendas until the Lord gets their undivided attention and full cooperation. It can take decades to develop a fully mature, functioning prophet of God. The

Father has taken me through many seasons of life lessons, experiences, and encounters, which led me into my own personal wilderness places to strengthen my ability to move in the spirit, teaching me not to depend on natural and worldly appetites and passions. God did not want me to function as a prophet in a familiar spirit, intellect, emotions, and intuitions but to obey and trust the voice of the Father. The Lord trained Jeremiah's five natural senses to discipline his spiritual senses and to teach him not to mix them together. Likewise, the Lord had to develop my temperament, which most prophets and prophetic people must learn how to control, balance, and master.

For example, I am the type of person who is very passionate, determined, and goal oriented when it comes to getting things done on time. Due to the fact that I am always on the go and moving forward, at times I can be very strong willed in my own plans; God allowed me to be challenged to learn how to wait and take my time with wisdom and not youthful zeal. While God was training me as a youth in the prophetic, He would cause me to go and grow through seasons of long suffering. (See Ephesians 4:2.)

The Lord was teaching me patience and wisdom. It was a necessity for me to learn how to hear the voice of God as a young prophet as well and to heed His instructions in order for me to be an effective communicator or orator. One thing that I needed to learn was the wisdom of God, and any prophetic servant must learn the principle of fearing the Lord, which is key to the beginning of prophetic maturation.

Wisdom and Humility Is Key to Prophetic Training

If a believer does not learn to increase in their ability to listen, hear, and obey, biblically they are considered a fool by not walking in the fear of the Lord. God has to teach His prophets how to hear His voice, His ways, and to know Him intimately. To know God personally and prophetically is having divine access to the all-knowing one who is omniscient.

In prophetic temperament training, God would actually train a person's character in an opposite way. For instance, if someone is very bashful, shy, introverted, reserved, timid, and fearful, God would allow that person to go through situations and circumstances where the individual would have to be social, interactive, and interpersonal with others. Furthermore, the Lord would cause this person to be surrounded by people who are bold, candid, extroverted, confident, and risky for the purpose of causing that person to have balance and be unmovable, like a tree, in any type of situation. As another example, if a person has a problem with being on time, then God might cause people to enter the person's life to help them to be more responsible and time conscious.

God creates people, places, and things to cause us to become more like His Son Christ Jesus so that we can walk in godly character and integrity. There are people who use excuses and statements such as, "This is the way I am," or, "This is how I was raised," or, "I have always been like this and you have to just deal with it." But in reality the person cowardly does not want to change, grow, and increase in godly wisdom and understanding. We must understand that this process of character development does not change your personality, but He does changes areas of our character that may be contrary to His nature. If an emerging prophet has pride, rebellion, or stubbornness in their heart, then God will break and work on those character traits, taking the student through severe training to purge from them those negative attributes so that the prophet can operate in humility, love, submission, and obedience.

There are character patterns, flaws, and personalities that we have received from birth that were inherited from our natural parents, and these traits can be good or bad. There are people in our families that can identify ways in which we are like our father, mother, grandfather, grandmother, brother, sister, cousins, friends, etc. In the same way that in the natural people can recognize certain character traits and personalities, there are also ways of the Father that we must adopt and take ownership of when we are born again by the Spirit.

The culture of the kingdom is the way and spiritual lifestyle of a believer and citizen of the kingdom of God. Paul the apostle in the Book of Galatians talked about Christ being formed in you. He would compare himself to a mother in travail and in labor at childbirth until Christ is formed in them—in other words, so that Christ's character, fruit, and that paradigm shift is evident in the life of every born-again believer.

The word *formed* is from the Greek words *morphoo* (mor-fah-oh) and *morphe,* which mean "1. the form by which a person or thing strikes the vision; 2. external appearance."[8] Galatians 4:19 speaks of a change in character, becoming conformed to the character traits of Christ Jesus in actuality, not merely in semblance. Prophets and prophetic people must have Christ formed in them, and when they prophesy the hearer of the prophetic word can feel the weight of glory and love of Christ. Believers alike should want to be more like Christ in word and in deed. It is a spiritual transformation that takes place on the inside first and manifests secondly on the outside of a believer. Jeremiah had to overcome personal inadequacies and false perceptions of his calling by learning through one-on-one encounters with the Father to understand his prophetic future role as a prophet called to the nations.

THE INITIAL CALL OF THE PROPHET

Furthermore, as I was learning how to hear the voice of God at a very young age, I did not know like Jeremiah how to speak or prophesy because I grew up in the Baptist denomination. Their paradigm and belief system of contemporary prophets and the prophetic ministry were only limited to the prophets of the old covenant. Even today in the twenty-first century, there are many religious denominations and ecclesiastical structures within the church that do not support, operate, embrace, understand, recognize, ordain, set, and commission fivefold ministry gifts given to the body of Christ.

I truly believe that spiritual reformation is coming in a whole new way to the body of Christ, and God is birthing *karios* moves of His Spirit around the world. Nations and many religious cultures are coming into present-day truth of the prophetic and the supernatural power of God. However, in spite of being a part of a Baptist church as a child, I would have many personal divine and demonic encounters,

---

8   Strong's Greek Concordance, #3444, http://www.studylight.org/lex/grk/gwview.cgi?n=3444 (accessed July 10, 2013).

visitations by angels and demonic spirits. I remember several times having a visitation of Christ in my dreams and in my prayer time with Him. Regardless of my Baptist foundation, which gave me little understanding of modern-day prophets and the role of prophets in the local church, God encountered me as I pursued what I was born to become. It was the Lord who sovereignly called me to the prophetic ministry office before my birth—not by man or through the Baptist denomination did this calling occur.

These personal, one-on-one dialogues that I had with God at the age of seven in prayer confirmed and validated that it was in fact the Lord who said that I was His and that I would do a mighty work for Him in due season. I could remember one time I was praying to the Lord in the closet of my bedroom at the age of twelve. I went on a three-day extreme fast without water and food, and on the first day of the fast I had a vision of the Lord.

On the second day and third day the Lord spoke to me in a loud, thunder-like voice saying, "Hakeem, Hakeem!" I can remember being in awe and in fear, running under the covers of my bed. I was so frightened that I heard the voice of the Father calling me a second time in my bed, "Hakeem, Hakeem." This time the Father's voice sounded like the voice of my very own mother calling me out loud. I answered Him by saying, "Yes, Mommy," and the Lord said, "It is I, Christ Jesus, who is calling you, Hakeem, and I have called you from your mother's belly. I love you, and I am your Father. I will use you to speak for Me one day."

After that encounter from the Lord, all I wanted to be at twelve years old was a judge, police officer, doctor, singer, and preacher. I did not know fully what the Lord was calling me to be because I was too young to comprehend at the time what a prophet was and his function. All I knew was that I wanted to be a judge, police officer, doctor, singer, and preacher, but God knew that He was going to use those unsure occupations of mine as a child to cultivate and shape me into the prophetic future vessel that He promised.

Like Jeremiah, I doubted my ability to speak for Him because of age and inexperience in the prophetic. In God's timing, the Lord would come to me and share with me His will and intentions and assist me through the process of becoming what I was born to be.

Those words from God echoed in my spirit for many years as a teenager, as well as at the time of receiving them. God confirmed His word over and over again until I knew without a shadow of a doubt that in fact He called me from and before birth.

By the age of fourteen I had received dozens of prophecies confirming the call of a prophet on my life. At the same time my prophetic gift was working mightily. I was able to see, sense, feel, know, dream, and encounter things in the spirit without any prior knowledge of them or insight. I would share things with my peers, and they would not understand how I knew what I knew. But, like Jeremiah, my childhood was not so bright. I would find myself in a place of deep anxiety, depression, lamentation, and sadness.

Overcoming Personal Obstacles

There were times as a child that I had to confront and challenge a lot of injustices that would go on in my family and personal life; in those cases I would suffer internally until I spoke out against it. But when I finally spoke up for myself and what was not right as a child I would be punished severely by authority figures in my life. It was the process and making of a prophet. God would use those life circumstances and issues to be the training tool and vehicle for me as a prophet to address, like Jeremiah, ungodly practices, injustices, and corruptions in my generation.

There were times growing up that I didn't want to live anymore due to the fact that I experienced tremendous rejection from those whom I loved the most. There were seasons in my life when I felt like a loner and isolated from the world, even though I had a large, close-knit family. My father was not in my life growing up. I was raised by a single mother and other strong women, such as my grandmother, Ruth Collins, who was the bedrock and matriarch of the Collins family. In addition to that I was raised in one of the roughest communities in the city of Wilmington, Delaware, called the Southbridge and Riverside Projects, where drug dealing, prostitution, murders, gang banging, and poverty was the culture.

There were times that I found myself fist fighting other kids in the neighborhood just about every other day to gain respect. As a prophet in training, as I call it, my life was riddled with broken-ness, suffering, and humility. Living in those types of demonic and worldly environments and atmospheres, it was hard for one at the age of seven to remain righteous and holy before God. The only outlet and peace that I found was in Jesus Christ.

Interestingly, those places became fertile grounds for cultivation, grooming, budding, purging, and training for me. I have learned to establish an intimate relationship with Daddy God and know Christ as Lord and King over my life. As a child I would face challenging moments and life-altering circumstances, but through it all I came to the realization that Jesus the Prophet was my ultimate source, provider, and protector. It was Jesus the Prophet who was speaking to the prophet on the inside of me. We must understand that Jesus Christ the Prophet dwells on the inside of the believer by the Holy Spirit. He is always speaking.

As I was faithful, transparent, and obedient to the Lord, He would make His voice so clear to me. The Lord's voice echoed in my spirit even when I was living in sin or disobedient at times. His voice became more real as I prayed and studied the Word more. The Bible says, "My sheep listen to my voice" (John 10:27), and the voice of "a stranger they will not follow" (John 10:5, KJV). Daddy God would put me on His lap in the spirit and share secret things concerning His will for my life. Likewise, Jeremiah had to find who he was born to be, which was found in Daddy God, the Creator of all things. God would be his Father.

Growing in the prophetic gift as a child my mother would say that I had a big mouth, and with that big mouth that I would always find myself putting my foot in it as well. Some prophets know what I am talking about. When growing up as a prophetic child life is very unique in itself. I was very charismatic, sensitive, extra emo-tional, and was sometimes labeled as bipolar and rebellious because I wanted to do things my way. In my own mind, I was the boss. One of the things that I had to learn in the prophetic is being delivered from the human spirit of men and agendas of men. Rejection comes so that one may become like Jesus, who was the Stone that the builder rejected.

I had to learn that what one may not want now, they will need later. As prophetic people and prophets of the Lord, we must understand that Jeremiah was not called by man, but by the Lord. What Jeremiah feared was his inability to speak and the rejection of men. Jeremiah was born to be a prophet who would prophesy as the Lord commanded him, regardless of what people thought or said.

As I stated earlier, Jeremiah's name means, "Yahweh establishes." The powerful thing about God is that He was going to use the meaning of Jeremiah's name, which spoke of his nature, and establish him as prophet to the nations while putting His word in his mouth to kings, princes, and governors of nations and kingdoms. Simply put, God (Yahweh) established Jeremiah as His spokesperson before conception. A person cannot want or desire to become a prophet, but prophets are born; Jeremiah was born to be a prophet. He did not afterward seek to be something that was not in his prophetic origin.

One cannot desire to be in the office of a prophet, but one can covet spiritual gifts. A person can desire to prophesy by the gift of prophecy or minister in one of the prophetic administrations through the gifts of the Holy Spirit. The frustrating part about the whole call to the prophet's office to me as a child was that I had no idea how to be what I was born to be for the Lord.

I am reminded of a baby first learning to know the voice of their parents. One interesting discovery is that when the parents start calling the baby its birth name, the baby doesn't know at first that it is his or her name, but the parents continue to speak it until the baby, over time, understands that in fact that is his or her name. How did you know your own name? It took someone calling you that name. It took several years as a child to fully respond and react when your name was spoken by the person who gave it to you.

Regardless of whether or not you liked what your parents or someone named you, it's still your name. Prophecy can function just like that; when spoken to a person, the hearer will hear that same prophetic word over and over until the time that the person responds and walks in prophetic fulfillment.

You Are Qualified to Be Used by the Lord

Similar to the prophetic call on someone's life, the Father will declare and confirm it as what you were born to be through others many times until the time that you understand, embrace, respond, and react to that call. Jeremiah had that same encounter with the Father and had to embrace that he was appointed, anointed, chosen, and sent before he was born. God desires that His people know and occupy that which they were created to be. Jeremiah, like many of us, felt inadequate and inexperienced to prophesy or speak. Jeremiah felt that his inability to perform was going to change God's mind, but in fact, he was to be used to prophesy extensively because God knew he was ready and able to prophetically speak to the nations. You may not be as eloquent and skilled in the area that you are called to, but know that by the Spirit of God you will be someday.

In Jeremiah's early ministry he was primarily a preaching prophet, going where the Lord directed and sent him to preach and prophesy. Jeremiah was used of the Lord through a holy indignation and dis-contentment against idolatry, the greed of priests, paganism and false prophets, including corrupt governments and worldly king-doms. Many years later God instructed Jeremiah to write down these early oracles and other messages. Jeremiah's perception of himself as an unqualified prophet caused the Lord to share with him about His will for Jeremiah's life and the purpose of his birthing.

Have you ever thought about why you were created and what was the purpose of your birth and life? I know I have many times and even as I continue my walk as a kingdom believer in the Lord. Those thoughts are still at the center of my mind and heart. I have been born to make an impact on my generation and leave a legacy for future generations to benefit and enjoy. Jeremiah, like many of us today, asked that question. He felt that he was not the man for a tre-mendous service of the Lord. God knew that he was the man and that he was going to speak for Him. God knew it was necessary for Jeremiah to be born in that generation to address an apostate nation who had turned from the true and living God.

We must understand that our very own birthing in the earthly realm serves a purpose for humanity to reap the benefits from. Many of us today have been birthed out of prophetic words and prayers that were prayed centuries or even decades before we came into being. Some prayer warrior, intercessor, prophet, grandmother, and nation cried out to the Lord to bring forth the eternal purposes of God in their time and generation.

BORN FOR SUCH A TIME LIKE THIS

In times past I recall thinking and wondering why the Lord would birth me in the time and generation age that He did. I remember an account when I was about twelve years old. My mother and grandmother told me that during the birthing of me and my twin brother, Naim, in August of 1981 there was an assassination attempt upon President Ronald Regan. At that time the HIV/AIDS epidemic had started in the United States. Also during the early eighties other nations around the world were going through many governmental leadership transitions, and some nations were revolting in revolutionary ways. During the time of my birth there were governments around the world that were being overturned and overthrown by rebellion of the people. Key leaders in those nations were being assassinated as well. In addition, there was a surge of technological breakthroughs and discoveries during the late seventies and early eighties. I truly believe that in times of transition, restoration, and reformation, God knows what is needed and who He can use to play a key role in His redemptive plan of reconciliation.

Throughout history and in every generation of men, God has always and will always continue to raise up men and women to radically shift, alter, and transform their world and society. The Bible says, "The earth is the LORD's, the fullness thereof; the world, and they that dwell therein (Ps. 24:1, KJV; see also 1 Cor. 10:26). Before we are born God sees the beginning and ending of a thing, because Christ Jesus is the Alpha and the Omega, the beginning and the ending. There is no beginning and ending without or outside of God. So, that being said, you are important to the time, season, age, or generation that the Father births you into. You must understand that your generation needed you to be born in the time that you were conceived.

Chapter Two

GOD'S PROPHETIC PURPOSE

And we know that all things work together for good to those who love
God, to those who are the called according to His purpose. For whom
He foreknew, He also predestined to be conformed to the image of His
Son, that He might be the firstborn among many brethren. Moreover
whom He predestined, these He also called; whom He called, these
He also justified; and whom He justified, these He also glorified.
—ROMANS 8:28–30, NKJV

GOD HAS PROPHETIC promise and eternal purpose for those He calls. We see that there are those who are predestined, called, justified, and glorified by the Lord. We also see Jesus being preeminent of many brothers. Regardless of personal hardship, sufferings, disappointments, and bad news, believers can know that God will work in the midst of our circumstance to fulfill His good, eternal purpose in His people. Even if the circumstance or situation doesn't change, know that God will get the glory out of the situation, and He will guarantee success and good outcome as a result.

We are called to be conformed into the image of His Son, Jesus Christ. It doesn't matter what our calling may be as ministers of the Lord. Our destinies are linked in Christ, and we are to be like Him in the earth as His ambassadors, ultimately destined to be with Him eternally when our earthly ministry and purpose is fulfilled. There is a divine purpose on earth, but also there is a glorified purpose as Sons of God. If Jesus is the firstborn of the many brethren, then there are those who have been chosen, predestined, called, and justified before the world came into existence to be glorified with Christ.

I Am Not Eloquent To Speak

There are people who make excuses about their earthly calling and do not realize their divine purpose. Jeremiah complained about his inexperience to speak because of his age, and Moses complained about his inability to speak due to his speech impediment. There are many things that we might not like about ourselves, but God overlooks those things and uses them for His eternal purpose. Just imagine if every called leader in the Bible complained about their circumstance, personal issues, or flaws and let those things keep them from fulfilling the call of God. I don't believe we would be here.

I like the story of Moses, for instance, because he was one that God used regardless of his past and personal imperfections. He was one that God's purpose was fulfilled through, and that's what is imperative. He was used by God as His prophet to bring deliverance and salvation to a people. They needed the Lord to rescue them from the hand of Pharaoh. They needed salvation, and God sent a prophet to do it.

The Bible indicates that Moses had a speech impediment, which caused him to fear the mission that God gave him. In the Book of Exodus, just after Moses had been called by God and told to go to the Pharaoh and lead the Israelites out of Egyptian enslavement, he appeals to the Lord, saying, "Pardon your servant, LORD, I have never been eloquent…I am slow of speech and tongue" (Exod. 4:10). Later in Exodus 4:13 he says, "Pardon your servant, Lord. Please send someone else." God reassures Moses and instructs him to go meet his brother, Aaron, the Levite Priest, who is eloquent and would speak to the people for Moses.

Moses felt that he was unable to speak because of his speech impediment, but Aaron was going to be Moses' prophet, and Moses was going to be like God. Moreover, Moses' excuse was the very thing God judged. The excuse that Moses used became the instrument that God used, which was his mouth to speak to Pharaoh. Moses did not have to declare much but just say to Pharaoh by the authority of God, "Let God's people go." Moses had to prophetically stutter out the word of the Lord to Pharaoh, because his inability, like Jeremiah, was a personal problem, issue, and concern to him.

God used the very thing that he complained and made an excuse about to be the very instrument to cause a nation to be emancipated from Egyptian bondage. The very thing that the devil uses against you, the very thing that you may dislike about yourself, is a secret weapon that the devil uses against a believer to hinder them and cause them not to fulfill what they were born to fulfill.

LACKING CONFIDENCE TO COMMUNICATE

Jeremiah felt insecure about his ability to prophesy because of his age and inexperience, and Moses felt that same way about his speech. I can relate to both of these men. I can remember when I was in middle school I had a very hard time speaking very well. It wasn't that I was not a bright kid; it was just that I lacked self-confidence. I used to mumble frequently, and my mother used to get on me about my speech problem. My mother would always tell me to speak clearly and speak up. I had no self-esteem whatsoever. I was in desperate need of validation due to the fact that I was the middle child and my natural father was not present in my life to cultivate my identity. Therefore, I did not really have any sense of security or purpose. Growing up in a single family home, at times, was like living in my own world. I really did not know how to connect and relate with other people. I was different and peculiar.

I can recall a time that I was in junior high school and my classmates would tease me about my speech problem. When I would speak in front of the class I would talk very fast or talk under my breath. I was the smallest guy in my class, and because of that people would badger, bully, and control me. Little did they know that this little guy from the projects could stand up for himself when challenged. When I would get into fights I would always seem to win, and many would be surprised. People who witnessed the fight were not surprised of my victories but by the profanity that came out of this little guy.

Ironically, I could only speak well when confronted by enemies, but when it was time for me to be heard, I was timid and bashful. I had to realize that God was using circumstances and situations to develop my temperament, character, and personality to be that prophet that He has called me to become. I had to come to the realization that I was *born to speak,* and those who know me, know that I love to share what's on my heart and talk.

The enemy uses those things that I call personal flaws to become giants in my life so that he could silence my voice. I remember receiving a prophetic word from a prophet that God was going to use me to be a great speaker and prophetic orator. I laughed inside about that prophecy when I looked at my current issue, but God was going to make me an eloquent speaker by His Spirit and not by what it looked like then. So, like Jeremiah and Moses, I understood that the very thing that I felt was insignificant was the very thing that God was going to use to be significant for His glory.

That being said, it did not matter what my personal flaws and complexes were. In God's eyes they were not flaws and complexes. They were His perfection and mastered handiwork. We must be careful what we think about ourselves. According to the Bible, "Out of the abundance of the heart the mouth speaks" (Matt. 12:34, NKJV; see also Luke 6:45). That is why we must guard our hearts; out of it flows the cares of life.

YOU HAVE A RIGHT TO SPEAK!

The devil uses what a person says against them. The biggest lethal weapon and enemy of a believer, especially prophets, is ignorance. Why? Because the Bible says that people perish because of the lack of knowledge (Hos. 4:6). I do not believe it is information that people lack, but it's the knowledge of themselves and their purpose in life. The things we sow can be the very things that we reap.

I am reminded of police officers who, when they make an arrest because of probable cause, read the suspect their Miranda rights. If there is anything that causes them to make an official arrest, they begin to read those rights, saying that you have the right to remain silent and that anything you say can and will be used against you. This is what the adversary does to a believer of Christ when he or she makes excuses and complains about something they do not like about themselves or something they were born with. The enemy uses what a person says as an arsenal against the person, but the Lord does the opposite. He uses what you say as a weapon of war on the enemy once the person comes into the revelation that they were born like Christ to destroy the works of the enemy.

One major lesson that every prophet has to grow in and go through is the school of humility. God will take a prophet and prophetic leader through their personal wilderness to overcome pride, conceit, haughtiness, and ignorance in their life. Humility and obedience to the Lord is something that any believer cannot shortcut. Humility is key to honor and promotion. We must understand that we were born on purpose, and God has everything to do with your success here on earth.

Whenever a person is birthed into the earth it is because the earth has need of you and what you are purposed to change in it. God, the Maker of the earth, created it to be inhabited. God did not waste His time creating the earth, nor did He create mankind in vain. It's our kingdom responsibility to see through heaven's lenses to know what's on the heart of the Father and realize His eternal purposes for our lives.

Interestingly, I came across a passage of Scripture that blessed me while writing this book. This verse reveals the heartbeat of God in creating, making, forming and birthing anything. Isaiah 45:18–19 (NKJV) says, " For thus says the Lord, Who created the heavens, Who is God, Who formed the earth and made it, Who has established it, Who did not create it in vain, Who formed it to be inhabited: I am the LORD, and there is no other. I have not spoken in secret, In a dark place of the earth; I did not say to the seed of Jacob, 'Seek Me in vain'; I, the LORD, speak righteousness, I declare things that are right." Isaiah 45:18–19 (THE MESSAGE) speaks of it as, "God, Creator of the heavens—He is, remember, God. Maker of earth—he put it on its foundations, built it from scratch. He did not go to all that trouble to just to leave it empty, nothing in it. He made it to be lived in."

This is the very purpose why the Creator created humanity and wanted a spiritual family to reflect His image and implement the culture of His kingdom into every generation, era, age, and society. The overall plan and destiny of man is that Christ is conformed in us and that we walk in the original purpose, plan, inheritance, godly qualities, and characteristics that the Creator designated to us. Our inheritance is one of dominion only when one has been fruitful, multiplied, filled the earth, and has subdued whatever needed to be put under our subjection in the earth.

We have to realize that before humanity was ever created and birthed out of the Creator's mind and mouth, the Lord created a natural atmosphere for man and created the spheres of dominion for man to rule, function, live, and prosper in. It does not matter if one does not have a calling to be a prophet, apostle, evangelist, pastor, teacher, etc. We must understand that all mankind was given kingly dominion in the earthly realm by God before the earth ever existed and manifested in time (Gen. 2:7–9).

God, who is not locked into time, space, and seasons, planned outside of time and space the destiny of mankind in the natural realm. Before we were born we were predestined to become a kingdom, a chosen people, and a royal, spiritual race to populate the earth with the glory of the Lord. We have been birthed out of prophecies of the Lord. The word of the Lord was spoken on purpose to define man's purpose for living on earth.

A Sure Word of Prophecy

The Father had you on His mind, just like He had Jeremiah on His mind when He called him to prophetic ministry. The word of the Lord came down from heaven supernaturally and manifested itself in earth naturally. Have you ever received a prophetic word and forgot about it, and years later that same word came back full circle? Have you ever received a word from the Lord, and you were so busy doing the work of God that it hit you that you were walking in prophetic fulfillment of that word that was spoken? Have you ever needed a word from the Lord, and it didn't come the way you would like, but it came?

Usually the word of the Lord comes at a time when a person really needs it the most. Jeremiah experienced that same thing. Moses was in the midst of his own wilderness, and the Lord spoke to him by a burning bush. Mary, Jesus' mother, was in need of a word as well, and an angel of the Lord came with a prophetic word.

The word of God will find you just like the word of the Lord found Jeremiah; it took on a prophetic dynamic and function. That word from God was a sure prophecy that solidified his calling and removed all of Jeremiah's doubts about speaking on the Lord's behalf. Moses couldn't use his stuttering complex as an excuse not to prophesy to an Egyptian leader who ruled with an iron fist.

It is very important to understand the dynamic of the prophetic function and how the Spirit of God operates and flows. The word of the Lord came to Jeremiah to do what? It came to lift him up, throw him into, and establish him. That is usually what prophecies or the prophetic word does when it comes to an individual, city, nation, or system. It will lift you up, thrust you into, and establish you by confirmation and revelation.

The word *before,* according to Merriam-Webster's Dictionary, means, "in advance, ahead, at an earlier time, previously."[9] I always say that I would rather know something before than after the fact. There is a saying that goes, "What you don't know will not hurt you," but I believe that what you don't know will hurt you. The Bible says that the people perish because of lack of knowledge (Hos. 4:6). Jeremiah needed to know what God had thought of him before he was born in the Earth. Jeremiah needed to know he was born on purpose.

In addition, God had already in times past knew, appointed, chosen, ordained, commissioned, anointed, and released him into public prophetic ministry; it's just that in due season God made known to Jeremiah His will for his life, and it was up to Jeremiah to answer that call in the timing that God had revealed it to him. Jeremiah's understanding of his prophetic potential had to be altered by a divine encounter by the Lord Himself. In order for Jeremiah to embrace this high calling he needed to be personally trained, mentored, governed, and monitored by the Lord, who called him on purpose.

Being born on purpose, a prophet will go through *intense* personal development, character adjusting, pride, and ego-breaking challenges and deliverance from the fear of man. Prophets encounter almost every condition and realm of society that they will soon face in their own prophetic ministry to confront, contend, transform,

---

9 *Merriam-Webster Dictionary Online,* s.v. "before," http://www.merriam
-webster.com/dictionary/before (accessed May 26, 2013).

deliver over to, and change. Prophets have to first encounter the God of heaven and their Creator and fall out of agreement with what they were used to and come into agreement with their King.

There is more to prophesying than just proclaiming the word of the Lord or being an oracle used of God; prophets communicate with precision and accuracy the mind of God in plain language. In other words, prophets hear, see, smell, feel, sense, taste, and know things in the spirit world, and they are commissioned to translate and transmit what heaven is saying, revealing those things that cannot be seen and releasing them into the natural realm of what God is about to do.

LIVING ON PROPHETIC PURPOSE

To know the purpose of being born, we must understand that we are children of the Most High God, and we are not to walk in darkness. When a person does not know who they are and which direction to go, they are living in darkness, meaning without purpose. We can see in Scripture that at times the people of God knew nothing and understood nothing. They need to be reminded that they were gods, which means that they were spiritual representatives of the Lord in the earth. God is your Father, and we are His spiritual offspring. We have to live life on purpose. If a person doesn't know their purpose, then it is impossible for them to fulfill it. Whatever God created as Creator of the universe was not done by accident but on purpose. When the Father spoke you into existence, your purpose was birthed. Everything in life serves a specific purpose and assignment. Regardless of Moses' speech impediment or Jeremiah's age and inexperience with prophecy, they were born on purpose. We cannot make excuses for why we cannot accomplish anything in life and for the Lord.

Jeremiah 29:11 (GW) says, "I know the plans that I have for you, declares the LORD. They are plans for peace and not disaster, plans to give you a future filled with hope." Jeremiah had a personal encounter with the Lord through a divine intervention and through the counsel of God, and the Lord revealed to him what he was born, assigned, and purposed to do. Jeremiah had to get acquainted with the prophetic ministry by God before he could ever walk as a prophet sent to the nation of Israel. In other words, Jeremiah had to understand his purpose first and know that God had commissioned him to a public prophetic office before he could be ready.

As believers we carry the purpose of God and the DNA of heaven on the inside of us. The Holy Spirit wants to consume our very being and empower us with the necessary power to fulfill that purpose in the Earth and for our generation. I truly believe that the prophetic ministry is instrumental in the plan and purposes of God. God, who is the Creator, used the power of prophetic creativity by faith to bring things into divine order. We have the same prophetic creativity by the Holy Spirit as believers; it is resident in us. We must prophesy and speak those things that are not as though they exist. But first we must by faith possess the prophetic Spirit of God.

Chapter Three

POSSESSING THE PROPHETIC SPIRIT

But Moses asked him, "Do you think you need to stand
up for me? I wish all the LORD's people were prophets
and that the LORD would put his Spirit on them."
—NUMBERS 11:29, GW

P OSSESSING THE PROPHETIC spirit is something that is not limited to those who are sovereignly called to the office of the
prophet, but to those who possess the Holy Spirit indwelling
and habitation. The Holy Spirit is a prophetic spirit, and since every
believer is regenerated by the Spirit of God at the rebirth, each
believer has the innate ability to prophesy to each other.

Nonetheless, due to the fact that there is limited education available on higher levels of the gifts of the Spirit, prophecy, the office of
the prophet, and the supernatural power of God, today in society
we see multi-media campaigns and marketing strategies proclaiming
demonic literature and publications. These materials are usually
about psychics, fortune tellers, new age doctrines, tarot card and
palm readers, astrologers, pornography and adult entertainment,
money schemes, and get-rich-quick systems, which influence the
minds of people and make it difficult for the gospel of the kingdom
to be preached.

I truly believe that the church has seen tremendous breakthroughs
in her ability to integrate its kingdom methods and dynamics to
invade cultures of society and reclaim those pillars for the purpose
of kingdom advancement, colonization, and expansion. Prophetically
the church is expanding in how she engages these cultures and sub-
cultures with heavenly strategies and Holy Spirit–led technology. No
longer will there be a misconception about true prophecy versus

false prediction and readings, the demonic world and angelic spiritual world, prophets of God and false prophets and psychics, the natural versus the supernatural.

In the world most people would think that the prophetic and other Holy Spirit operations are the same as physic perceptions or spiritualist readings. Both are quite different in function and source. Prophets receive supernatural revelation, insight, knowledge, and wisdom *from* God, which is eternally inspired communication media from the Spirit of God, while psychics receive their revelation from familiar and seducing spirits, which gather information about a person that is earthly, carnal, and demonically motivated by gossip, slander, tale-bearing, charm, and greed for money.

I have shared a prophetic word several times to unbelievers by walking in prophetic evangelism, including detailed information about past, present, and future events in their lives, and one of the many questions that I would from unbelievers and unbelieving so called believers would be, "How did you know that? Who told you that about me? How did you do that? And are you a psychic?" I would get very upset about the last question labeling me a psychic. However, I realized that they did not know the difference between a prophet and a psychic. Sadly, the world is familiar with witches, warlocks, psychics, and other demonic and secular terms, but they have no knowledge or idea of prophets, apostles, the prophetic, or knowledge of the Holy Spirit or other biblical realities of the spiritual realm.

JESUS REVEALED IN PROPHETIC EVANGELISM

While I was growing in the prophetic gift and ministry, the Holy Spirit would give me a strategy when I would prophesy to someone who was not a believer and follower of Christ Jesus. When I would do prophetic evangelism, I needed to use Jesus' name frequently in my prophecies. God wanted me to show them the difference between a psychic and myself; I would display, by using the name of Jesus, that my information doesn't come from seducing spirits but the Father of all souls and spirits.

By using this different prophetic strategy in prophesying I would no longer receive questions about me being a psychic, but I would be asked if I was "a prophet or something." The world may not have much knowledge about the prophets, but they know that they're different. A person can sense the prophetic function is Jesus revealing their heart and destiny to them. After prophesying to these unbelievers, I would see the power of God change their lives right before me. I would witness them getting instant deliverance, breakthroughs, and salvation through a prophecy. I call this the power of prophecy. This is what happens when one is consumed with the prophetic Spirit of God and uses the name of Jesus while ministering in love. There is power in the name of Jesus, and I also believe there is power in prophecy when released from a Holy Ghost–filled individual.

Moreover, there are misconceptions regarding the difference between one who is a prophet and one who can prophesy. I will cover that as well later, but this chapter is focusing on possessing a prophetic spirit. Possessing a prophetic spirit will give believers discernment in distinguishing between what is godly and the profane, between truth and error. Upgrading in knowledge, information, and education on spiritual gifts like prophecy and its function will remove and clarify much mysticism, spookiness, and the flakiness that can be prevalent in the prophetic. What a person does not understand, they usually reject. We should not throw out the baby with the bath water without researching and getting a full understanding of the matter.

The prophetic ministry and office has always been misunderstood. Furthermore, I have read many great books written on the subject. I believe now in the twenty-first century that people from around the world have access to thousands of books and resources on the prophetic, and with that we are going to see a major paradigm shift in the prophetic ministry. This paradigm shift is going to happen as God continues to use and raise up genuine apostles, prophets, teachers, and Holy Spirit–filled believers who have a passion for the prophetic and the word of the Lord to impact nations, systems, governments, and earthly kingdoms. There will be concise and foundational truth in the prophetic administration of these gifts. In addition, the Lord is going to continue to raise up in every generation kingdom believers, prophets, and prophetic people who will not only worship God in spirit and truth but also prophesy in spirit and truth.

Furthermore, as we come into more present-day truth and revelation of the significance of possessing a prophetic spirit and the paradigm of the prophetic operation, we are going to see Samuel, Moses, Jeremiah, Elijah, and Elisha-type mantles being activated in new ways in the twenty-first century and in the church today.

YOUR PROPHETIC NAME IS YOUR ASSIGNMENT

One of the biblical patriarchs that I have been intrigued with was Moses, who was the first official prophet of Israel, as well as a shepherd, godly lawyer, legislator, and judge. He was one that instituted Israel's judicial system, new legislation, government, leadership, and their religious system. The prophetic spirit, authority, and anointing upon Moses caused things to shift atmospherically and aquatically while existing in Egypt. Moses was used by the Lord to deliver His people from the merciless regime of Pharaoh and the Egyptian government of the Hebrews.

Even though Moses was being raised in the courts of Pharaoh, who considered him a son, Moses possessed a prophetic name. He was drawn out of water, and his name means "drawn out." Just like Jeremiah's name, which was prophetic in nature to his prophetic assignment to nations and kingdoms, Moses was sent by God to "draw out" the people of Israel from the wilderness. It's interesting that Moses was drawn out of the water when he was a baby, but God would use him to draw the children of Israel out of the desert place as an adult.

Moses was taken out of water, which water represents symbolically the Word of God, refreshing, growth, and is essential for life. One of Moses' assignments as a prophet was to draw the nation of Israel out of enslavement, through water (the Red Sea), which signifies the prophetic word of the Lord delivering them. We can see according to the Book of Exodus that water was the vehicle that became the death penalty for Pharaoh and his army. The prophetic word of the Lord through Moses to Pharaoh became a bridge of crossing for God's people and the cemetery for Pharaoh and his people.

Moses was sent to prophesy the judgment of the Lord to Pharaoh while at the same time bringing salvation through freedom to God's people. Water is equated to the life-giving power of redemption, and Moses was used like a type of Christ and apostle who brought healing, deliverance, redemption, and salvation.

Moses is one prophet that I admire in particular because he was meek, humble, and possessed extraordinary power in the Spirit, which caused deliverance and emancipation for an entire nation that was in bondage. When the prophetic is delivered, it brings deliverance. The prophetic word given to Pharaoh by Moses was the Lord signifying His word with accompanying signs, wonders, and miracles. Moses was the possessor of the prophetic spirit, authority, and power of God as a prophet.

Even though Moses was a prophet, my emphasis is that God used the prophetic to bring deliverance for a people. I have received many personal prophetic words that brought me deliverance and became a bridge to cross over into destiny—and those very same words were a funeral for my past. Moses had a tremendous anointing on his life, so strong that even the Lord wanted him to delegate some of the honor, which in Hebrew means "authority, weight of responsibility, and glory," upon his leadership team. Moses took ownership over the prophetic call and did as the Lord commanded him. (See Numbers 11:24–30.)

A HEART TO IMPART THE PROPHETIC SPIRIT AND AUTHORITY

If a person is not called to stand in the office of a prophet, this does not mean that a believer cannot prophesy or minister the heartbeat of God to another. We must know that the gift of prophecy, spirit of prophecy, the governmental office of the prophet, and other gifts of the Holy Spirit are for the sole purpose of assisting one another in love. This was Moses' burden in regard to the prophetic function. Numbers 11:24–30 is the fulfillment of God's prophetic word to Moses, that he should have assistance in the government of Israel. Moses was an Old Testament type of an apostle and would impart what was on his life and transfer the prophetic spirit to the eldership team. The prophetic spirit is transferable, in contrast to the office of a prophet, which is not transferable. I believe that we all can be prophetic in spirit, but not all are prophets. Moses wished that all of God's people were prophets.

In Numbers we read that, Moses was instructed by the Lord to give a measure of his prophetic spirit to the seventy elders, which were a part of Moses' apostolic team and prophetic presbytery. They discoursed of the things of God so that all who heard them might say that God was with them. Two of Moses' elders, Eldad and Medad, were found in the tabernacle as the rest of the leadership team realized and were aware of their own insecurities and unworthiness. To their surprise the Spirit of the Lord found them in the camp, and there they exercised their gift of praying, preaching, and praising the Lord; they prophesied as moved and possessed by the prophetic Spirit of God.

Prophecy is largely despised today in the twenty-first century because of lack of biblical knowledge and revelation of this gift. I have heard many different teachings on the gift of prophecy, prophets, and the prophetic ministry that brought much confusion, fear, and misunderstanding. But we must see from God's perspective, which is emphasized in the Scriptures, that the gift of prophesying is the most important spiritual gift. Paul considers it vital to the upbuilding of the church at large.

In response, we must ask this serious question, What is the sole role of prophecy for the church today? Prophecy has been despised before. Moses was persuaded that the Lord desired to delegate his governing apostolic authority to a vast number of leaders and called seventy elders to a leadership meeting at the tabernacle. Two of them were absent. The prophetic Spirit of the Lord fell on the sixty-eight who were in attendance. Surprisingly, the Spirit of God also came upon the two who were found left in the camp, and they began to prophesy as well. The people who heard these two elders, Eldad and Medad, reported them out of jealousy and being uncomfortable, since they wanted them to stop prophesying.

Moses' wish that all of the Lord's people were prophets (prophetic) began to be manifest corporately on the Day of Pentecost when the Spirit of the Lord fell on the baby church and prompted them to speak out in tongues, which were the manifestation of the Lord's might. Peter, under the inspiration and influence of the Holy Spirit, interpreted the miraculous outpouring:

> This is what was spoken by the prophet Joel: "In the last days, God says, I will pour out my Spirit on all people. Your sons and daughters will prophesy, your young men will see visions, your old men will dream dreams. Even on my servants, both men and women, I will pour out my Spirit in those days, and they will prophesy."
>
> —ACTS 2:16–18 (QUOTING JOEL 2:28–29)

Peter describes the Pentecost manifestation of tongues as a variety of the prophetic gift at work. The New Testament Scriptures make it clear that the Spirit is a universal gift to the body of Christ and that prophecy is the characteristic gift of the Holy Spirit. The apostle Paul outlined specifically that the ministry gift of prophesying was for every believer: "For you can *all* prophesy one by one" (1 Cor. 14:31, NKJV, emphasis added; see also v. 5, 24). I believe that there is a spiritual renewal and awakening coming to the twenty-first century church in her expectation of the universality of prophecy among those of the kingdom of God.

When we try to start and establish ministries, churches, and believers without this gift being active, it is like trying to swim across the Atlantic Ocean dog-paddling: it can be done, but it will take a lot of time and will be harder to accomplish. We should take in serious consideration Paul's epistle to the Corinthians, in which he writes that the gift of prophesying is indispensable to the church. In this passage the importance of the ministry gift of prophesying is viewed from Paul's passion for it. He goes on to admonish the Corinthian church to "desire earnestly to prophesy" (1 Cor. 14:39, NKJV; see also 12:31 and 14:1).

In all the various lists and discussions of the gifts in Paul's letters the only constant gift is *prophecy*. Whenever Paul makes a point to classify and identify the gifts in terms of importance, prophecy is given preference over all the rest. (See 1 Corinthians 14:1; 1 Thessalonians 5:19.) Only in the two passages of Scripture where Paul speaks of gifted men (prophets) rather than of the gift of prophecy do prophets fall into second rank behind apostles. (See 1 Corinthians 12:28; Ephesians 2:20; 4:11.)

The Spirit of God is not constrained, confined, limited, or restricted to the tabernacle of Moses, but the Spirit of the Lord desires to tabernacle as a covering, protector, and revelator to His people. Just like the wind blows sovereignly where He will, it's up to a believer to move where the wind blows and have an ear to hear what the Spirit of the Lord is speaking. The Bible says to "whoever has ears, let them hear" what the Spirit of the Lord has to say (Matt. 11:15).

Having an understanding of the prophetic and how to operate can be difficult at first, and once the training wheels come off there may be times one may hit and miss through trial and error, but know that with much exercise in that ability to hear and speak, prophesying will become *second nature*.

Never Cease to Prophesy

The two elders of Moses had enough faith to prophesy, sing the song of the Lord, and minister before the Lord within the camp. When the Spirit of the Lord comes upon a person, they are empowered. We can also see in Numbers 11:25 that God came down in a cloud and spoke to Moses and took of the spirit that was on him and mantled the seventy elders with the prophetic spirit. While it rested on them all, they began to prophesy. This passage of Scripture also states that they did not prophesy again; it is discouraging to know that after having an encounter with the Lord and receiving the prophetic spirit to prophesy, they did not prophesy again.

I believe that they couldn't prophesy outside of divine authority, which was placed in Moses. The prophetic spirit needed to be governed, and Moses was the lead elder of Israel. The elders couldn't prophesy without Moses' oversight, and they needed to possess Moses' meek and humble spirit. Just imagine giving a powerful prophetic word for someone in your church or ministry and being moved by the inspiration and unction of the Holy Spirit to minister, but later on, because of unbelief, fear, insecurities, and unworthiness, you do not prophesy ever again from that point on.

I have witnessed in the past that prophets and prophetic people stop prophesying because of past sins, struggles, circumstances, situations, and proclivities that cause their anointing, gifting, and ministry to become inactive or dormant. The enemies of the prophetic are unbelief, fear, pride, rebellion, self-condemnation, a religious spirit, and covetousness. I cannot count how many times God used me to minister to broken, defeated, wounded, prideful, rebellious, bitter, and rejected prophets. The Lord would use the power of prophecy to restore their self-worth, honor, dignity, identity, purpose, and respect. The same Holy Spirit that gives one the unction to function is the same Holy Spirit that can allow a person to overcome personal issues.

Most of the prophets I relate and connect to all tell the same type of story: they were not given the opportunity to prophesy or speak what was on their heart because of something personal. Their current leadership did not understand prophets or the prophetic ministry. This type of negligence done by the senior leader of a church or the prophet themselves can cause internal damage if not addressed quickly. We are not to neglect any gift that has been given to us. We are to be stewards over that which the Lord has given.

PROPHETIC NEGLIGENCE

To neglect your spiritual responsibilities is to deny your own inheritance and birthright as God's ambassador. In the local church, a prophetic culture is established when those with unique gifts of the Holy Spirit are operating under authority. First Timothy 4:14 encourages believers not to neglect the gift that was given by prophecy and with the laying on of hands of the presbytery (eldership team). Holy Spirit gifts are transmitted or transferred through impartation, as we see with Moses and his eldership team receiving the spirit of prophecy.

The Holy Spirit needs to be imparted first before one can prophesy by the Spirit of God. Without the Spirit of God, impartation will be limited in its function, because prophecy is inspired by the Holy Spirit. As gifts are imparted through godly leadership and through the laying on of hands and prophetic words, a person is legally able to operate within the areas of grace, calling, and the measure of rule given by God and confirmed through other authorized witnesses and leaders in the church.

The gift of prophecy is limited in function to exhortation, edification, and consolation, which brings encouragement and strength. The spirit of prophecy is simply sharing the heartbeat of Jesus Christ. We must not operate outside our measure of rule and grace. Every believer can minister prophetically, not just in a capacity limited to words only but through the arts, such as prophetic song, dance, music, and drama.

There should be a prophetic culture established in every local assembly, church, ministry, and nation. I love the prophetic ministry just as I love and need to eat and drink. Why? Because food and drink are essential to our health, well-being, and life. So is the prophetic function, because the prophetic gift is the only gift that brings life and prosperity. The prophetic spirit brings life and nourishment to areas that may be desolate, deprived, and isolated. The prophetic spirit empowers you to do and say things that in your own natural ability and strength you could not do.

I can only imagine what a believer with the prophetic gift can do when they prophesy. The prophetic strength and faith like Samson will be on you to prophesy with power by the Spirit of God. It will have to take humility to operate on this level. I believe a prophet is dangerous to the kingdom of darkness when he or she prophesies, but prophets are more potent when they are silent as well. A prophet's mantle, grace, measure of rule, and jurisdiction are accompanied by an arsenal of angelic ministering spirits. When a prophet or someone with a prophetic anointing prophesies, there are angels released to carry out the word of the Lord. Prophesying is the least a prophet in the office does.

This book is written specially for those who desire to prophesy and to discover their prophetic voice, gift, nature, and spirit. If we as humans all can speak and communicate, even though there are different dialects, accents, and languages, what we have in common is that we can communicate. With that being said, we all are not prophets, but we can all prophesy to communicate what God is saying. Regardless of one's gifting, this book will help believers become sons and daughters of the kingdom who can operate in the prophetic oil and Spirit of God with power and confidence.

ESTABLISHING THE PROPHETIC SPIRIT ON THE LEADERSHIP

Moses wanted to see the elders function in the prophetic because he knew it impacted his own life. How many leaders today have a heart like Moses to give what they have and impart some of it to the next leadership? Moses was not afraid of any such effects from the prophetic spirit that was placed on the seventy by God. Moses desired that the Lord's people were prophets. In other words, Moses desired that they be possessed by the prophetic spirit. It should be every leader's desire and passion to see their people, congregation, leadership team, and spiritual sons and daughters move in the prophetic dimension.

Moses wished that every individual person among the people of Israel were prophets. These prophets were to be either extraordinary or ordinary as ministers of the word. Since if all became prophets there would be none to prophesy to or to teach and instruct (likewise, all would be not rulers or helpers and assistants in government, for then there would be none to be governed), Moses' statement is to be taken comparatively and is designed to show how far Moses was from an envious spirit in regard to the gifts of others. His wish, if it was the will of God and consistent with the order of things, was that every man had as great or greater gifts than he had, therefore qualifying them for public service and usefulness. This was the modesty and meekness of Moses. There is a sense indeed that all the Lord's people, all good men, are and should be prophets, and by the grace of the Spirit of God they are qualified.

Senior leaders, if you are raising up an apostolic and prophetic house, start equipping, training, recognizing, activating, and releasing those called to the prophetic ministry and office of the prophet. The prophetic is vital to the growth and spiritual climate or temperature of a local church. Things are birthed when we speak what God desires to speak; it will happen through prayers, fasting, and worship unto God. God wants to speak to His people on an individual level and corporate level. God loves to deliver His word to people who are ready to transition and go beyond the mundane and familiar.

Eagles' Wings

In Exodus 19:3–5 (NKJV) it reads, "And Moses went up to God [Elohim], and the LORD called to him from the mountain, saying, "Thus you shall say to the house of Jacob, and tell the children of Israel: 'You have seen what I did to the Egyptians, and how I bore you on eagles' wings and brought you to Myself. Now therefore, if you will indeed obey My voice and keep My covenant, then you shall be a special treasure to Me above all people; for all the earth is Mine.'"

This bird is the king of the heavens and has keen vision and the ability to soar to great depths and heights. The Lord is all-knowing and all-seeing, and like the eagle's vision, the Lord's prophetic vision for the children of Israel was their full release and liberty. One of God's burdens for His people was that they would come unto to Him again and not worship any other gods. The primary function of the prophetic is to redeem and turn the people's heart back to the Lord. I call this "prophetic deliverance." It was the power of the prophetic spirit and the Holy Spirit upon Moses that brought transition to a depressed and restricted people.

In the days of Samuel the prophet we see that King Saul was being inaugurated in the kingly office. Samuel was instructed by God to anoint Saul as king over His people. God wanted to be their king, but they wanted to be like other nations, so God chose Saul. After being commissioned as king by Samuel, Saul encountered a company of prophets, and the Spirit of God filled him. He began to prophesy with the other prophets. One doesn't have to be a prophet to prophesy, but King Saul prophesied like the prophets he encountered at Gibeah. He was possessed with the prophetic spirit and prophesied without any prior or former experience.

This Holy Spirit impartation and these encounters are something God desires His people to take ownership of. Moses gave some of the honor that was upon him to Joshua, who was full of the spirit of wisdom through the laying on hands and the prophetic word. As

Moses laid his hands on Joshua and charged him, Joshua received the impartation of the Spirit of God and walked in the authority of Moses.

Joshua was possessed by the Spirit of God through the power of impartation, which caused him to possess authority. We must understand that Joshua already possessed the spirit of wisdom before he was commissioned by Moses. Moses, being an Old Testament type of Christ, was used as a deliverer for God's people. There is deliverance, healing, and freedom through the word of the Lord.

Chapter Four

DELIVERANCE, HEALING, AND LIBERTY THROUGH GOD'S WORD

You have seen what I did to the Egyptians, and how I bore you on eagles' wings and brought you to Myself. Now therefore, if you will indeed obey My voice and keep My covenant, then you shall be a special treasure to Me above all people; for all the earth is Mine.
—Exodus 19:4–5, NKJV

THE PROPHETIC WORD of the Lord will always bring deliverance from strongholds, struggles, yokes, and religious or worldly bondages. God promised that He would deliver His people through His word and used a mediator (Moses) as the prophet, intercessor, and judge to deliver the word of God to Pharaoh. The children of Israel were sold into slavery and were harshly oppressed by the Egyptians for over four hundred years. They continually cried out to God, and He heard them each time they lifted up their voices to Him.

When it was time for them to be delivered, just as God promised beforehand, He used the imagery of an eagle to refer to Himself delivering them from the Egyptians' grip. Three months after they were delivered God reminded them of His quick deliverance by calling their attention back to the imagery of the eagle. He said, "You have seen what I did to the Egyptians, and how I bore you on eagles' wings and brought you to Myself" (Exod. 19:4, NKJV). The nourishing and all-seeing eye of the Lord, like an eagle's, is swift and focused to deliver, bringing justice and emancipation to those who have faced demonic, civil, societal, domestic, and religious injustices. God delivered the children of Israel by His word, just like the prophetic does when it comes to an individual. The prophetic word comes with the power to deliver as it is being delivered to the recipient.

SEASONS OF RENEWED STRENGTH

The prophetic brings deliverance to people who may be in a season of transition or in a valley of decision; they may even be in a place of bondage or enslavement personally, mentally, economically, socially, financially, domestically, relationally, psychologically, physiologically, spiritually, religiously, and emotionally. The prophetic is like eagles' wings to bear one up and bring them into another dimension that they have not been to or known before. The prophetic brings change, freedom, and restoration. Simply, deliverance is going from one state to another or one place to another. In addition, the prophetic nature and dimension of God is that one is being prophetically transformed and reformed.

Isaiah 40:31 says, "But those who hope in the LORD will renew their strength. They will soar on wings like eagles; they will run and not grow weary, they will walk and not be faint." The prophetic word of the Lord gives a person new life, because the words that Jesus said that He speaks are spirit life or spirit and life. Have you ever received a powerful prophetic word and felt like you could soar and go higher? Or perhaps the prophecy made you feel anew and refreshed. God's prophetic word gives strength to run, walk, and do things supernaturally by faith in God, without unbelief and doubt. The prophetic strength usually comes at times when one is faint at heart and weary.

Exodus 19:4–5 (NKJV) says, "You have seen what I did to the Egyptians and how I bore you on eagles' wings and brought you to Myself. Now therefore, if you will indeed obey My voice and keep My covenant, then you shall be a special treasure to Me above all people; for all the earth is Mine." You can see that God was reminding the children of Israel of His word and His covenant for them to keep. When a person receives a prophetic word from the Lord personally and/or through a prophet of God, one must understand that it's conditional. At times it may be unconditional, but typically most prophetic words are conditional. God is requiring complete cooperation and obedience to fulfill His eternal purpose for your life.

Moreover, God told the Israelites to obey His voice, meaning serving no other gods or substitutes and to keep His covenant, meaning His Word, commands, and will. That scripture makes it clear that once they had done what the Lord had commanded, then they would be marked as a special treasure to God above all nations and people in the earth, because the earth is the Lord's. When I am going through and I am weary, I always have to mediate on past prophetic words and promises of the Lord and do a self-audit for the purpose of walking in obedience, thereby discerning the right season and timing of the Lord. Some prophetic words can take years to fulfill and some a lifetime. Even so, some prophetic words may be through the next generation or your natural and spiritual posterity, which is called a legacy.

When I go back in my mind and recall old prophetic words that I have received from seasoned prophets and prophetic leaders, the words give me new strength and new wings to soar to greater levels in God. In addition, the previous prophetic words still have a tangible anointing on them, as when I first received it.

HEALING IN HIS WINGS

Malachi 4:2 (NKJV) says, "But to you who fear my name The Sun of Righteousness shall arise With healing in His wings; And you shall go out And grow fat like stall-fed calves." The Sun of Righteousness is no other than Jesus Christ. Jesus arose with healing in His wings. Jesus came and delivered His healing to you on the day that you decided to dedicate your life to Him. What healing did He bring to you? Jesus came to you with more than just physical healing.

Please remember that Jesus delivered it to you, but that does not force you to accept it! It is like a parcel delivery. The courier company brings it to you. The parcel is only yours once you sign for it, reach out and accept it. This is why so many are still hurting and sick; Jesus already delivered their parcel, but they have never taken the actual delivery of it.

The first healing that Jesus brought to you was the healing of your soul. He set your soul free from the torment that it had experienced at the hands of the evil one. Jesus totally healed and renewed your soul. In doing that, Jesus removed all the hurts of the past. He mends the brokenhearted as anointed by the Holy Spirit. He sets us free from the curse of death that hangs over the soul of the unbeliever.

The second healing is the healing of the mind. Jesus came into our lives, and we were made a new creation. He changes the way that we think and the way that we view things. He renews our mind. Have you ever received a word from God through a prophet or someone with the resident gifting, and those words echoed in your spirit and mind? It's like regardless of the current circumstances or issues that seemed contrary to the prophetic promise over your life, that word brought assurance, peace, healing, and confidence. The Bible says that "God is not slack concerning his promise" (2 Peter 3:9, KJV).

Finally, the third healing is the healing of our body. He removes all of our sickness away from us. He came that we should have life and life in abundance. Psalm 107:20 says, "He sent out his word and healed them; he rescued them from the grave." We are to be blessed, and one of the greatest blessings of all is to walk in total health and wellness. There is no sickness that is too bad or too far progressed that it cannot be healed through Jesus. The Bible shows us many examples of the healings that Jesus performed while He was on the earth. I have witnessed physical healings and miracles through a spoken word, and I myself have given prophecies to hundreds concerning total healing.

A prophetic word can bring healing to the mind, soul, and body. The eagle is symbolic of independence, but the bird's function is also interdependent with the wind; likewise, the eagle was God's reminder to His people that the children of Israel needed Him for freedom, liberty, and emancipation. The prophetic power of prophecy does that through the power of the Holy Spirit. It is the wind of the Holy Spirit that carries us on eagles' wings to the place of promise and greatness.

LORD, JUST SPEAK THE WORD!

There was a man, a centurion, who had authority in the Bible. He had heard about Jesus and the spiritual authority that He possessed. He traveled to meet Him because there was someone who needed healing or an instant miracle in his house. The man with authority understood that when a person with authority and influence speaks, something has to change, happen, and align itself with that authority.

Moreover, the man met Jesus and told Him about the situation. He asked that Jesus would just speak the word. He understood that because of His authority the person in need of a healing would be healed. Jesus, seeing this man's great faith in all of Israel, spoke the word of healing, and at that very hour the person was totally healed. When the centurion got back to his house the person was healed completely. (See Matthew 8:6–13.) The prophetic word that brought healing was activated in Jesus due to this man's faith in Jesus' authority in speaking healing.

The prophetic had to obey what He said. Faith and the prophetic go hand in hand. In other words, it takes faith to prophesy and declare life to a dead situation. It is really a person's belief system or paradigm in regard to healing, faith, and the word of God that brings deliverance. Jesus had a reputation of healing by His words. The word of the Lord doesn't just bring freedom, but there is transformational power by the prophetic spirit that comes upon a believer and changes their heart and life.

Chapter Five

THE POWER OF PROPHETIC TRANSFORMATION

The Spirit of the Lord will come powerfully upon you, and you will prophesy with them; and you will be changed into a different person.
—1 Samuel 10:6

S AMUEL THE PROPHET was one who instituted the prophetic university and was Israel's last judge. King Saul was in route looking for his father's lost donkeys, but in the process he encountered the prophetic personality of Samuel, who at a very young age was flawless in the prophetic. The whole northern and southern parts of Israel recognized him as an honorable prophet whose words did not fail. King Saul was the people's choice for king, with the sanction of God, who selected him, anointed, and commissioned him through Samuel. King Saul was chosen to be a king and not a prophet, but he himself encountered the spirit of prophecy and was transformed.

First Samuel 10:5–6 says:

After that you will go to Gibeah of God, where there is a Philistine outpost. As you approach the town, you will meet a procession of prophets coming down from the high place with lyres, timbrels, pipes and harps being played before them, and they will be prophesying. The Spirit of the Lord will come powerfully upon you, and you will prophesy with them; and you will be changed into a different person.

King Saul needed to be changed into what he was now going to embrace. There was a prophecy and declaration through Samuel, who represented the voice of God to Saul. Before Saul could carry out such a kingly assignment and mandate he needed to be empowered, employed, and deployed by the Spirit of God. It was prophecy that preceded his position as king over Israel. Moreover, Saul was about to encounter a sudden change that would radically happen in the presence of prophets who were prophesying. This change of heart that he was going to experience would also change the way he was going to govern the people. Saul's heart needed to be changed in order for him to be a godly king and not like other kings of other nations.

Transformation was something that needed to be done. God didn't want Saul to have the same nature as other kings, which caused the people to want to have their own king instead of God being their King.

SPIRIT OF TRANSFORMATION

According to the Merriam-Webster Dictionary, of *prophecy* is "an inspired utterance of a prophet…a prediction of something to come."[10] The verb form, *prophesy,* means "to speak or utter by divine inspiration" and "to predict with assurance."[11] Again, we see that in 1 Samuel 10:5–6 Samuel gave Saul detailed words of knowledge, wisdom, and insight into who Saul was going to see at the next city, that he was going to see a group of prophets with musical instruments prophesying or ministering in prophetic songs of God.

> After that you will go to Gibeah of God, where there is a Philistine outpost. As you approach the town, you will meet a procession of prophets coming down from the high place with lyres, timbrels, pipes and harps being played before them, and they will be prophesying. The Spirit of the LORD will come powerfully upon you, and you will prophesy with them; and you will be changed into a different person.

---

10   *Merriam-Webster Dictionary Online,* s.v. "prophecy," http://www
.merriam-webster.com/dictionary/prophecy (accessed May 27, 2013).
11   *Merriam-Webster Dictionary Online,* s.v. "prophesy," http://www
.merriam-webster.com/dictionary/prophesy (accessed May 27, 2013).

The passage of Scripture above states that Saul was going to cross paths with a procession of prophets coming down from the high place ministering in prophetic worship. They would be prophesying, and the Spirit of God would come on him in power. He would prophesy with them and would be changed into a different person due to this encounter. Samuel prophesied accurately the intentions and purposes of God to a king who needed to be anointed for this great work. We see in this passage of Scripture that it is the Spirit of God that causes change in a person's life. It took a prophetic word to align Saul with heaven's plan. He needed to be employed and deployed by the Spirit of God. Being a king of Israel wasn't a job or career opportunity, but now it was a lifestyle that God needed him to embrace, understand, and walk in.

As king of Israel, Saul needed the prophetic spirit, wisdom, and counsel of the Lord. I have witnessed in my own life how prophecy has changed the very existence of my heart and destiny. There have been times when I wasn't clear about a specific assignment and what I needed to be doing in a particular season. The prophetic word came and brought clarity. It is as if Saul went to a prophetic gathering and conference, and after leaving that conference he was changed into another person.

The prophetic encounter changes the hearts of men. Have you ever received a prophetic word that changed your life? Have you ever been in a meeting of prophetic minstrels, musicians, prophets, psalmists, and leaders that stirred something on the inside of you to speak? If you have never experienced the prophetic or prophecy by the Spirit of God, I would recommend that you be baptized by the Holy Spirit to receive this gift from God. The prophetic function is imperative when one receives the Holy Spirit. In the Bible, when a person received the Holy Spirit they would speak in tongues, and they would prophesy.

Moreover, when a person encounters the ministry of the Holy Spirit, usually tongues follow first and then prophetic utterance. I have seen Pentecostal believers and different denominations operating only in tongues but being limited in prophecy. I remember challenging a person in the prophetic who was a Pentecostal. This individual had a genuine call to the prophetic ministry and also spoke in tongues quite frequently. However, when I asked that person to give me a prophetic word, they got offended and stated that they were a prophet of God and did not need to prove themselves to me. My reply to that person was that prophets of God hear and speak what is on the heart of God to His people. I cannot understand tongues, but I can understand prophecy in my native tongue.

I also went on to say that tongues are a sign for unbelievers, but prophecy is a sign for the believer (1 Cor. 14:22). I believe that comment from the young man was an excuse not to prophesy, further exemplifying the limited understanding of the gifts of the Spirit in general and how these gifts operate within the church or for the believer. The way this individual developed a mature prayer language in tongues is the same faith needed to mature in prophecy or prophesying. In other words, it took a yielding vessel to speak in other tongues, so it takes a yielding vessel to minister in the prophetic.

Prophecy Is a Sign to Believers

First Corinthians 14:22–25 (NKJV) says:

> Therefore tongues are for a sign, not to those who believe but to unbelievers; but prophesying is not for unbelievers but for those who believe. Therefore if the whole church comes together in one place, and all speak with tongues, and there come in those who are uninformed or unbelievers, will they not say that you are out of your mind? But if all prophesy, and an unbeliever or an uninformed person comes in, he is convinced by all, he is convicted by all. And thus the secrets of his heart are revealed; and so, falling down on his face, he will worship God and report that God is truly among you.

We can see clearly that tongues are a sign to unbelievers, but prophecy is a sign for believers. The apostle Paul's use of Isaiah 18:11–12 notes how the harsh, unknown tongues of foreign invaders during Isaiah the prophet's day was a sign of God's divine judgment upon Israel that they completely scoffed at and rejected. So Paul was making a comparison of tongues during Isaiah's day and noted how tongues in operation in the Corinthian church could have the same effect of hardening believers who were present whose response and receptivity to the sign of tongues might be, "You are out of your mind or insane." We can see the same type of reaction and expression from unbelievers witnessing the move of the Spirit and birth of the church on the Day of Pentecost in the Book of Acts. (See Acts 2:13.)

However, prophecy, on the other hand, is a sign to believers, leading them to repentance. I believe that with the infilling of the Holy Spirit we can witness a dual function and manifestation of tongues followed by prophecy. My point to the young man was that one who speaks in a tongue does not speak to men but to God, for no one understands him; however, in the spirit he speaks mysteries. Accordingly, he who prophesies speaks edification and exhortation and comfort to men. In addition, the Scriptures tell us that he who speaks in a tongue edifies himself, but he who prophesies edifies the church (1 Cor. 14:2–4). As Holy Spirit-filled believers we must move beyond just tongues only and into the prophetic dimension to edify, exhort, and comfort others as well (the church).

We read in 1 Corinthians 14:5 (NKJV) says, "I wish you all spoke with tongues, but even more that you prophesied; for he who prophesies is greater than he who with tongues, unless indeed he interprets, that the church may receive edification." In other words, Paul wanted this gifted church to be in order when it comes to gifts of the Holy Spirit, tongues and especially prophecy. This church was so gifted that they needed to be governed by the Holy Spirit in love and under apostolic supervision. They needed to know the purpose of operating in these gifts, and he wished that this church would be a prophetic community, assembly, or local church.

TONGUES AND PROPHECY

The prophetic element was needed because it edifies, exhorts, and comforts the church as a whole. While tongues are necessary to edify oneself in the faith and in worship, the gift of prophecy is greater because everyone can hear, learn, and be encouraged. If a person speaks in a tongue and there is no interpretation following, then prophecy is greater for the purpose of edification. There is no reason to speak exclusively in inspired tongues if there are not any prophetic words following.

Tongues exercised in a church gathering must therefore be interpreted. So if one decides to yell out in tongues in a public meeting, that person bears the responsibility of interpretation. (First Corinthians 12:10 permits diversity in these two gifts of the Holy Spirit.) If no interpreter is present, the tongue is to be restrained, as we read in 1 Corinthians 14 and verse 28 (NKJV), which says, "But if there is no interpreter, let him keep silent in church, and let him speak to himself and to God." What this is saying is that you can speak to yourself and God in tongues, but there has to be an interpreter; but if there is not, keep silent and minister to God in tongues. We have to understand the operation of these gifts in the church and how to use them properly. The gift of tongues has its place privately, but the gift of tongues *along with* prophecy has its place publicly or corporately.

There have been times when I have heard people speak in tongues and give little or no prophetic words at all. I would not discourage them because the desire is there to minister the word of the Lord, but I would tell them to worship the Lord with some holy anointed music, go into the spirit (speak in tongues), and wait on any strong or light impression on their senses. Then share what they saw, heard, felt, discerned (sensed), and tasted. It's important for prophets and prophetic people to learn to stir up the gift of God on the inside of them, and usually worship in music, word, and in the tongues will uncap the prophetic gifting by the Spirit for a Holy Spirit-filled believer to prophesy.

Notice that I said Holy Spirit-filled believers; you must believe that you can prophesy for God. Prophecy is the result of being filled with the Holy Spirit. In Luke 1:67, we read that Zacharias had been stricken unable to speak because of his confession of unbelief. He was dumb until his tongue was loosed through the infilling of the Holy Spirit. In addition, he not only spoke a few words for the first time in several months, but he also prophesied.

There have been times when I have prophesied to people through friendly evangelism out in the marketplace, and I have seen the convicting power of God touch unbelievers and believers alike. I've come to realize that the prophetic gift is a gift that builds people up. When

Saul came into a prophetic community of prophets, he became prophetic. In other words, if Saul, a future king of Israel, can prophesy, so can you!

The Holy Spirit anoints a person's tongue to speak through more ways than just mere words. I have received prophetic warnings that caused me to escape judgments, sicknesses, and even death. That is why I love the word of the Lord so much when released by anointed vessels; it helped me to change. That is the power of prophetic transformation. Just imagine if I did not take heed to the warning signs and prophetic words to confirm the wrong direction I was going. If I had a rebellious heart and didn't believe the word of the Lord for my life, I might have been incarcerated or even dead. Personally I would rather receive words of correction, rebuke, exhortation, and adjustment that will challenge me to live circumspectly and upright before a Holy God.

LOVE IS ESSENTIAL IN THE PROPHETIC GIFT

First Corinthians 13:2 (NKJV) states, "And though I have the gift of prophecy and understand all mysteries and all knowledge, and though I have all faith, so that I could remove mountains, but have not love, I am nothing." The gift of prophecy and other gifts of the Holy Spirit are null and void without love. A person cannot operate in any gifting of the Holy Spirit without love. It's impossible to minister by the power and authority of God without the love of Christ. A changed or transformed heart will cause a person to minister in love by the grace of God and be moved with compassion. How can a person minister in love and vocalize the heartbeat of God if they know not love and possess love? God is love. The Bible says, "Love never fails, but whether there are prophecies, they will fail; whether there are tongues, they will cease; whether there is knowledge, it will vanish away. For we know in part and we prophesy in part" (1 Cor. 13:8–10, NKJV).

Prophetic warnings and rebuke can transform and change a person's heart, motives, and intentions. Just imagine if one did not heed the warnings of the Lord, which is God's unconditional love toward those He loves and those that are His. The Lord chastens those He loves. If God didn't love you and want you to escape from the power of sin, He would never have sent His only begotten Son to save us from the law of sin and death. A prophetic word given in love is a blessing and not a curse.

If the prophetic wasn't important to God, He wouldn't have used and raised up prophets in the Old Testament to declare, foretell, and forth-tell His plans and purposes. I have borne witness and ministered to people who were once unemployed and became employed, were barren and then able to conceive children, sick and made whole, poor who became wealthy, depressed who became happy, in religious bondage or captivity and became liberated and transformed by the prophetic word of God. Prophecy can radically change a person's life in twenty-four hours. The word of the Lord transforms lives. It did for Saul when he left the presence of Samuel the prophet and encountered God through the prophetic atmosphere created through worship by the prophets.

Acts 1:8 says, "But you will receive power when the Holy Spirit comes on you; and you will be my witnesses in Jerusalem, and in all Judea and Samaria, and to the ends of the earth." This indicates that when the power of the Holy Spirit comes on a person, that person is immediately changed, transformed, and different by nature. Moreover, we see in Acts 19:1–7 that in the early church Paul, an apostle of Jesus Christ at Ephesus, found some religious persons who looked to Jesus as the Messiah. They had not been led to expect the miraculous powers of the Holy Ghost, nor were they informed that the gospel was especially the ministration of the Spirit. Paul disclosed to them that John never planned that those he baptized in water, or what I call "John's baptism," would stay there, but he told them that they should believe on Him who should come after him, that is, on Christ Jesus. They accepted the infilling of the Spirit and experienced new discovery of truth, and they were baptized in the name of the Lord Jesus.

UNDER THE PROPHETIC INFLUENCE

The Holy Ghost came upon them in a surprising, overpowering manner. They began to speak with tongues and prophesied, as the apostles and the first Gentile converts did. The people that received an infilling by the Spirit of God and the message that was presented to them by Paul were under the influence of the Spirit, and they were immediately changed. This was evidence that the power of the Spirit caused them to speak with tongues and prophesy as moved by the Spirit of God.

These believers of Christ received the baptism of Christ, which was by the Holy Spirit and not through John's baptism by water, which they formerly experienced. They were filled by and through the hands of Apostle Paul. They received the full measure of the Spirit of God. Acts 19:6 (NKJV) says, "And when Paul had laid his hands on them, the Holy Ghost came on them, and they spoke with tongues and prophesied." Paul, through apostolic impartation, laid his hands upon them. It seemed proper that these men should not only enjoy the ordinary influence of the Spirit but that some supernatural, spiritual gifts would be transferred and imparted as well. Their lives were transformed when they encountered the supernatural nature of the Spirit, which caused them to speak in other languages and prophesy. (See Acts 8:17; Romans 1:11.)

HIS DIVINE WITNESS

The Holy Spirit comes to change the nature of a person and superimpose His prophetic spirit on them. In the Book of Acts there was also a prophetic word in regard to the promise of the Holy Spirit and the birthing of the church in the first century. In Acts 1:8 the prophetic promise was that when the Holy Spirit came on an individual, he or she would be His witness. It took this prophetic dimension to birth the church. The Holy Spirit was sent to those first believers in the Upper Room, and they were transformed when there was a sound of a mighty rushing wind (Acts 2:2).

We become divine witnesses when we are endowed by His Spirit. It is the spirit of holiness that comes on us and dwells on the inside of His people that makes them witnesses of His power and love in the earth. King Saul needed the transforming Spirit of God to anoint and appoint him as king over His people Israel. When Saul encountered the transforming prophetic spirit, which was the Spirit of the

Lord, empowerment came for him to prophesy in worship like the prophets that came down from the high place. He was so transformed that others who knew him formerly thought he was a prophet.

Note that Saul was a king and not called to be a prophet. Even though Saul prophesied, he was not a prophet and did not walk in the same authority as that of Samuel. I have come across dozens of people who think that they are prophets because they prophesy, but this assumption is biblically incorrect. The prophetic office takes on a greater capacity and anointing than simply the possessing the spirit of prophecy and the gift of prophecy. If that were the case, the whole church at Corinth would have been loaded with prophets. There are senior leaders who may not be prophets but desire to come in contact with a prophetic environment by ministering first to the Lord, and then the gift of prophecy will be able to flow like a river the words from God.

I am reminded of someone who smokes cigarettes. If a person who doesn't smoke themselves but comes in contact with the smoke, the person can experience the same results as if they took the cigarette up to their own mouth. They call it secondhand smoking, and secondhand smoking is just as dangerous as smoking yourself; the effects are more or less the same.

So, Saul the king came in contact with the prophetic glory cloud that was created by the company of prophets. When he came in contact with that prophetic culture and environment, it was secondhand prophecy that kicked in. I call it a "prophetic hangover."

Ministering Unto God Releases His Voice

The prophets came down from the high place, which was the place of worship, so they were in a realm that caused anyone that came in contact with that prophetic climate to be radically and externally transformed. Prophets know how to minster unto the Lord first before they come out and give prophetic words. Samuel was a young, emerging prophet who ministered unto the Lord. Samuel ministered before the Lord and did not know Him personally. He served and ministered unto the Lord faithfully. He was found before the ark of God at Shiloh (1 Sam. 2:18; 3:1–21). Jesus ministered unto His Father in prayer. Paul ministered unto the Lord in prayer and with tongues of angels (1 Cor. 13:1). Prophets learn how to serve the Lord before they minister to others. The word *minister* simply means "to serve."

It is important to know that what prophets prophesy comes from the place of intimacy with the Father. There is no way a true prophet of God can come out of intense worship, prayer, fasting, and devotion in the Word with an inaccurate word. During ancient times, if a prophet would come out and give a word and it wasn't from the Lord, they would be stoned to death. Before any leaders come before the people to minster they must first minister to the Lord.

The word minister is simply to serve the Lord. Every believer is called of the Lord to do something and must learn how to minister to the Lord first before they are used to minister to people. Usually, I see people minister to people, and then when in times of trouble they go running back to the Lord to be ministered unto.

A person can discern when a person is changed, even if it's bad or good. The point I am making is that prophets are changed and transformed. In other words, the person's nature changes, and they are not the same person. The prophetic Spirit of Jehovah manifested itself in the prophesying of the prophets who Saul encountered, and it passed over to Saul so that he would prophesy along with them (1 Sam. 10:13).

Furthermore, Saul was entirely transformed by the Spirit of God. What is transformation biblically? Romans 12:2 (KJV) says, "And be not conformed to this world: but be ye transformed by the renewing of your mind, that ye may prove what is that good, and acceptable, and perfect, will of God." In fact, the traditional meaning of the word can be found in Matthew Poole's commentary from the 1600s, which exhorts: "Be you regenerated, and changed in your whole man; beginning at the mind, by which the Spirit of God worketh upon the inferior faculties of the soul."[12] Matthew Henry's commentary further expounds, "The progress of sanctification, dying to sin more and more and living to righteousness more and more."[13]

---

12   Matthew Poole, *Matthew Poole's Commentary on the Whole Bible* (Edinburgh: Banner of Truth Trust, 1700, 1990), s.v. "Romans 12:2."
13   Matthew Henry, *Exposition on the Old and New Testaments* (1706), s.v. "Romans 12," accessed May 27, 2013, at BibleStudyTools.com.

Spiritual Renewal and Transformation

The Greek word for "transformation" is *metamorphoo*, from which we get the English word *metamorphosis*, which refers to a complete change, such as a caterpillar turning into a butterfly. The New Testament Greek word *metamorphoo* is a verb founded in four places meaning "to transform" and "transfigure."[14] We can see its meaning in Mark 9:2 and Matthew 17:2 in regard to biblical transformation and transfiguration. Prophetic transformation can be a spiritual *metamorphoo* through prophecy that a believer receives through spiritual renewing of the mind and being transformed into the likeness of Christ. (See Romans 12:2; 2 Corinthians 3:18.) One of the dynamic aspects of prophecy is that it brings renewal and refreshing. Biblical transformation, then, applies to an individual believer's progress in sanctification.

According to the Merriam-Webster Dictionary the word *transform* means "to change in structure...appearance...[or] character."[15] It has a more distinct definition in regard to Saul, who was converted by the Spirit of God. The Holy Spirit gives believers an extreme makeover by the Spirit. One is changed internally, and then the change is witnessed by others externally. Prophecy, as I shared before, can cause a person to receive deliverance, healing, salvation, and a transformed lifestyle. Jesus Himself depended on the Holy Spirit to empower, anoint, and enable Him to do great signs and wonders.

The Spirit of the Lord Empowers, Equips, and Anoints

Jesus proclaimed in Luke 4:18, "The Spirit of the Lord is on me, because he has anointed me to proclaim good news to the poor. He has sent me to proclaim freedom for the prisoners and recovery of sight for the blind, to set the oppressed free." Jesus declared that the Spirit of God was upon Him. When the Spirit of God is on an

---

14 New Testament Greek Lexicon, BibleStudyTools.com, s.v. "metamorphoo," accessed May 27, 2013.
15 *Merriam-Webster Dictionary Online*, s.v. "transform," http://www.merriam-webster.com/dictionary/transform?show=0&t=1369672069 (accessed May 27, 2013).

individual, His Spirit covers and mantles them where others will not see, hear, or feel them but sense the presence of God instead. This was true of Saul. Others who knew him personally saw him as different person. He was changed by the Spirit of the Lord. The spirit of prophecy came on him to prophesy. The spirit of prophecy was activated while worship took place at the high place.

There had to be something significant and unique that caused those who looked on to question if Saul was among the prophets. When one encounters the Spirit of God and is regenerated by the Holy Spirit, there is a heart change that takes place immediately, and one is not the same after that encounter in the presence of the Lord. Jesus experienced and understood the importance of being anointed from on high to do what He was sent to do. John the Baptist, the prophetic forerunner of the King Christ Jesus, came in the spirit of Elijah. That type of spirit was a prophetic, transformational spirit that turned the hearts of the fatherless to their fathers and vice versa.

We read in Luke 1:13–17 (NKJV):

> But the angel said to him, "Do not be afraid, Zacharias, for your prayer is heard; and your wife Elizabeth will bear you a son, and you shall call his name John. And you will have joy and gladness, and many will rejoice at his birth. For he will be great in the sight of the Lord, and shall drink neither wine nor strong drink. He will also be filled with the Holy Spirit, even from his mother's womb. And he will turn many of the children of Israel to the Lord their God. He will also go before Him in the spirit and power of Elijah, 'to turn the hearts of the fathers to the children,' and the disobedient to the wisdom of the just, to make ready a people prepared for the Lord."

THE SPIRIT OF ELIJAH

The spirit of Elijah was the prophetic spirit or the prophets' spirit. Elisha asked for a double portion of Elijah's spirit. What was he asking for? Elisha, a son and successor of Elijah, asked for a double portion of Elijah's prophetic spirit to carry out his own prophetic ministry. Elisha followed this man's ministry. He left his family and business behind to pursue his destiny. Elisha needed the impartation and blessing of Elijah to fulfill his calling as a miracle-working prophet.

With any calling a person needs to be trained, monitored, groomed, prepared, challenged, aligned, tutored, mentored, and fathered. Elisha asked not just for Elijah's spirit, but he asked for his inheritance, favor, endorsement, honor, and affirmation as a spiritual son. He wasn't just one of the sons of the prophets at the prophetic university, but he was his protégé. Elijah validated and commissioned Elisha into his ministry. Elisha's ministry was never the same after receiving the double portion of the spirit. He possessed the same spirit of Elijah but in a greater measure. We knew that he received his inheritance because when he hit the water with the mantle it supernaturally parted ways, just like it did for Elijah when he was on earth. When the sons of the prophet saw Elisha from afar, they perceived, discerned, and saw the spirit of Elijah on him (2 Kings 2:6–18).

The spirit of Elijah does what a man could not do on his own; it turns his own heart toward God and toward his family. We must understand that the spirit of Elijah is a prophetic spirit signifying an Old Testament type of the power of the Holy Spirit represented in the New Testament.

John the Baptist came in the spirit of Elijah, and his message was a message of repentance, which means to turn away from, make a decision, to change, reform, to reconsider, to reevaluate and to change in one thought, paradigm, heart and attitude. His message, accompanied with the Holy Spirit, was a message of transformation and reconciliation. Even though there is no record biblically that John the Baptist operated in miracles like Elijah of old, the urgency of his message to that first century generation to reform, change, or make an immediate decision was miraculous in itself.

A CHANGE OF HEART

Then the Spirit of the LORD will rush upon you, and you will prophesy with them and be turned into another man. Now when these signs meet you, do what your hand finds to do, for God is with you. Then go down before me to Gilgal. And behold, I am coming down to you to offer burnt offerings and to sacrifice peace offerings. Seven days you shall wait, until I come to you and show you what you shall do." When he turned his back to leave Samuel, God gave him another heart. And all these signs came to pass that day.

—1 SAMUEL 10:6–9, ESV

King Saul is one of the most memorable characters in the Bible. Even as a youth Saul was the kind of guy you'd choose to be a leader. He was tall, handsome, and well liked. He was the son of a powerful Benjamite called Kish. The first time we encounter Saul he is searching for some of his father's donkeys that had wandered off. He was gone so long and so far on his search that he became concerned that his father would worry about him (1 Sam. 9:3–14). As a last resort, Saul and his servant enter the city where Samuel, the man of God, is living and worshiping, and that is where Saul's life is changed.

At the beginning of Saul's story we don't see the enraged enemy of young David, nor the prideful king who rejects God's commandments not to keep the spoils from pagan enemies. What we see here in this First Book of Samuel is a young man chosen by God to be the first king of His people, a man destined to unify the tribes and conquer the Promised Land of Canaan. This thoughtful young man Saul is to become King Saul of Israel. God alone is the one able to make the necessary changes to turn him into someone who would accomplish God's will.

Then I will give them one heart, and I will put a new spirit within them, and take the stony heart out of their flesh, and give them a heart of flesh, that they may walk in My statutes and keep My judgments and do them; and they shall be My people, and I will be their God. But as for those whose hearts follow the desire for their detestable things and their abominations, I will recompense their deeds on their own heads," says the Lord GOD.

—EZEKIEL 11:19–21, NKJV

God desires to give us a living, beating heart for Him. That's what He did for Saul, transforming the young Saul into a king worthy to lead Israel. The Lord will bless those who embrace their new heart and know that God is the one true, living God. When we follow the signs God sends us, when we meet His Word at the intersection of our will and His, then we will be changed into a new creation (2 Cor. 5:17) and whatever we do, God will be with us.

The above Scripture gives a picture of how the Lord will deal harshly with those who refuse their God-given heart and who return to their fleshly desires and appetites. When we depart from God's will to follow our own desires, when our hands are led by our head instead of our God-given heart, then God will not be with us to strengthen us nor protect us.

That is what happened to Saul. He allowed his heart to return to its old form, following his own pride. God withdrew His blessing and gave it to the shepherd boy David. Although David also had his personal problems, he kept his humility and his heart toward God. David was able to come back to the Lord because he knew that God would forgive him.

So when the Lord calls us and offers to change our hearts, how will we respond? When He says, "Follow Me," will we drop everything and keep following Him no matter what may happen? Will we put aside our pride and our earthly desire for wealth, power, or success? Will we take up our cross daily to follow Christ? Is it our desire to walk in the ways of the Lord and to heed to His voice?

After Saul left Samuel that day, he went among some prophets and started prophesying, too, just as Samuel had foretold. When Saul's friends saw him prophesying, they were amazed at the change in him. They even wondered if Saul was going to stay among the prophets. Saul's friends recognized that this was a brand-new Saul. Are we so transformed that our family, peers, coworkers, and others hardly recognize us? Once we are transformed, then we can be on the prophetic cutting edge of what God is doing in the earth.

Chapter Six

BEING ON THE PROPHETIC CUTTING EDGE

And the sons of the prophets said unto Elisha, Behold now, the place where we dwell with thee is too strait for us. Let us go, we pray thee, unto Jordan, and take thence every man a beam, and let us make us a place there, where we may dwell. And he answered, Go ye. And one said, Be content, I pray thee, and go with thy servants. And he answered, I will go. So he went with them. And when they came to Jordan, they cut down wood. But as one was felling a beam, the axe head fell into the water: and he cried, and said, Alas, master! for it was borrowed. And the man of God said, Where fell it? And he shewed him the place. And he cut down a stick, and cast it in thither; and the iron did swim. Therefore said he, Take it up to thee. And he put out his hand, and took it.
—2 Kings 6:1–7, KJV

THOUGH LIFE CAN sometimes throw a curve ball when we least expect it, we still have to remain consistent to what our passions are and what we've been born to accomplish. There may be times where we are toiling and laboring in a particular area of our lives and sometimes feel that what we are trying to accomplish is not getting us anywhere. We can become fatigued, restless, and drained if we don't have the necessary reinforcement and resources to be successful. I know personally in my own Christian walk that I have not been so successful and faithful to what life expected. At times people, places, and things became a priority and not my God-given assignment.

Many believers have found themselves, like I once did, working to pay bills and working to make someone successful; meanwhile your dreams, desires, and passions sit on the back of the shelf until you receive a revelation that it's time to dust off those dreams and breathe on them again. There are also people who are in their sphere of activity and love what they are doing, but at the same time life throws them a curve ball, which can put that big project or dream on halt until further notice. There are people who have left the very thing they loved and were passionate about only to find themselves in awkward situations and circumstances.

Losing Your Passion and Zeal

The world is constantly evolving, changing, and upgrading to keep up with current trends and the competition. These things can be demanding on a person who has been doing the same thing for years and doesn't embrace change very well. Meeting high demands in the marketplace and the workplace to reach your own business goals, as well as those in the workplace to assist your employer's personal and corporate goals, can be discouraging. How many people have felt like resigning, retiring early, or moving on to something else? Well, we have been there, and it's not good to be doing something great for God and lose your zeal in it. Across the world there are families, marriages, businesses, ministries, churches, leaders, etc. losing their edge because of life struggles.

Usually finances are the key to losing that edge, when in reality God should be the center of one's joy and strength. The Bible says in Nehemiah 8:10, "The joy of the LORD is your strength." My question is, If a person has all the money in the world, would that guarantee success, happiness, fruitfulness, and longevity? My answer is no, if it's without God, who owns the earth, the world, and those who inhabit it. Have you ever lost something and couldn't find it or fell into a particular sin or struggle and felt like you would never recover from that? Have you ever experienced success and literally overnight lost all that you worked so hard for due to a fire, flood, catastrophic events, or just the unexpected death of a relative, friend, or business partner? Whatever it may have been, we all need some level of peace and joy. It's not a good thing to build and labor in something and suddenly lose interest in it.

Something had happened in the process of building, laboring, and advancing in that thing that was so important to you. Losing your effectiveness and edge can cause you to become dull, ineffective, irrelevant, and even obsolete. Regardless of what we may endure personally, we must never lose our edge in the midst of personal setbacks, dilemmas, and problems.

Preparing for Great Expansion

The thing I find interesting about the function of the prophetic is that even if things may seem lost to man with God there is nothing hidden. The prophetic anointing and spirit has the potency to resurrect anything dead, lifeless, and unproductive.

In 2 Kings 6:1–7 Elisha talked about the sons of the prophets, who were understudies and mentees of the Elisha, who I like to think of as the dean, provost, and president of P.U. (Prophets University). The sons of the prophets were in a season where they were preparing for a new construction project and expansion to their residential dormitory to help facilitate critical mass. In addition, in their service and training for their prophetic ministry they had to learn discipline, teamwork, and laboring. While the sons of the prophets were on the job building a new dormitory and cutting wood with an ax, the head of one of the axes fell into the water.

The man who had lost the ax head became distraught because it was borrowed. He cried out to Elisha, and the great prophet performed a miracle. The axe head floated to the surface. The man put out his hand and picked it up as instructed by Elijah.

Now, lest we be too harsh on this poor man who lost the ax head, let us remember that he was engaged in a great work. He was busy! Yet, if there is a flaw in his activity, it is found in this: he was working, but he was not watching! Consequently, he lost the ax head and was unable to continue his work. He had lost his prophetic cutting edge.

THE PROPHETIC BATTLE-AX

In ancient times axes were not just used for cutting wood, but they were used a weapons as well. A prophet has a battle-ax in the realm of the spirit, and when they war, they are very skillful and cunning in their work. A prophet must not lose his ability to fight and contend. The prophet's ministry and mantle can be mass destruction on the kingdom of darkness and anything that opposes the advancement of the kingdom.

Jeremiah had a weapon of war like the battle-ax. It is prophetically outlined in Jeremiah 1:9–10:

> Then the LORD put forth His hand and touched my mouth, and the Lord said to me: "Behold, I have put My words in your mouth. See, I have this day set you over the nations and over the kingdoms, To root out and to pull down, To destroy and to throw down, To build and plant."

We can see in this passage of Scripture that the battle-ax was used "to root out, pull down, destroy and throw down" first before one could build and plant something new. You see, the ax head represents the authority and power to finish the job. No individual can cut down trees by swinging at them with an ax handle. It will take a razor-sharp blade and power to cause the tree to fall. In the church, we need to realize that without our cutting edge, that is, the power of the Holy Spirit, we will never be able to serve the Lord properly, nor will we be able to make an impact in the world and bring societal transformation. We need the strength of the Holy Spirit and His power to get the task done for His glory and cause the kingdom of darkness to be plundered.

Unfortunately, Christianity has become so tied to its traditions, religious manmade systems, and its programs that, for the most part, the cutting prophetic edge has been lost. In addition, there are denominations that refuse to shift gears from the old into the new. This shift is called a paradigm shift. We must change the patterns of our old thought processes and shift into a new, innovative thought process. As kingdom believers, we have to shift from a my-church-only mentality and to a His-kingdom mentality. It's imperative that we stay on the front line of what God is doing in the earth. We serve a God of the new. I believe that we must be relevant in the twenty-first century and move in the power of the Holy Spirit to advance the kingdom of God through new kingdom technologies.

It is imperative that the church move along with the times that we are living in to evangelize the world with the message of the kingdom, not the message of our religious systems and governments. The world is out-thinking the church. We must not become obsolete in what we are doing for God.

THE ISSACHAR ANOINTING: PROPHETIC FORECAST

Due to the fact that there are people who will never experience the spirit of liberty in the Holy Ghost, there will be a form of godliness, but they will deny the power thereof. It's a necessity to have a sons-of-Issachar type of anointing, mantle, and discernment to know what to do in certain seasons and when to act. Let us first define the key words in 1 Chronicles 12:32 (KJV) says:

> And of the children of Issachar, which were men that had understanding of the times, to know what Israel ought to do; the heads of them were two hundred; and all their brethren were at their commandment.

- Issachar: The meaning of this name is "he will bring a reward, man for hire."[16]

- Men: a person, people (Strong's Heb582).

- Understanding: Strong's Concordance explains that *understanding* means "to separate mentally, to distinguish, be cunning, diligently, deal wisely, be prudent" (Strong's Heb998), while Merriam-Webster's Dictionary defines *understanding* as "a mental grasp, the power of

---

16   *Holman Illustrated Bible Dictionary* (Nashville, TN: Holman Bible Publishers, 2003), 852. See also Blue Letter Bible, s.v. "sakar" http://www.blueletterbible.org/lang/lexicon/lexicon.cfm?strongs=H7939

comprehending, esp. the capacity to apprehend general relations of particulars."[17]

- Times: "fortunes, occurrences";[18] *fortunes* mean "portion, abundance of valuable material possessions, resources, prosperity, destiny, fate, wealth and riches," and *occurrence* means "an event, an incident, happenings and circumstance"[19]

- Know: *biynah*, "to discern, understand, perceive and consider" (Heb998)[20]

The Hebrew word for "know" in this verse is *yada*, which is a word that means God gives the personal understanding and revelation, and it is not a knowing that comes from reading someone's book for example.[21] Merriam-Webster's Dictionary defines the word *know* as "to perceive directly, having understanding or direct cognition of, to recognize the nature of, to be acquainted or familiar with, to be aware of the truth of, to have practical understanding of and possessing confidential information."[22]

Furthermore, from the meaning and authority of the name Issachar we see prophetically that those who walk in the character and vocation of Issachar will deliver a sure reward to the Lord, as well as a reward to the sphere of activity they are called to. Their mind is cunning, with the ability and capacity to mentally distinguish between that which is wise and unwise, good and evil. They diligently pursue the comprehension needed to prosper and survive well before the Lord. The prophetic Issachar type of people will

17 *Merriam-Webster Dictionary Online*, s.v. "understanding," http://www.merriam-webster.com/dictionary/understanding (accessed May 27, 2013).

18 *Old Testament Hebrew Lexicon*, s.v. "6256," BibleStudyTools.com (accessed May 27, 2013).

19 *Merriam-Webster's Dictionary and Thesaurus* (Springfield, MA: Merriam Webster Inc., 2007), s.v. "fortunes," "occurrence."

20 Blue Letter Bible, s.v. "biynah," www.blueletterbible.org/lang/lexicon/Lexicon.cfm?strongs=H998 (accessed June 4, 2013).

21 Blue Letter Bible, s.v. "yĕda`," www.blueletterbible.org/lang/lexicon/lexicon.cfm?strongs=H3046&t=KJV (accessed June 4, 2013).

22 *Merriam-Webster's Dictionary and Thesaurus*, s.v. "know."

receive understanding and divine revelation from the Lord Himself, because they know their Lord intimately.

The Issachar prophetic types are wise and diligent. They are able to perceive and seize opportune times of acquiring wealth, success, and favor. Another key word found in 1 Chronicles 12:32 is the word *commandment,* which means in the original Hebrew, "the mouth as the means of blowing, particularly speech; to puff; blow away."[23] As the sons of Issachar walk in revelatory understanding conceived out of direct relationship with the Father, the words of their mouth will possess tremendous power, authority, and a measure of grace, which carries the weight of responsibility to lead others.

Let us look at the father, Issachar, the progenitor of the entire tribe. In Genesis 49 Jacob prophesies to his twelve sons, including Issachar, beginning the prophecy in this way: "Gather yourselves together, that I may tell you that which shall befall you in the last days" (Gen. 49:1, KJV). Jacob was very prophetic and a type of an apostle because he was thinking generationally. He prophesied and blessed his sons. He wasn't only prophesying to them but also to the generations that lived within them, as Jacob was concerned about his posterity and the legacy that would be birthed through them.

Genesis 49:14–15 contains Jacob's prophetic word for his son Issachar, which we, the church, must grasp. The Issachar type of paradigm will accelerate people to move into the next moves of God's Spirit without reservation and hesitation. If the church in the twenty-first century does not upgrade in how she ministers the gospel to the world and stay relevant, innovative, and creative, the church will soon be outdated in her efforts to evangelize effectively and bring in a great harvest of souls in this hour. There have to be prophets and apostles working together as a team with evangelists, pastors, and teachers to advance the purposes of the kingdom. We must stay current to the fresh new moves of the Spirit of God. Having an Issachar mind-set invites the revelatory anointing from the Father.

---

23 Strong's Exhaustive Concordance, s.v. "peh," 6310. See also NAS Exhaustive Concordance of the Bible with Hebrew-Aramaic and Greek Dictionaries, Copyright © 1981, 1998 by The Lockman Foundation — All rights reserved — http://www.lockman.org; http://biblesuite.com/hebrew/6310.htm (accessed July 10, 2013).

Never Remain Dull

Just like the sons of the prophets at "Prophet University," we must know what time it is and accommodate the tremendous growth that is coming. In the midst of building and working, one of the sons of the prophets lost their zeal, strength, authority, power, position, and head. How many leaders have taken a swing at something with all that was within them, and while hitting their target, lost themselves in the process? It is our kingdom responsibility to remain sharp and ready for the next move of God. There are many believers around the world who have lost their edge and have remained stuck in one place, church, teaching, job, etc. They lost their ability to find themselves and get back in the race.

This causes the church, the lives of the believer, and anything we do to lose power. We cannot lose our cutting edge. To be prophetic is not just speaking for God; it is also knowing what to do next. If a person knew what they were to do next, I believe most people would get there faster. Unfortunately, there are times we do not have all of the answers to our destiny, but those answers reside in God. God's prophetic promises are a sure word of prophecy, and we must walk in prophetic fulfillment of them. To stay relevant, we must stay in relationship with our heavenly Father, who will keep us current. Sadly, most of what we do in the church can be done without the agency or the power of the Holy Spirit. We are so good at what we do that we can operate in the power of the flesh and no one notices the absence of God. I believe that God is going to connect people with different kinds of iron, which represent people who are sharper than you. The Bible says, "As iron sharpens iron, so one man sharpens another" (Prov. 27:17). The prophetic will keep you moving forward and keep you sharp as understanding of the Word of God comes to you.

Let's take a look at a few scriptures that reveal the power of the spoken Word of God.

> For the word of God is alive and active. Sharper than any double-edged sword, it penetrates even to dividing soul and spirit, joints and marrow; it judges the thoughts and attitudes of the heart.
>
> —Hebrews 4:12

He made my mouth like a sharpened sword, in the shadow of his hand he hid me; he made me into a polished arrow and concealed me in his quiver.

—ISAIAH 49:2

Take the helmet of salvation and the sword of the Spirit, which is the word of God.

—EPHESIANS 6:17

May the praise of God be in their mouths and a double-edged sword in their hands.

—PSALM 149:6

"Is not my word like fire," declares the LORD, "and like a hammer that breaks a rock in pieces?"

—JEREMIAH 23:29

In his right hand he held seven stars, and out of his mouth came a sharp, double-edged sword. His face was like the sun shining in all its brilliance.

—REVELATION 1:16

The double-edged sword can be the double-edged ax head. The prophetic authority and strength is in the ability to prophesy His will and mind. It is very important that any believer, especially prophets of God, know and understand the Word of God. It is useless to hear a prophecy from a prophet who gives you his own words and not the word of God. Prophets are to be interpreters of God's divine message.

As I was stating, when the sons of the prophets at the prophetic university of Elisha were laboring and working in the ministry, one of them lost his ax head while they were cutting trees. The ax head fell in the water, and then the sons of the prophet knew who to contact. They contacted this prophetic leader, mentor, and prophetic dean to restore that which was lost. The apostolic anointing and grace releases divine godly wisdom, strategy, and patterns to build, while the prophetic anointing gives direction, adjustment, and forecasts what season to build and when to build in the timing of the Lord.

While the sons of the prophets were building to accommodate present and future expansion of the Prophetic University, one of the sons of the prophet lost his fire, edge, his ability to continue to work and establish a place to live. So he sought the prophetic Professor Elisha, who had a reputation in the supernatural and walked in the prophetic inheritance with the supernatural mantle of his father, Elijah. Elisha decided to go to the place where his student lost his prophetic edge and ax head.

Don't Lose Your Head

The axe head also represented the prophetic student. He lost his head! Don't lose your head in this season. You need it to think spiritually with the mind of Christ. You must not lose control and lose your God-given burden and passion in this hour. This is the season where you have to go back to the place where you may have fallen, repent, and seek the Lord in regard to the prophetic word and promises that He has spoken to you personally and through apostolic and prophetic leadership that God sent you in the past. Go back to the prophetic words and dreams that you may have had in the past. You must go back and meditate on them and allow the word of the Lord to revive you and re-establish to the place of authority and power in the Holy Spirit.

The sons of the prophets lost their prophetic cutting edge, and the prophetic causes a person to live in a new place and move into greater degrees of movement. The prophetic causes you to expand, stretch, and enlarge from the place of comfort and move in a greater place to enlarge in ministry, personally, economically, domestically, spiritually, financially, and mentally. We must enlarge our mental capacity, like the prayer of Jabez in 1 Chronicles 4:10, and prophetically release the decrees of the Lord to see that which you have spoken come forth suddenly.

It is also important to note in the account of the prophets' sons and the ax head that what they lost was something that was borrowed. This must mean that the prophets depended on the prophetic provisions of the Lord. The sons of the prophets must have been poor. Regardless of the status quo economically, or if you are in ministry, business, have a church, or are building, you must understand that God is going to provide for you. You will get your edge back and be sharper than you have ever been before. Even though you may not have the finances to finish what you have started, if it's a God vision, then God will provide the provision.

There is a saying of mine, "If it is God's will, then it is God's bill." In other words, if God said it through His prophetic voice, then it's God's invoice. This is the season that God is going to provide supernaturally the resources that are needed for you to continue that which you have been building, and you will get your restoration.

Prophetic words of knowledge, wisdom, and discerning of spirits can identify people, places, and things that may have caused us to lose heart and our edge. The prophetic gifting can target with bull's-eye precision to bring us back to the place where we fell and cause us to get our footing again.

We see this in the biblical account. The sons of the prophet took Elisha to the place where the man lost his edge (ax head). The prophet Elisha asked the sons of the prophet, "Where did the axe head fall?" and he showed him where it fell in the water Jordan. Elisha showed them *all* how to trust in the God of heaven, the provider of all, and demonstrated with an on-the-job lesson, as Jesus did with His twelve disciples in regard to the five loaves of bread and two fish, which supernaturally fed five thousand, including women and children. The prophet Elisha cut a stick and threw it in the water where the ax head fell, and the iron floated to the top of the River Jordan supernaturally.

God is going to prophesy to you and will ask you where you have fallen or where you have lost your prophetic cutting edge, fire, passion, identity, calling, burden, and godly zeal. Then He will send His word to find, bring, and cause you to experience restoration, and you will float back up to the top. I believe that you will get your edge back and be on the prophetic cutting edge of what God is doing, like the sons of Issachar.

PROPHECY

I prophesy to you in this season and seasons to come that you will connect with true prophets and apostles who have the word of the

Lord resident in them to help bring you into the place of destiny and prophetic fulfillment. I speak prophetically to every leader and Holy Spirit–filled believer that has started something, whether it's a building project, ministry endeavors, business, music, entertainment, government, arts, commerce, family, or in any areas of society. Know that with God all things are possible.

This is the season of the second wind to come to you and give you momentum. Don't lose your edge, but be on the prophetic cutting edge! It's a season to find seasoned men and women in your area of ministry, business, or field that are new and different types of irons (people) that will sharpen your edge and will cause you not to be irrelevant in your generation. It is not time to be dull but sharp again. Not only will you will be restored and redeemed back to the place of kingdom advancement and work, but you will be able to prophesy to others, restoring their lives.

It is time to prophesy and speak decrees of blessings over your life and area of influence. Do not wait for a prophet like Elisha to come and restore things prophetically in your life. You have the Holy Spirit, and you all can prophesy the will of the Lord.

Chapter Seven

YOU CAN ALL PROPHESY

For you can all prophesy one by one, that all
may learn and all may be encouraged.
—1 CORINTHIANS 14:31, NKJV

A S I HAVE traveled across the country ministering in the prophetic, I have come across many people who are still puzzled,
perplexed, and somewhat confused about prophecy, the gift
of prophecy, the prophetic anointing, the spirit of prophecy, and prophetic teaching and preaching, as well as the office of the prophet.
There are dozens of questions that I have to answer in regard to the
difference of these prophetic administrations.

In the modern church, people who witness someone prophesying,
someone working in miracles or as a healing evangelist or an apostle
mistakenly but automatically assume they are a prophet. The prophetic ministry and gifts have been misunderstood for centuries.
There are many books written on this subject that have been an aid
in defining the role of the prophet in the church, in the world, and in
the twenty-first century.

However, there are still denominations and religious organizations that still believe that there are not modern-day apostles and
prophets because we have the Holy Spirit and the Bible. I totally dis-
agree with that paradigm and belief system, because these two minister together, along with the other five-fold ministry offices, which
are vitally essential to the equipping of the saints for the work of
ministry and maturation of the many-membered organism in Christ,
according to Ephesians 4:11–13.

Prophets, Prophecy, and Prophetic Ministry Are God's Ideas

I have read dozens of books on these subjects. Some of them are great educational tools that will bring foundational truths to the prophetic work. A few of the books have been written by people who are not prophets or prophetic at all but cessationist theologians who deny the continuation of the ministry office of the apostles and prophets. Cessationists or charismatic (Pentecostal) cessationists hold the doctrine and view that there was a restoration of the gifts of the Spirit, like tongues and the baptism of the Holy Spirit, but refuse to believe the restoration of the governmental offices of apostles and prophets for today. They believe that it was only for the first-century church and that it has ceased, but I believe they are incorrect. If that were the case, then why are there still evangelists, pastors, and teachers? They believe those offices are still available today but feel apostles and prophets are not, essentially removing them from Scripture, though we were warned not to omit and add to the Word of God (Deut. 12:32).

Furthermore, many of their religious debates, arguments, and paradigms stem from John 16:13 and 1 Corinthians 13:8–10, which they interpret as saying that the charismatic gifts outlined in the Book of Acts and Paul's letters in the first century were replaced by the Holy Canon of the New Testament Scripture. We have many different views and belief systems in regard to the restoration of the ministry of contemporary apostles and prophets of today. This type of view and doctrine is still prevalent in today's church and among many denominations.

Sadly, these types of teachings cause many to deny present-day apostolic and prophetic leaders, therefore causing many to reject anyone who claims apostleship and the prophetic gift. I truly believe in the restoration of apostles and prophets today, as I have encountered the benefit of receiving from those set, appointed, called, chosen, and sent by the Holy Spirit to equip the saints to do the work that they have been born to do. There are many church leaders today in the twenty-first century who hold to their own traditional and religious views as modern-day cessationists or charismatic cessationist.

We need Holy Spirit–inspired believers who understand the importance of interpreting the Holy Scriptures, and more importantly, who understand that Scripture should not be interpreted using our own belief systems, schools of thought, or religious mind-sets and paradigms.

THE PROPHETIC IS GOD-BREATHED

Second Timothy 3:16–17 (NKJV) outlines that all Scriptures are given by inspiration of God.

> All Scripture is given by inspiration of God, and is profitable for doctrine, for reproof, for correction, for instruction in righteousness, that the man of God may be complete, thoroughly equipped for every good work.

The term *given by inspiration of God* is translated from the Greek word *theopneustos,* which literally means, "God-breathed."[24] In other words, God-inspired words are God's creative breath, and all Scriptures are the byproduct of His will. Therefore, being God's own utterance, the Bible is properly called the Word of God, which is prophetic in nature. The word of God given in prophecy is related, because when prophets and prophetically gifted individuals prophesy, even in part, they are ministering under the inspiration of the Holy Spirit and declaring the word of God.

Second Peter 1:20–21 says, "Above all, you must understand that no prophecy of Scripture came about by the prophet's own interpretation of things. For prophecy never had its origin in the human will, but prophets, though human, spoke from God as they were carried

---

24 *New Spirit-Filled Life Bible* ©2002 by Thomas Nelson, Inc., the Holy Bible, New King James Version ©1982 by Thomas Nelson, Inc. In the reference section on page 1714 of the Greek definition *"theopneustos,"* which literally means "God-Breathed." See also Blue Letter Bible, s.v. "theopneustos," www.blueletterbible.org/lang/lexicon/Lexicon.cfm?strongs=G2315 (accessed June 4, 2013); s.v. "emphysaō," www.blueletterbible.org/lang/lexicon/lexicon.cfm?Strongs=G1720&t=KJV (accessed June 4, 2013). "God breathed" taken from James White, "God-Breathed; Breathed Out By God; Theopneustos," Alpha & Omega Ministries Apologetics Blog, January 3, 2006, https://aomin.org/aoblog/index.php?itemid=1193 (accessed July 10, 2013).

along by the Holy Spirit." When the true prophet of God speaks forth the word of God through *prophecy* it is God breathing on the hearer of the word. Second Peter 1:20–21 elaborates this divine truth and adds that none of what was given was the opinion, ideology, and concept of the writer or author of the Scriptures (verse 20) and that each writer involved in the production of the Holy Scriptures was "moved by" (NKJV, literally, "being borne along") the Holy Spirit. It was the Holy Spirit at work in the author of the Holy Canon and not their own thoughts and paradigms.

The Scriptures that I will present throughout this book are for cross-referencing and for your own study time. Whatever your present belief system is in regard to this gifting and ministry, I will challenge you to have a noble Berean spirit and research the Scriptures with an open heart to get the full understanding and heart of God in regard to the prophetic, as it is a ministry of the Holy Spirit that is being restored for present and future generations to benefit from.

According to 1 Corinthians 14:31 (GW) says, "All of you can take your turns speaking what God has revealed. In that way, everyone will learn and be encouraged." This passage of Scripture states that all who have the gift of prophecy or resident gift of prophecy can prophesy within the church so that all who hear will learn, be encouraged, edified, comforted, and strengthened. That is the purpose of the gift of prophecy being released in the congregation. This specific scripture is not saying that everyone in the church can prophesy at will but only designated to those who have the prophetic gifting.

THE PROPHETIC GIFT MUST BE GOVERNED BY LEADERSHIP

I have been in churches that were very gifted, like the church of Corinthians, who loved the gift of prophecy and tongues, but there was no order established when it came to prophets ministering one-by-one what God had revealed to them for the benefit of the church to be blessed and encouraged.

Paul endeavored to set the church in apostolic order when it came to the function of this gift. The Corinthian church was very charismatic but lacked order. He was governing and overseeing the operation of the moves of the spirit of prophecy there. Paul, being their spiritual father, established order so that all who heard would be instructed and built up in the gift of prophecy.

Moreover, during those times, they were living in what seemed to be the last days. There was much persecution and opposition, and they needed to be encouraged, edified, and comforted. The only hope was in Christ and in His promises to save them. Consequently, what God had revealed through His prophets and believers with the gift of prophecy was very important. The prophetic function was encouraging to the one who had the gift and also to the hearer of the divine utterance.

Colossians 2:2 (NLT) reveals the heart of the apostle Paul and his understanding of the mysteries of God being revealed through prophecy and divine messages:

> I want them to be encouraged and knit together by strong ties of love. I want them to have complete confidence that they understand God's mysterious plan, which is Christ himself.

We can see that prophecy will bring hearts together in love, unity, and establish a believer in complete confidence in God's divine plan in a way that they understand. Prophecy that is being revealed by the Lord is God's divine plan, which is Christ revealing Himself to an individual. In other words, when God is speaking to you through His word by prophetic utterance and dreams, visions, or encounters, Christ Himself is being revealed. Proverbs 20:12 (NKJV) says, "The hearing ear and the seeing eye, The LORD has made them both." The Lord has created our ears and eyes for the purpose to see and hear, not only naturally but spiritually as well. So, we have the ability to hear and perceive (see) through our spiritual senses the voice of the Lord.

Any believer that has the Holy Spirit can and should be able to hear and see (perceive) the voice of God when He speaks to them personally. With that in mind, if a person can hear, see, feel, taste, and smell with their five human, natural senses, then in the spirit realm there are the same prophetic spiritual senses. If a believer can hear the voice of God personally, then they can speak prophetically corporately. Many people in the church have a problem hearing the voice of God, but once they learn how to hear the inner, small voice of the Lord, then the second problem that follows is confidence to speak for the Lord.

God Speaks in Various Ways

First Kings 19:11–12 (NKJV) says:

> Then He said, "Go out, and stand on the mountain before the Lord." And behold, the Lord passed by, and a great and strong wind tore into the mountains and broke the rocks in pieces before the Lord, but the Lord was not in the wind; and after the wind an earthquake, but the Lord was not in the earthquake; and after the earthquake a fire, but the Lord was not in the fire; and after the fire a still small voice.

Elijah the prophet was accustomed to seeing and recognizing the signs, wonders, and miraculous power of God throughout his ministry. He was used to getting divine revelation from the Lord through the wind, earthquakes, and fire, but God decided to do something different. The Lord revealed Himself to the prophet in a small, still voice.

We must understand that God does speak through various ways and methods. Consequently, we can neither limit, nor put God in a box and think that He is going to speak or reveal Himself the same way all the time. God does bring revelation and answers to life circumstances and problems. I have discovered that when there is much confusion, turmoil, and many problems getting the best of me and I'm in search of an answer, it is best for me to stop what I am doing and get quiet before the Lord, and then He will speak to me by His small, still voice.

Have you ever looked for something and could not find it? Literally you searched everywhere for it, and when you calmed down and got quiet, you found the thing that you were looking for. It was right in front of you the whole time. This has happened to most of us. Likewise, God is always speaking and giving us answers to our problems. He speaks prophetically to us by His Spirit if we would just be still and know that He is God.

Moreover, people do hear the voice of God all the time, but recognizing it can be a challenge. Usually a person's first instinct or "gut feeling" is usually the Lord speaking to them. One of the ways I've learned how to hear the voice of God is that usually His voice is a familiar voice and typically sounds like your own voice in your spirit. Have you ever had a conversation with yourself and answered yourself? We all have done that before (though if we do it out loud people will ask if we are talking to ourselves). But in all actuality you were having a conversation with the Holy Spirit and Jesus, the prophet's voice on the inside of you.

We see there are some believers who can hear the voice of God but have trouble relaying what God is saying to others. Then we have those who don't have a problem speaking what God is saying to others but refuse to hear what God is saying to them personally.

In his book called *Spirit Talk, Hearing the Voice of God*, Larry Randolph writes:

> I believe the human conscience is in some ways synonymous with the voice of the Holy Spirit. This is apparent when you consider that the conscience of man is God's implant—the oracle of right and wrong. Basically, conscience is a person's inner awareness of conforming to the will of God or departing from it, resulting in a sense of what is correct and incorrect in one's conduct or motives. Although, the term "conscience" does not appear in the Old Testament, the concept does.[25]

This reminds us of Romans 9:1-2 (NKJV), which says, "I tell the truth in Christ, I am not lying, my conscience also bearing me witness in the Holy Spirit, that I have great sorrow and continual grief in my heart." Paul was writing about the matters of a person's conscience and stated that we as believers should be led by a holy, sanctified conscience as the Holy Spirit witnesses within our hearts. I

---

25 Larry Randolph, *Spirit Talk* (Wilmington, NC: Morningstar Publications, 2005), 72.

believe there has to be a balance in discerning the voice of the Lord and speaking prophetically.

Growing in the prophetic, I have come to learn that our Lord loves to share secrets, facts, and detailed stories with those who are in relationship with Him. Amos 3:7 (The Message Version) says, "The fact is, GOD, the Master, does nothing without first telling his prophets the whole story." In the New International Version, Amos 3:7–8 says, "Surely the Sovereign LORD does nothing without revealing his plan to his servants the prophets. The lion has roared—who will not fear? The Sovereign LORD has spoken— who can but prophesy?"

God will do nothing without revealing His plans to His holy prophets. Since we have the Holy Spirit, we must know the nature of God, who loves to talk to those who will listen and even speak through his chosen vessels as an oracle to share His plan, will, and purpose in the Earth. Daddy God holds the master plan and blueprint for your life; therefore you are the key to the doors of destiny.

DADDY GOD LOVES TO SPEAK TO HIS CHILDREN

Daddy God loves to communicate. Everything He did in times past was through His words. God wants to communicate to us and wants to communicate through us. You can prophesy! Note what I just said, that you *can* prophesy. I did not say you could not prophesy. Those who are anointed by the Holy Spirit and have the gift of prophecy resident in them can prophesy to edify, exhort, and comfort other believers.

In Numbers 12:6–8 (NKJV) the Lord says:

> Hear now My words: If there is a prophet among you, I, the LORD, make Myself known to him in a vision; I speak to him in a dream. Not so with My servant Moses; He is faithful in all My house. I speak with him face to face, Even plainly, and not in dark sayings; And he sees the form of the LORD.

The Lord can speak in various ways. We see that God speaks to His prophets in a vision, dreams, and mouth to mouth, like He did with Moses. God can speak in dark sayings, in which case the prophet would have to wait on the Lord for specific instruction, direction, interpretation, clarity, and understanding.

The term *dark sayings* refers to the various times when God communicates in mysteries or parables. Remember in John 16:29 when the disciples where happy that Jesus was speaking plainly and was not using figures of speech. We all have used figures of speech when communicating with each other. The disciples said to Jesus, "Now you are speaking clearly and without figures of speech." Moreover Psalm 78:2 (KJV) declares, "I will open my mouth in a parable; I will utter dark saying of old." This passage of Scripture reveals that God prophesied in dark sayings, parables, or figuratively.

There have been times when I have prophesied to people figuratively or in a dark saying. For example, I would say, "For son, know that you are going to be like a tree planted by the rivers of living water, and this is a season when you will give birth to that baby on the inside. You have been pregnant with this baby, but now your water will break and you will give birth." This prophecy should not be taken literally in regard to the prophetic language or figure of speech used. This individual was a male and cannot get pregnant, nor is he a tree but a person, and there is no baby on the inside of him.

This prophecy may be accurate, and the word of the Lord should be taken seriously but with spiritual understanding. I told the man that he is going to be "like a tree planted by the rivers of living water" and that in this season he would give birth to a baby, which speaks of a spiritual baby. This is not a real baby but may be speaking of vision, something new or fresh—ideas, ministry, business, or whatever has been on his heart. When I stated that he has been pregnant, it doesn't mean that he has a belly but that in his heart there is a something big or great that he is about to implement and walk out regarding the prophetic vision that is in him.

JESUS UTILIZED THE PROPHETIC ADVANTAGE TO EVANGELIZE

Jesus, as our role model, used wisdom when operating in the gifts of the Holy Spirit. He often used the gift of words of knowledge, which is one of the gifts of the Holy Spirit. We see this type of example with Jesus and the Samaritan woman in John 4:9 (NKJV). When she said to Jesus, "How is it that You, being a Jew, ask a drink from me since I am a Samaritan woman?" Jesus did not respond to her question, but rather He discerned her spirit and saw that here was a woman in need of refreshing and in need of to be revived by the living water that He could provide her. Therefore, Jesus said to her in verse 10 (NKJV), "If you knew the gift of God, and who it is who says to you, 'Give Me a drink,' you would have asked Him, and He would have given you living water." He didn't answer her initial question, nor did He disclose His heavenly identity as the Son of God, but He talked to her as a gentleman engaged in friendly evangelism with words of knowledge about her marital status, past, and current relationships, revealing what was going on in her life; therefore, she perceived Him as a prophet (John 4:17–18).

Jesus' word of knowledge regarding the woman's past and present caused her to receive the gift of the Spirit, which was really salvation. I will explain the difference between the gifts of the Spirit and the gift of the Spirit.

Jesus, figuratively speaking, called Himself the living water, and He is the living water. He used this type of prophetic language to cause her to think. She understood later, but He caught her attention by confirming through prophetic words what was on her mind, heart, and spirit at Jacob's well. He used the prophetic to win her heart.

God wants to use you to prophesy. Sometimes prophets can prophesy things to a person, and others may be listening to the prophecy and do not understand what is being spoken, but the individual receiving the word will understand exactly what is being revealed. There are times where the person receiving the prophetic word may understand pieces of the word but does not understand the rest. Upon taking their prophecy home and listening to it or reading over it later, the understanding may come. The Bible says that now our knowledge is partial and incomplete, and even the gift of prophecy reveals only part of the whole picture (1 Cor. 13:9)

I believe we were conceived out of the word of the Lord, so likewise we were born to prophesy. What am I saying? We were born to communicate and fellowship with God and each other. Could you imagine the world with people not communicating with each other? Could you imagine people walking around quiet and mute? This world would be pretty boring. I know how it feels not to speak to someone because of an issue or argument, and I know how it is not to be spoken to. Communication is imperative to understanding what is on the mind and heart of a person. Whether God speaks to you mouth to mouth or figuratively, you can prophesy by the gift of prophecy.

The keys to successful relationships, regardless of what level they are established on, are love and communication. Without proper communication, accountability, trust, transparency, and mutual respect, the relationship will fail. God loves us so much that He communicated that by sending His Son (His Word) to bring us back in right fellowship, relationship, accountability, and right standing with Him.

It is God's heart for us to communicate with Him and to hear His voice in various ways when He chooses to speak to us. Like a loving Father, when He speaks to His spiritual offspring, He desires to have an intimate relationship with us. Any successful and loving relationship must by its very nature involve two-way communication. He is very much interested in what you are doing. The Lord is not an absentee Father or a seed donor, but He is your heavenly and loving Father. It's His good pleasure to give you the kingdom as your inheritance. The Lord is not an Indian giver but a loving Father who loves to give good gifts to those who ask Him. The gifts of the Holy Spirit can be given to those who ask for them.

As I stated before in the previous chapter, if God used King Saul, Israel's first king, to prophesy when he was introduced to the prophetic team coming down from the high place of worship, then a prophet and prophetic minister must be a worshiper and lover of his or her God. This prophetic team cultivated the prophetic atmosphere that allowed ordinary men, when connected to the prophetic stream, to became extraordinary and prophesy. The prophetic was released through worship to God and music, and the spirit of prophecy caused Saul to prophesy like the prophets. He wasn't a prophet, but he could prophesy like the prophets.

Even though he was chosen king, there was a prophetic dimension of the Spirit of God that came on him to transform him into an oracle of the Lord. Therefore, it does not matter if you are not a prophet, but you can prophesy like the prophets. All are not called to be prophets, but all can prophesy in varying degrees (1 Cor. 12:7).

NOT ALL ARE PROPHETS, BUT ALL CAN PROPHESY!

Are all apostles? Are all prophets? Are all teachers? Are all workers of miracles? Do all have gifts of healings? Do all speak with tongues? Do all interpret? But earnestly desire the best gifts. And yet I show you a more excellent way.

—1 CORINTHIANS 12:29–31, NKJV

We see that not all are called to the same specific office, nor does everyone possess the same gifts of the Holy Spirit. But *all* can desire the best or greater gifts, which is suitable and needed at the time to minister within the church. For example, prophecy would be more suitable over tongues to operate in because it needs no interpretation. In other words, prophecy would be the best gift to use in some cases because it brings edification to the corporate body, as compared to tongues that need interpretation. The gift of prophecy is a building gift.

Prophecy and other gifts, along with tongues, should be done in a more excellent way. We must operate in faith, love, and hope when operating in the gifts of the Holy Spirit. Operating in these gifts should promote love and unity among believers, not division, confusion, dishonor, and pride. All may not be prophets, apostles, teachers, etc., but all have a part to play as His body and in His kingdom. I believe that if we have the Holy Spirit, which is the holy nature of God, then we can prophesy holy, inspired words of life as well. The Holy Spirit is an apostolic spirit, prophetic spirit, evangelistic spirit, pastoral (shepherding) spirit, and teaching spirit. A person does not have to walk in any of these ministry gifts given to the church to function in the Spirit and in different operations and administrations.

God's various gifts are handed out everywhere; but they all originate in God's Spirit. God's various ministries are carried out everywhere; but they all originate in God's Spirit. God's various expressions of power are in action everywhere; but God himself is behind it all. Each person is given something to do that shows who God is: Everyone gets in on it, everyone benefits. All kinds of things are handed out by the Spirit, and to all kinds of people! The variety is wonderful:

wise counsel
clear understanding
simple trust
healing the sick
miraculous acts
proclamation
distinguishing between spirits
tongues
interpretation of tongues.

All these gifts have a common origin, but are handed out one by one by the one Spirit of God. He decides who gets what, and when. You can easily enough see how this kind of thing works by looking no further than your own body. Your body has many parts—limbs, organs, cells—but no matter how many parts you can name, you're still one body. It's exactly the same with Christ.

—1 Corinthians 12:4–12, the message

Teamwork and Synergy Is Key to Ministry Effectiveness

It's very clear that regardless of the different parts of the body, it is still one body working together and making sure that every joint does its part. We need each other to function and survive. The eyes are a part of the body, and the eyes cannot say to the feet, "We have no need of you," because the feet are also a part of the body. Both function differently on the body, but they are members of the same body, regardless of each other's function in the body of Christ. For example, if the feet are damaged, then the eyes are affected as well, because it's a part of the body too. Without each part doing their part, the body is not completely whole and functioning as it was ordained and originally made to function by the Lord.

We are the body of Christ, and God has need of you in His body. Jesus is the Head of the church, called the body of Christ. God placed Him as Head of the church and set Him over all things concerning the church. Christ Jesus is concerned about His body in the earth, called His church. Every part in His body plays a major and key role. There are no big *I* and little *you* in the Kingdom of God. You are not insignificant but significant.

A Spirit-filled believer can prophesy in the body and not be called to be a prophet in the body of Christ *per se*. One can work miracles and not be an apostle, healing evangelist, or miracle worker *per se*. Offices and giftings of the Spirit work through each person differently. We are all one body, and it is the same Spirit and Lord working in and through us all. We have the Holy Spirit to give the expression of God in the earth to His people and through His people.

God has created us for a specific purpose with a unique calling and destiny. We have not been born to fill church pews and listen to sermons for the rest of our lives, but each of us collectively contributes in the advancing and expansion of the kingdom of God in our words and deeds. I come to encourage you that God passionately wants to speak through you, and you can do just that. Just believe, have faith, and prophesy.

IF GOD USED A DONKEY TO SPEAK, HE CAN USE YOU TO PROPHESY!

Interestingly, in the Bible God used a donkey to speak literally to Balaam, a rebellious prophet who compromised his prophetic ministry to give false predictions and became a people pleaser and not a pleaser of the Lord. Numbers 22:28 (NLT) says, "Then the LORD gave the donkey the ability to speak. 'What have I done to you that deserves your beating me three times?' it asked Balaam." Balaam gave his own presumptuous words that came from his own mind and heart, which was coerced by the people and not given by God. He was labeled a false prophet.

We must understand that Balaam started out as a genuine prophet of God, but due to greed and power he became a false prophet. How many people do you know who are genuinely prophets, but during their life or ministry they became flakey, mystical, and presumptuous? Ultimately this can be caused by pride, erroneous teachings, poor belief systems, lack of accountability to godly authority, scandals, worldly fame, greed for money or power, perversion, immorality, rejection, unforgiveness, and bad character. All of these, just to name a few, can cause a person to be stigmatized as a false prophet. A false prophet does not mean that a person was not originally a true prophet of God at one time but only signifies that their character identifies the god or deity they worship. In other words, you know a person by the fruit that they bear.

We must understand that there were prophets who did not serve God, but they were prophets of their own god. How you know a prophet of God is that what they say comes to pass by the authenticity of their words. My point here is that if God can use an animal to speak to a lying prophet, then God can use you as well to speak for Him.

I always wanted to know why God needed to use a donkey to speak to someone who was called a prophet. Were there an abundance of false prophets during the time of Balaam? Was there a short supply of true, genuine prophets to use? I believe that God put that in the Bible to demonstrate His sovereignty in choosing who He desires to use to speak for Him. By any means necessary—God used Balaam's transportation, the donkey—God was going to speak a word Balaam.

Could you imagine hearing your family pet speaking prophetically to you? Most people would think it was demonic or from Satan. Imagine yourself driving in your car as you are heading to do something that you know God isn't pleased with or just in plain rebellion. You set out to do something in your own willpower, and suddenly your car breaks down. Most people would, again, blame it on Satan.

Or imagine instead maybe you are doing something for God and have become very zealous in your pursuit. You think you were doing God a favor or helping Him out, and then your car breaks down or something hinders you. Again, most Christians would blame it on the enemy, when in actually it can be the warning signs of the Lord prohibiting you from doing something unlawful or self-righteous.

Paul, like Balaam, on his high horse of pride, zeal, haughtiness, and religious indignation, was persecuting the church with all that zeal and religious self-righteousness; he thought he was doing the Lord a favor, but he was breaking the heart of God (Acts 9:3–8). Paul needed to be the donkey (humbled, meek, walking in humility and lowly of spirit) to see from the heart of Christ Jesus who he was persecuting.

I cannot imagine my pet turtle or dog speaking prophetically, but in the days of Balaam it happened. Luckily, we have been made in His image and according to His likeness, and I don't have to be a donkey or cat for God to use me to speak for Him.

The Holy Spirit is a prophetic spirit; therefore, we should be prophetic by nature, discovering our own prophetic voice. In the next few chapters I will be sharing on what prophecy is, how to discern true prophets and false prophets, prophetic desire, activating in the prophetic, how to discover your own prophetic voice, spiritual gifts, supernatural gifts of the Holy Spirit, and many more keys that will help you discover your gifts, thereby encouraging you to walk in a greater level of the prophetic and deeper understanding that you were born to prophesy by the Holy Spirit!

Chapter Eight

PROPHETIC DESIRE

Pursue love, and desire spiritual gifts but especially that
you may prophesy.... Therefore, brethren, desire earnestly
to prophesy, and do not forbid to speak with tongues.
—1 CORINTHIANS 14:1, 39, NKJV

D ESIRE IS SOMETHING that can be good or bad based on the
motivation of one's heart. Many of us through life have
desired things, whether it be a new car, house, job, husband
or wife, children, money, clothes, food, or whatever it may be personally. Everyone in life has at one time or another desired something
that someone else may have. Regardless of the reason for wishing for
something, that particular desire was something on your heart and
mind.

Most people fulfill what's on their heart and passionately pursue
their desires by any means necessary. There are godly desires and
demonic desires. Even throughout the Bible, God warns us about
having earthly, fleshly, carnal desires, called lusts of the flesh, passions, a spirit of covetousness (Gal. 5:16–25). These things are contrary to His spirit and war against the spirit. Because the spirit is
against the flesh—they are contrary to one another—that a person
will not do the things that they wish. There are godly desires, burdens, and appetites that a person can possess by the Spirit. Godliness
and moral purity is needed to operate in any gift.

In Romans 8:5 it says, "Those who live according to the flesh have
their minds set on what that flesh desires; but those who live in accordance with the Spirit have their minds set on what the Spirit desires."
This Scripture reveals that a person will do what is in their heart
and mind. A kingdom believer must fix their mind to be passionate

about the desires of the Lord. Does God give you the desires of your heart? Yes, and even more. It may be different plans or desires than you ever thought you wanted. He has extraordinary plans when you simply put Him first in your life, but you must be cooperative with the Spirit of God. He will cause you to walk by the Spirit and fulfill the desires of the Spirit. So in other words, if one is sinful, then they will commit acts of the flesh. Consequently, those who are spiritual will mind the things of the Spirit, committing to pleasing the Lord in their lifestyle and conduct.

A Holy Desire

The prophets of old were holy men of God. The messages and prophetic words in them carried a holy indignation, discontentment, righteousness, and burden of the Lord. Note that I said they were holy men of God. A person may have desires and passions, which is the Greek word *epithumia*.[26] This word is from the Greek word *thumos*,[27] from which *thermos* and *theromostat* are derived. These words combined indicate a "temperature" that may rise to the degree that these burning desires and passions must be regulated and directed for proper spiritual investment into godly purposes instead of carnal and fleshly desires. We must redirect and channel our passions and desires for the glorification of God.

If one is going to desire anything, it should be for spiritual things and not carnal things. We must walk in the spirit and not fulfill the lusts (desires or passions) of the flesh.

In other words, *to walk* in the Greek (*stoicheo*) means to "walk in line."[28] As believers, we must walk in line of the Spirit, and with prophesying it must also be in line with the *logos*, the written Word

---

26   Blue Letter Bible, s.v. "epithymia," www.blueletterbible.org/lang/lexicon/ Lexicon.cfm?strongs=G1939 (accessed June 4, 2013).

27   See http://www.biblestudytools.com/lexicons/greek/nas/thumos.html; http://www.biblestudytools.com/dictionaries/bakers-evangelical-dictionary/ desire.html; http://en.wikipedia.org/wiki/Thermostats. See also *Baker's Evangelical Dictionary of Biblical Theology*, edited by Walter A. Elwell (Grand Rapids, MI: Baker Books, 1996).

28   Blue Letter Bible, s.v. "stoicheō," www.blueletterbible.org/lang/lexicon/ Lexicon.cfm?strongs=G4748 (accessed June 4, 2013); "to walk in line," http:// preceptaustin.org/galatians_524-26.htm (accessed July 10, 2013).

of God. When a person prophesies, those prophetic words also must be backed up by the Word of God. Have you ever received a prophetic word and it didn't sound right in your spirit? You knew that it was not in line with God's Word, and something was unsynchronized. Likely, this individual's prophesying life may not be in line with the Spirit and with the written Word of God. In other words, you know that they were in their flesh, or they gave a carnal, familiar, or sensual word that was contradicting to God's Word. It is imperative for prophets and prophetic people to have sound biblical doctrine. If one's doctrine is off, more likely they have limited revelation of God's Word. In such cases the prophecy will be off, sounding flakey.

In addition, you can tell when someone is walking in the Spirit and has foundational truth. When they prophesy, it carries the authority of God. I will address later in the book the connection with false prophets, prophecies, and how to recognize them. In this chapter we will talk about having a prophetic desire to prophesy.

No Selfish Personal Prophecy

Trust in the LORD and do good; dwell in the land and enjoy safe pasture. Take delight in the LORD, and he will give you the desires of your heart. Commit your way to the LORD; trust in him and he will do this: He will make your righteous reward shine like the dawn, your vindication like the noonday sun. Be still before the LORD and wait patiently for him.

—PSALM 37:3–7

We must desire what God desires, so that He can give us the desires of His heart and not just ours. The Bible says that God wants to give us the desires of our hearts; He didn't put any restrictions on that statement other than we understand the desires cannot be sinful. What might be one person's desire, another person might judge as sinful based on their belief system or religion, as in the eating of meat or working on another man's sabbath.

I remember prophesying on the prophetic team at my local church along with my twin brother. We were ministering to these women, and God had given me a word of knowledge about a man who had left her. I went on to say that God was going to send her another who would make her happy and that this relationship would be the will of the Lord.

The woman stopped me dead in my tracks while I was prophesying and began to ask us questions about her ex-husband who had left her for another woman. She stated that she was hurt but that she wanted him back. She wanted to know if the Lord was going to send him back to her. At first I was upset because I had never had this happen to me before; usually I would take questions after the ministering if a person had a question or wasn't clear on the prophetic word.

Furthermore, this woman's only reason for coming in the prophetic line was to hear a word about her ex-husband and not about her calling, destiny, and purpose. She was more concerned about him leaving her for another woman and was asking dozens of questions as if we were physics. I told the lady that God is her husband, and He wanted her back. In addition, I told her that God was going to send her another who would love her and make her happy. If she would have listened to the prophetic word and the instructions that followed, she would have heard that God was doing a new thing in her life, to include that He was going to send her a new husband who would love her the way she was meant to be loved.

God does restore marriages and whole families, but my point is that the woman's desire and focus was directed on the past and on someone who did not want her anymore. God was using my brother and me to reveal the Father's desire to this woman. The words of knowledge about a man leaving her triggered a sensitive area and caused her to focus on that and not what God desired for her future.

A prophetic word from the Lord has the power to realign and redirect our passions to the Lord's passions. Our desires have to be God's desires, and His desires must become our desires. Accordingly, we come to desire that which He desires for our lives. Sounds like a tongue twister, huh?

What is most interesting to know is that out of all the spiritual gifts, prophecy is something that a believer should desire, especially while pursuing love as the purpose and intention to operate in these giftings. The Bible says that we can desire earnestly to prophesy. In other words, with a pure, genuine, and loving heart a believer can covet the gift of prophecy.

It is very profound to me that prophecy is one of the gifts of the Holy Spirit that can be desired. My point here is that we have been given the Holy Spirit as a gift from the Father, and along with the Holy Spirit's gifts, one of them is prophetic utterance. Prophesying is unique in itself in that a believer should be able to function in this because we have the Holy Spirit working on the inside of us. If a believer can yield his or her natural faculties to the Holy Spirit's unction, then they can function in prophetic utterance. The Holy Spirit has a desire as well, and that is to be used by you to empower others.

LOVE SHOULD BE THE MOTIVATION TO PROPHESY

The Bible says it God's good pleasure to give us the kingdom. In other words, it is the Lord's desire to give us our inheritance. It is the Father's heart to give His children good things, if they ask for them. Even a wicked father knows how to give good gifts to their children; they will not give them something evil, even though they may be wicked at heart, if their children ask for something good from them. Moreover, it's the Lord's desire that we will not perish but that we have eternal life. God did not create hell for His people; hell was created for the fallen angels and those who desired to live independently without God. That decision became the very place that the spiritually disconnected will spend eternity.

Love is the primary character of prophecy. First Corinthians 14:1 says, "Pursue love and desire spiritual gifts but especially that you may prophesy." One chapter back, 1 Corinthians 13:4–7 reveals the primary character of personal and corporate prophecy. It can be found by substituting the phrase "personal and corporate prophecy" for the word *love* in 1 Corinthians 13. What would be the pretense for doing this? Personal and corporate prophecy is particularly connected to the person, testimony, and Spirit of the Lord Jesus Christ. We know this from reading the following verse:

> And I [John] fell at his feet [the angel] to worship him. And he said unto me, See thou do it not: I am thy fellowservant, and of thy

brethren that have the testimony of Jesus: worship God: for the testimony of Jesus is the spirit of prophecy.

—Revelation 19:10, kjv

Jesus is Lord, God is love, and the spirit of prophecy is the testimony of Jesus Christ, who is God and who *is* love. Therefore the truth about Daddy God is that He *is love*. This needs to be understood, because much of the prophetic is released in a harmful, harsh, and bitter way. Here is a basic test for all personal and corporate prophecy: Is it spoken in the spirit of love and in the integrity of God's Word as defined in the thirteenth chapter of 1 Corinthians? We must define love this way, because there are many definitions of love. I've have witnessed familiar, presumptuous, blasphemous, and unkind denunciations given prophetically as "tough conditional love" when it had nothing to do with the love defined in 1 Corinthians 13.

First Corinthians 14:1–3 outlines to us that prophecy is simply for edification, exhortation, and comfort—not rebuke, correction, reprimand, or repudiation. The only example biblically we have of this other kind of prophecy was when the disciples of Christ wanted to rebuke some people who weren't following them. Jesus proceeded to tell them they didn't know what spirit they were of. This is because these disciples were operating under an old covenant mind-set and the paradigm of the law of sin and death, not the new covenant mind-set and paradigm of grace and truth.

First Corinthians 13:4–7 shows what personal prophecies should entail when given:

- Personal prophecy should bring hope, unity, and peace of God.

- Personal prophecy is given in the Spirit of truth.

- Personal prophecy is honest.

- Personal prophecy offers clear instruction, directives, and wisdom.

- Personal prophecy is direct.

- Personal prophecy is anointed.

- Personal prophecy is patient.

- Personal prophecy is kind.

- Prophecy does not attract attention to self but to God.

- Personal prophecy should not be for financial gain as the sole purpose.

- Personal prophecy does not deceive.

- Prophecy does not condemn, discourage, discomfort, or tear down.

- Personal prophecy is not condescending.

- Personal prophecy does not bring envy, division, or jealousy.

- Personal prophecy does not boast and draw attention to oneself.

- Personal prophecy is not proud, arrogant, conceited, or puffed up.

- Personal prophecy does not dishonor, belittle, or take advantage of others.

- Personal prophecy is not self-seeking.

- Personal prophecy is not easily angered or short tempered.

- Personal prophecy always protects, perseveres, covers, and enlightens.

- Personal prophecy reveals Christ and His love.

As we can see, as a kingdom believer we are instructed and admonished to desire spiritual gifts of the Holy Spirit, along with pursuing love. One cannot operate in the spiritual gifts of the Spirit without love at the forefront. With the pursuit of love come the gifts of the Spirit.

JUDGING PERSONAL AND CORPORATE PROPHECY

In 1 Corinthians 14:39–40 Paul was addressing the abuse of spiritual gifts in the Corinthian church and explaining how to operate in order during a service. Paul was not quenching the activity of the gifts of the Holy Spirit within the assembly of believers, but he wanted integrity and oversight to be in place. He desired them to operate in the gifts of the Spirit, as today we should also operate in all things decently and in order.

Furthermore, his word was specifically for those who were prophets and had the gift of prophecy resident in them. The spirits of the prophets are subject to the prophets. In other words, if two or three prophets believe they have an inspired, revealed word of the Lord and desire to share it openly before the congregation, they can do so in order one by one as the others judge. The spirit of the prophet is under the control of that prophet. The word *subject* in Greek is *hypotasso,* which literally means "to submit to one's control," and the word suggests obedience, submission, cooperation, subordination, subservience, and subjection.[29] In other words, the spirits of the prophets are to stand under the prophet who is prophesying within a local body of believers specifically.

The prophetic gift of utterance can also be put under the control and responsibility of the prophetic possessor. It is the prophet's spirit that can be governed and controlled at will.

I believe we shouldn't wait until we get fifty, sixty, or seventy years old to desire to prophesy. In my ministry we have activated three to twelve year olds in the prophetic and the supernatural. It is our desire to equip, train, activate, educate, and impart into the next generation the ability to move in the supernatural power of God and prophesy the word of the Lord. I have found in the younger generation that they are more open to releasing the word of the Lord and move in greater faith for miracles because they are not religious, nor too intellectual *not* to believe God for signs, wonders, and miracles.

This is a trait the early apostles shared. These apostles of the Lamb were unlearned men and had not been to the religious schools of Jesus' day. They were ordinary men who produced the extraordinary power of God, which drew the attention of the religious scholars, scribes, Pharisees, and Sadducees. This is good news for the body of Christ. Most people have not been to the schools of thought or

---

29   Blue Letter Bible, s.v. "hypotassō," www.blueletterbible.org/lang/lexicon/ Lexicon.cfm?strongs=G5293 (accessed June 4, 2013).

seminary on how to heal the sick, raise the dead, and prophesy. There is nothing wrong with further education in the area that one is called, but it's not the prerequisite to producing miracles. The only belief system and paradigm that a person needs is faith in God, who can do the impossible.

I love to see the next generation of radical youth minister before the Lord and observe the extreme faith they possess to believe God for unusual or unprecedented miracles. It's the adults with all that knowledge and information who struggle to just believe God for miracles. There is no chronological age to desire and to operate in the spiritual gifts of the Holy Spirit. The Holy Spirit's gifts are available to those who believe and have the faith to do the work of the Lord Jesus Christ. One does not need years of education in theology to operate in the supernatural power of God. It is only by faith that a person is filled with supernatural wisdom and the ability to act and speak as an oracle for Christ. Are you willing to prophesy at a greater level and release what is on the heart of our King? It is my prayer and desire, like Moses, that many will prophesy and be prophets by the Spirit.

All those in authority within the church should desire to see their people raised and mature in the gifts of the spirit, but more importantly there is love, faith, unity, peace, and joy. Bad character produces bad fruit and prophecies. Further, we must understand that our desires and passions should be for more of Christ in us than looking for signs, wonders, and miracles. If there is more Christ, the hope of Christ resident in us, then we can see tangible miracles daily.

We need to keep in mind that whenever you receive a prophecy from the Lord by a prophet or prophetic believer, the prophetic word is God's desire and thought toward you. What is the definition of the word *desire*? According to Merriam-Webster's Dictionary, the word *desire* means "strong wish, longing, formal request for action, something desired, long or hope for, exhibit or feel desire for."[30]

30　*Merriam-Webster's Dictionary and Thesaurus*, s.v. "desire."

Pursue Spiritual Gifts,
Especially to Prophesy

The biblical type of desire is expressed by the Greek word *zeloo*, meaning "to be zealous for, to burn with desire, to pursue ardently, to desire eagerly or intensely."[31] The negative definition of this word is associated with strong envy and jealously. (See Acts 7:9; 17:5; 1 Corinthians 13:4; James 4:2.) God is not calling us to be jealous, envious, and to covet each other's gifts and calling. Instead we should desire, pursue, covet, and earnestly desire spiritual gifts, especially the gift of prophecy.

Prophecy and the prophetic ministry was the life of the New Testament church. They were blessed by the presence of God when the prophetic utterances in operation released the gift of prophecy. As the apostle Paul states in 1 Corinthians 14:1, 39, pursuing love as our primary pursuit, prophecy is to be embraced for the edification, exhortation, and comfort of the congregation, both corporately and individually.

The practice and exercise of the gift of prophecy is encouraged by the apostle Peter in 1 Peter 4:11. I like this passage of Scripture because it encourages believers in prophesying as the oracles of God. First Peter 4:11 (NKJV) says, "If anyone speak, let him speak as the oracles of God. If anyone ministers, let him do it as with the ability which God supplies, that in all things God may be glorified through Jesus Christ, to whom belong the glory and the dominion forever and ever. Amen." The scripture says that if anyone speaks, let him speak as the oracle of God. In other words, if a person prophesies by prophetic utterance and inspiration of the Holy Spirit, let him speak like God is speaking or prophesy with the ability that the Lord supplies to you so that Christ is glorified through you. If a person is going to minister prophetically, one must prophesy with dominion in Christ and speak the oracles of God as if God is speaking. There is nothing like hearing a word of the Lord spoken through a prophet who speaks the oracles of God, as if God were speaking

---

31 Blue Letter Bible, s.v. "zēloō," www.blueletterbible.org/lang/lexicon/Lexicon. cfm?strongs=G2206 (accessed June 4, 2013). See also *New Spirit-Filled Life Bible* ©2002 by Thomas Nelson, Inc., The Holy Bible, New King James Version ©1982 by Thomas Nelson, Inc. found in the "Word Wealth" index section on page 1599.

Himself. There is a different effect when I prophesy to people like God is speaking. Usually there is a strength and strong authority on a prophet's words that is stronger than when they are speaking in third person. However, there is nothing wrong with speaking as a prophet or prophetic believer in the third person to share what God is saying through you.

Paul says in 1 Corinthians 14:31 that a believer has prophetic potential within them to prophesy. It is intended as means of a general participation among the believers, mutually benefiting each other with anointed, caring, loving words of edification, strength, insight, confirmation, affirmation, and revelation. Prophecy can also provide insight so that the hearts of men are humbled when ministering to the Lord in worship. The Lord can suddenly make one aware of His Spirit's knowledge of their need and readiness to answer it (1 Cor. 14:24–25).

There are specific guidelines for the operation of this unique gift, as with all gifts of the Holy Spirit, to ensure that one gift does not supplant the practice and exercise of others or usurp the authority of the spiritual leadership governing its activity. All prophecies are subordinated to the plumb line of God's infallible Word, the Bible—in which is the standard and foundation to all prophetic utterance in the church, which is to be judged and screened according to 1 Corinthians 14:26–33.

THE WORD OF GOD IS GOD REVEALED

Prophecy is more than just mere words spoken by a yielded vessel and prophet of God. Prophecy is the spirit of revelation being released. The Book of Revelation is a prophetic book that simply says in Revelation 1:1 (KJV), "The Revelation of Jesus Christ, which God gave Him to show His servants—things which must shortly [quickly, swiftly and imminently] take place. And He sent and signified it by His angel to His servant John." The Book of Revelation is simply about our King and His kingdom, and it was intended for those in the first century who heard this prophecy and needed hope to endure times of persecution and continue to be servants of God until the end of that age.

"Revelation" is translated from the Greek word *apokalypipsis,* which is an unveiling or disclosing of a reality that previously has not been perceived.[32] This apocalypse came from God through Jesus Christ, whose past and present work and position in heaven at the right hand of the Father is the content of the revelation communicated to John by an angel. (See Revelation 22:16.) The purpose of that prophecy and this book was to show His servants, genuine believers, and followers in that age what must take place and the events that would occur shortly, imminently, or quickly.

The Spirit of Wisdom and Revelation

My point is that Paul prays in Ephesians 1:17–19 that the people will receive the spirit of wisdom and revelation with the dual objective of their knowing Christ and understanding His purpose and power working in their lives. *Revelation* refers to an unveiling of our hearts that we may receive insight into the way God's word is intended to work in our lives. That is what I believe prophecy does; it discloses God's original intention and thoughts about you so that you can understand God's plans and purpose for your life. The preaching and teaching of the Word is also used prophetically in aiding people to see the glory of Christ, His purpose, and power for them.

The Holy Scriptures are called the "revealed Word of God." The Bible declares that God's Law and the Prophets are the result of His revealing work, essentially describing the whole of the Old Covenant as "revealed." Moreover, in the New Covenant this word *revealed* is used in writings as well. (See Romans 16:15 and Ephesians 3:3.) We have to be clear that prophetic insight into the Word should not be considered equal to the actual giving of the Holy Scriptures or *logos* (the written Word). As helpful as insight into the Word of God can be,

---

32   Blue Letter Bible, s.v. "apokalypsis," www.blueletterbible.org/lang/lexicon/ Lexicon.cfm?strongs=G602 (accessed June 4, 2013); s.v. "revelation," www .blueletterbible.org/search/translationResults.cfm?Criteria=revelation%2A+G602 &t=KJV (accessed June 4, 2013). See also http://en.wikipedia.org/wiki/Revelation; http://en.wikipedia.org/wiki/Apocalypse (accessed July 10, 2013).

the final authority of that revelation of God's Holy Word is the only sure foundation for establishing our lives. (See Matthew 7:24–29.)

Ephesians 1:17–23 (NKJV) says:

> That the God of our Lord Jesus Christ, the Father of glory, may give to you the spirit of wisdom and revelation in the knowledge of Him, the eyes of your understanding being enlightened; that you may know what is the hope of His calling, what are the riches of the glory of His inheritance in the saints, and what is the exceeding greatness of His power toward us who believe, according to the working of His mighty power which He worked in Christ when He raised Him from the dead and seated Him at His right hand in the heavenly places, far above all principality and power and might and dominion, and every name that is named, not only in this age but also in that which is to come. And He put all things under His feet, and gave Him to be head over all things to the church, which is His body, the fullness of Him who fills all in all.

It is the spirit of wisdom and revelation that we receive when prophecies are being released and when reading the Word of God. Until then we do not know what is the Lord's desire and heart toward His people. God wants to open the eyes of our understanding and bring enlightenment. We have the prophetic Scriptures and the Word of God as a sure prophecy. I am not saying that we put all our hope and trust in prophecy; it should be in God's Word first. If there is any prophetic utterance being released, it should be backed up by the Word of God.

The Bible is a prophetic and historical holy book that was written by Spirit-inspired individuals. The Law and the Prophets and Christ Jesus were the fulfillment of what was written and spoken (prophesied). Having the eyes of your understanding or heart being enlightened really means that your heart may receive the glorious light and brightness of hope resulting when the wealth of God's investment in you is understood and made clear by revelation of His Word.

Have you read the Word of God, received a prophetic word, or heard the teaching and preaching of the Word of God and the light-bulb came on, or you had an aha moment? That is a sign that your spiritual eyes and heart received revelation and understanding of God's purpose, which He will work in a believer. Having a prophetic desire is sharing the heart of God's desire for you to be all that He has desired you to be. Knowing your gifts and spiritual abilities can allow you to operate in the one or more dimensions of the prophetic.

Chapter Nine

DIMENSIONS OF THE PROPHETIC

*And it shall come to pass in the last days, says God, That I will pour
out of My Spirit on all flesh; Your sons and your daughters shall
prophesy, Your young men shall see visions, Your old men shall
dream dreams. And on My menservants and on My maidservants
I will pour out My Spirit in those days; And they shall prophesy.*
—ACTS 2:17–18, NKJV

THERE ARE FOUR distinct functions of prophecy according to the Word of God. This book is not an in-depth study specifically on the office of the prophets but on the function of prophecy and discovering one's prophetic voice, gifts, nature, and identity in Christ. The basic scriptural definition of prophecy, according to 1 Corinthians 14:3, is edification, exhortation, and comfort. This is a New Testament guide to prophecy in its simplest function. The office of the prophet is not limited to this function but goes more in-depth. The purpose of prophetic spoken words is to bring edification, which means "to build up" like a building or edifice.

We are the edifice and building of the Lord, called "the church" in the earth. That church is not a natural building with natural material or stones, but we are "living stones." The building grows in the Lord through prophecies. The word *edify* shares the same root as the word *edifice,* which means "to build." To *prophesy* means "to forth-tell, declare, and reveal the word of the Lord."[33] This function to prophesy acts as a predicting function of future events, as divinely inspired by the Holy Spirit's anointing.

Amos 3:7 says, "Surely the Lord GOD does nothing, unless He reveals His secret to His servants the prophets." I have seen that many

---

33   Blue Letter Bible, "prophēteia," www.blueletterbible.org/lang/lexicon/
Lexicon.cfm?strongs=G4394 (accessed June 5, 2013).

do not know about the ministry of the prophet, prophetic ministry, prophecy, or the gifts of the Spirit. I believe it is time for us to explore the four different realms or levels of prophetic ministry. Until we understand this, many will never know where they fit in. There are also four dimensions of prophetic ministry, which I will outline in an easy-to-understand form, and I will also expound more in-depth on the supernatural gifts of the Holy Spirit in a later chapter.

1. The Spirit of Prophecy

And I fell at his feet to worship him. But he said to me, "See that you do not do that! I am your fellow servant, and of your brethren who have the testimony of Jesus. Worship God! For the testimony of Jesus is the spirit of prophecy."

—Revelation 19:10, nkjv

This is the simplest level of prophetic ministry. The spirit of prophecy makes it possible for all people in a certain area to move in the area of the prophetic. Revelation 19:10 states that the spirit of prophecy is basically the testimony of Jesus. The Holy Spirit is a prophetic spirit, and He loves to pour Himself on those who will receive Him. In the Book of Acts 2:14–18, the spirit of prophecy caused those who were called sons and daughters ("servants and handmaidens," kjv) to prophesy. The spirit of prophecy enables people to function when there is a Holy Spirit–filled unction.

It takes an act of supernatural faith to operate in the spirit of prophecy when it manifests in a room or area. When the spirit of prophecy manifests in a room, all people within the dwelling have the anointing upon them. When the spirit of prophecy lifts, then the anointing to prophesy lifts as well in a room.

Any believer can yield to the spirit of prophecy and declare the testimony of Jesus. Have you ever been in a meeting and were asked by the pastor or someone if you would like to give a testimony of the goodness of Christ? Well, the spirit of prophecy is like Jesus coming in a meeting and standing up to declare what is on His heart and His goodness.

Moreover, the spirit of prophecy can be released through intense worship. In 1 Samuel 10:10 we see how King Saul came into direct contact with the spirit of prophecy. As he walked down the road of Gilgal and encountered a team of prophets, the spirit of prophecy came upon him, and he began to prophesy in the same prophetic vein as the prophets coming down from the high place. We can see in this specific account the manifestation of the Holy Spirit. When you come into contact with the spirit of prophecy, you have the supernatural ability to do as the prophets do.

2. The Gift of Prophecy

To another the working of miracles, to another prophecy, to another discerning of spirits, to another different kinds of tongues, to another the interpretation of tongues.

—1 Corinthians 12:10, nkjv

The gift of prophecy and the spirit of prophecy are similar, but the gift is on a more advanced level. The spirit of prophecy can be taken away and lifted, while the gift of prophecy remains. When God gives a gift to someone, He will not take it away. Romans 11:29 says that the gifts and callings of God are irrevocable.

Now let us look at the word *prophecy*. The Hebrew word for prophesy is *naba*, meaning to speak or sing by inspiration, and in the Greek we have *chazah*, meaning "to mentally perceive, to have vision of."[34] Prophesy means "to speak on behalf of another." When we speak on behalf of God, we are prophesying.[35]

Now, the second dimension or level of prophecy is the gift of prophecy, which mainly operates in the realm of the future. There are gifts that pass judgment and rebuke, like the word of knowledge, which I will explain in later chapters. The gift of prophecy can be stirred up by one who has the gift resident in them. In 2 Timothy 1:6

---

34 Blue Letter Bible, s.v. "chazah," www.blueletterbible.org/lang/lexicon/Lexicon.cfm?strongs=H2372 (accessed June 4, 2013). See also http://www.thefreedictionary.com/prophecy.

35 Blue Letter Bible, s.v. "prophēteuō," www.blueletterbible.org/lang/lexicon/Lexicon.cfm?strongs=G4395 (accessed June 5, 2013). See also http://www.thefreedictionary.com/prophesy.

(NKJV) we read, "Therefore I remind you to stir up the gift of God which is in your through the laying on of my hands."

In other words, even though the spirit of prophecy and the gift of prophecy are similar (but different when manifested), a believer can yield to the spirit of prophecy when present and prophesy from the dimension of the gift of prophecy as well. The only difference is that the gift of prophecy, when uttered, has added strength and power than prophecies given by the spirit of prophecy alone. There are dimensions of strength of the gift depending on the measure of grace received by the believer who possesses the gift. Believers who prophesy by the gift of prophecy will deliver words of edification, exhortation, and comfort, according to 1 Corinthians 14:3. Individuals who are not called to the ministry office of a prophet should operate only within the limitations of the gift of prophecy, which is edification, exhortation, and comfort.

There have been times when I have witnessed individuals that operate outside of their grace and try to prophesy and bring correction, rebuke, order, affirmation, direction, confirmation, impartation, revelation, and activation. These are functions of a prophet and, when spoken outside of that gifting, they only bring dissention, division, and confusion within the body of Christ. One must function in the grace that he or she was called and gifted in. In other words, a person who operates in the gift of prophecy must stay in their lane (grace), and if they illegally intrude into someone else's lane without permission, there is an accident waiting to happen. Believers who have been ordained, recognized, and released by the senior leadership of a local church or congregation as a prophet of God are the ones who have been given the godly honor, authority, and release to speak beyond the limitation of the gift of prophecy. God is not the author of confusion but of peace.

3. The Prophetic Anointing

The prophetic anointing is the third dimension of the prophetic. This type of anointing operates with a greater depth and dimension. A person can have the prophetic anointing on them and operate like a prophet but may not be called as a prophet in the office. The anointing is the measure of the spirit of the prophet that comes upon a person, which mantles them to operate in the authority of a prophet. In other words, the prophetic anointing allows a person to become a prophet for a specific time, season, moment, and period to prophesy with the authority of God. The prophecy anointing is a term that applies to a move of the Holy Spirit within a person to shift them to prophesy.

The mantle on a prophet is their equipment and tools for the official prophet or prophetic individual to function. When the Holy Spirit manifests in a believer, the prophetic anointing and words of wisdom and knowledge manifest Him.

Let's now take a look at 2 Kings 2:13 (NKJV), which says, "[Elisha] also took up the mantle of Elijah that had fallen from him, and went back and stood by the bank of the Jordan." Like Elisha, when someone picks up the mantle of the prophetic, they are endowed with a prophetic anointing. Now hear this clearly: not everyone with a prophetic anointing is a prophet. There is a thin line between the two, but nevertheless there is a line. To have a prophetic anointing means to bear a mantle upon your high calling. The prophetic anointing is tangibly discerned and sensed in the belly, abdomen, and in the heart like rivers of water. (See John 7:38.)

The prophets of old made reference to the fire in their bellies, which people may refer to as their "gut feelings" and fire in their bones and joints, like the prophet Jeremiah experienced. The prophetic anointing can be like electricity when the Holy Spirit moves through an individual. It's a manifestation of the Holy Spirit's power and utterance of prophecy.

There are prophetic pastors and prophetic teachers. Pastoring and teaching are the high callings, and the prophetic mantle or anointing is like icing on a cake. Therefore, there are different dimensions of the prophetic anointing. There can be dreamers, visionaries, prophetic apostles, prophetic evangelists, prophetic palmists, prophetic deacons, prophetic elders, prophetic musicians, prophetic worshipers, prophetic intercessors and watchmen, prophetic counselors, prophetic writers, songwriters, etc. We must understand that each of these can be prophets, but not everyone with these anointings are prophets.

4. The Office of the Prophet

And He Himself gave some to be apostles, some prophets, some evangelists, and some pastors and teachers.

—Ephesians 4:11, nkjv

And God hath set some in the church, first apostles, secondarily prophets, thirdly teachers, after that miracles, then gifts of healings, helps, governments, diversities of tongues.

—1 Corinthians 12:28, kjv

This is by far the most important and highest level of the prophetic dimension. This is the mighty office of the prophet. Without this office there would be no solid foundation in the church (Eph. 2:19–20). The office of the prophet is one of the most important offices in the body of Christ. The office of the prophet carries the strongest and most authoritative prophetic utterances because they speak using the spirit of prophecy, the gift of prophecy, the prophecy anointing, and also from the prophetic ministry office in which they stand.

Before we go into the attributes of this office, let us understand what a prophet is. A prophet, simply put, is the ambassadorial mouthpiece of God. There are women prophets in the Bible who were called prophetesses. A prophetess is simply a female spokeswoman and prophet of the Lord. Male or female, without the prophet, the church will miss out on a lot of what God is saying and doing in the earth.

A prophet prophesies with greater authority, capacity and depth than other Holy Spirit–filled believers who have not been sovereignly called to the office of the prophet. Moreover, when a prophet prophesies, they prophesy with greater precision, accuracy, insight, wisdom, knowledge, and scope of heaven's view for the earth. The office of the prophet ministers and administers the prophetic in the breadth, length, depth, and height of the prophetic dimension.

Now, there are many attributes to the office of the prophet:

- Prophets have the ability to set up that which is upset.

- Prophets place things that are out of line into line (order).

- Prophets declare and decree what God is speaking in every situation, circumstance, and arena of society.

- Prophets do rebuke, reproof, and pass godly judgment in love and wisdom.

- Prophets edify (to build up), exhort (to stir up), and comfort (to cheer up).

- Prophets bring into open view God's view, perceptive, heartbeat, and mind-set for His people, nation, or territory.

- Prophets give clear godly guidance, direction, and understanding.

- Prophets explain and expound on things in all facets of time, seasons, and elements for getting people to understand the spiritual side of them.

- Prophets keep leaders accountable to God and those under their leadership.

- Prophets stand in the gap as intercessors, seers, and watchmen (*shamar* prophets) for the people.

Prophets have a very unique place within the body of Christ. Their ministry is very important and cannot be neglected or despised. The prophet's ministry is the interpretation of everything from a spiritual standpoint. This ministry is used to bring spiritual implications of things past, present, and in the future before the people of God. This ministry also gets people to understand the significance of happenings in their spiritual walk and help them understand their value. There are three functions of the prophet's ministry:

- To hold things to the full thought of God, usually a reactionary thing

- To call back, redeclare, and repronounce of God's mind, therefore bringing into clear view again the thoughts of God

- To relate to the full, original, and ultimate purpose of God in and through His people

There are three gifts that naturally flow through the prophet:

- The word of knowledge or wisdom: a supernaturally inspired utterance of facts and knowledge, past, present, and future

- The gift of prophecy: a supernaturally inspired utterance from God

- The discerning of spirits: a supernatural ability to discern a person's spiritual character and the source of his actions and messages, such as from the Holy Spirit, demonic spirits, the human spirit, or from the flesh

In addition, prophets can flow and operate in most of the nine gifts of the Holy Spirit, which I will outline in the next chapter. The prophetic administration of a prophet is that they supervise the execution of, use of, conduct of, and manage the prophetic function. In retrospect to prophecy, there are different ways to administer and minister prophecy. Prophets have the power, authority, and grace by God to go beyond the first three dimensions of the prophetic or prophecy and administer the prophetic anointing through confirmation, affirmation, correction, rebuke, alignment, impartation, direction, counsel, activation, revelation, and birthing.

Prophets can walk in the supernatural like Moses, Elijah, Elisha, and Jesus, who operated in deliverance, miracles, healing, and helps. As there are different administrations to the office of the prophet, there are different types of prophets who had various assignments and callings. John the Baptist did not operate in miracles but was governmental. Jeremiah was a weeping prophet who was called to nations and kingdoms. Ezekiel and Zechariah were visionary prophets. Moses was a deliverer, judge, and shepherd. Samuel was Israel's last judge, priest, dean, and prophet of the school of prophets. Regardless of the dimension of the prophetic that a person will operate in, it is done through the supernatural gifts of the Holy Spirit or the ministry of the Holy Spirit.

Chapter Ten

SUPERNATURAL GIFTS
OF THE HOLY SPIRIT

Having then gifts differing according to the grace that is given to us,
let us use them: if prophecy let us prophesy in proportion to our faith.
—ROMANS 12:6, NKJV

WHEN OPERATING BEYOND one's fullness in the Holy Ghost it is necessary to comprehend the impact of the Spirit's full function of gifts in and through the life and witness of the believers, called the body of Christ. The Spirit-filled encounter is more than just speaking in tongues, shouting, and dancing in church; in reality it is entering into the fullness of the gifts and fruits of the Spirit, which is detailed in the New Testament. (See 1 Corinthians 12:7–11; Galatians 5:22–23.) Moreover, it has a broader dimension of exercising and demonstrating God's gifts of spiritual enablement, empowerment, and endowment, which is described in Romans 12:3–8 and Ephesians 4:7–12.

Romans 12:3–8 (NKJV) says:

For I say, through the grace given to me, to everyone who is among you, not to think of himself more highly than he ought to think, but to think soberly, as God has dealt to each one a measure of faith. For as we have many members in one body, but all the members do not have the same function, so we, being many, are one body in Christ, and individually members of one another. Having then gifts differing according to the grace that is given to us, let us use them: if prophecy, let us prophesy in proportion to our faith; or ministry, let us use it in our ministering; he who teaches, in teaching; he who exhorts, in exhortation; he who gives, with liberality; he who leads, with diligence; he who shows mercy, with cheerfulness.

We can see that we must serve the Lord in the spiritual gifts that He has given to us. The Lord wants us to use them according to the proportion or measure of faith that comes with that spiritual gift and call. If it's teaching, then use it by teaching. If it's ministry, then use it in ministering. If it's to exhortation, then use it by exhorting. And if it's prophecy, then use it by prophesying. In the passage above the apostle Paul was using himself as an example in his own apostolic function in the body as an authoritative apostle through the grace given to him.

The Measure of Faith to Operate

With any gift or calling there is a measure of faith that is given to an individual at birth to operate in that future call and gifting. The measure of faith is not talking about saving faith but the faith to receive and to exercise the gifts of God apportioned to the believer. When we hear the term *measure of faith* it is best understood as a synonym for *spiritual gift* (*charisma*). With any spiritual gift there is a measure of faith to operate, but there is also a measure of rule or influence as well. We cannot operate outside of the measuring line or boundaries that are established within the spiritual gift. There is a grace to operate within the sphere or limitation of the gift and call. This faith is not also talking about the gift of faith, but there is a measure of faith that is bestowed upon the person that possesses a particular calling and gifting.

Moreover, our unique and different gifts and abilities should cause a believer to love and depend more on one another. This should make us more united as *one* body in Christ Jesus. There should be a strong synergy and connectivity within the body of Christ, all working together in love. There is no gift greater or better than another, but love is to be pursued when operating in concert with the gifts of the Spirit.

Prophecy, especially as in Romans 12:6, refers either to those creative and creation gifts from the Lord that empower and enable the believer to view all aspects of life with special, continual prophetic insight, knowledge, understanding, and discernment. The discernment is independent of the public prophetic office or special use by the Spirit in giving public prophecy and of the manifestation of public prophecy in uttering a prophetic word that the Lord brought to a believer's mind spontaneously. (See 1 Corinthians 12:10.)

When the Scriptures say to prophesy in proportion to our faith, more likely it means that prophecy or the prophetic gift is to be exercised in accordance with the biblical integrity and maturity God has granted the oracle in recognizing that God is the originator of the gift. There are people who want the gift for the purpose of self-glorification but not for the Giver of that gift, which is the Lord, who should get all the glory. There should be a hunger as new covenant believers not just to want to prophesy or operate in the gift of prophecy (or any gifts of the Holy Spirit) but rather to want to operate and to hear God speaking, therefore declaring what the Father is saying, that He may be glorified as a result.

THE GRACE OF GOD

When we talk about the supernatural gifts of the Holy Spirit, what I am referring to is the Greek word *charisma* (singular) or *charismata* (plural), which are used to designate spiritual gifts in the most simple, practical, and technical sense of the word. They are graces of the Holy Spirit."[36] The gift of God on your life is the "holy grace" and "holy call" as well.

Have you met anyone who was very gifted or talented? It is because they are graced and called to a specific area. It doesn't have to be ministry *per se*, but whatever they are operating in causes them to be very charismatic. For a person to be charismatic basically means that the person is gifted. Usually prophetic and spiritual people are the most charismatic individuals. In the Book of Ephesians 4:1–13, there are words such as *doma* and *dorea* that are also used to designate gifts, referring to these gifts as "enablers" or "equippers" for personal service and as facilitators in the kingdom of God. The *doma* or *dorea* gifts that the Lord Jesus gave to the church today are the

---

36   Blue Letter Bible, s.v. "charisma," www.blueletterbible.org/lang/lexicon/
Lexicon.cfm?strongs=G5486 (accessed June 5, 2013); s.v. "charis," www
.blueletterbible.org/lang/lexicon/Lexicon.cfm?strongs=G5485 (accessed June 5, 2013).

fivefold ascension gifts of apostles, prophets, evangelists, pastors, and teachers.[37]

In *The Message* Bible, Ephesians 4:11–13 says:

> He handed out gifts above and below, filled heaven with his gifts, filled earth with his gifts. He handed out gifts of apostle, prophet, evangelist, and pastor-teacher to train Christ's followers in skilled servant work, working within Christ's body, the church, until we're all moving rhythmically and easily with each other, efficient and graceful in response to God's Son, fully mature adults, fully developed within and without, fully alive like Christ.

These are the *doma* or *dorea* gifts within God's body. We cannot mix them up with the nine gifts of the Holy Spirit. These are given by Christ to the church for the purpose of equipping the saints for the work of ministry. If one is called to the five-fold ministry, that person must know which one of these *doma* offices (gifts) they are called to and born to operate in.

In Corinthians 12:1 the word *pneumatikos* is used to also describe the gifts as "things belonging to the Spirit."[38] The point I am trying to make is that each of these words gives a contemporary meaning to the supernatural work of the Spirit in our lives as He prepares us for kingdom service and expansion in grace.

What Are the Supernatural Gifts of the Holy Spirit?

> Now concerning spiritual gifts, brethren, I would not have you ignorant.
>
> —1 Corinthians 12:1, kjv

The apostle was addressing the church at Corinth in regards to the spiritual gifts of the Holy Spirit. It was his heart and motivation

---

37   Blue Letter Bible, s.v. *"doma,"* www.blueletterbible.org/lang/lexicon/Lexicon.cfm?strongs=G1390 (accessed June 5, 2013); s.v. *"dōrea,"* www.blueletterbible.org/lang/lexicon/Lexicon.cfm?strongs=G1431 (accessed June 5, 2013). For more information, see http://nephos.com/Patriallpage73.htm.

38   Blue Letter Bible, s.v. "pneumatikos," www.blueletterbible.org/lang/lexicon/Lexicon.cfm?strongs=G4152 (accessed June 5, 2013).

to upgrade that church in the things of the Spirit. He stated that he would not have them be ignorant. As prophetic people we must understand the working of the Holy Spirit and must possess the spirit of love to flow effectively in the gifts of the Spirit. The Bible says that God gives severally as He sees fit, and that all the different gifts of the Spirit work in tandem by the same Holy Spirit (1 Cor. 12:11). Paul didn't want this gifted church to be misinformed on the different gifts, their operation, and also how to operate in them in love. The Corinthians' misunderstanding of the expression and operation in which the Holy Spirit works through them caused them to abuse the public usage of the spiritual gifts. This caused confusion within the congregation in regards to the gifts of tongues and prophecy. Paul responds with fatherly wisdom to the problem in the church by bringing clarity on the necessity of spiritual gifts operating in unity, love, and in order to alleviate disorder, dissension, confusion, and pride outlined throughout chapter 12 of 1 Corinthians.

In verse 1, we read that Paul did not want these gifted individuals to be ignorant of what they were operating in. There is nothing like operating in something that you have no knowledge of. The apostle Paul wanted to bring understanding and order in the Corinthian church.

In the Old Testament prophets operated in these gifts of the Spirit, and the difference in the New Covenant is that the same thing can happen potentially through every believer and not just through a few. Ephesians 4:12 tells us these gifts are given to prepare, train, educate, and equip God's people for holy service and for building up the body of Christ.

In Mary Fairchild's article on "What are Spiritual Gifts?" she states that the term "spiritual gifts" comes from the Greek words *charismata* (gifts) and *pneumatika* (spirits). They are the plural forms of *charisma*, meaning "expression of grace," and *pneumatikon*, meaning "expression of Spirit."[39]

We can see that spiritual gifts are expressions of the divine

---

39 Mary Fairchild, "What Are Spiritual Gifts?" About.com, http://christianity. about.com/od/holyspirittopicalstudy/a/spiritualgifts.htm (accessed July 10, 2013). See also Wikipedia.org, s.v. "spiritual gift," http://en.wikipedia.org/wiki/ Charismata (accessed July 10, 2013).

personality of the Holy Spirit through the Christian believer. In other words, there are various and multiple kinds of spiritual gifts, ministries, operations, administrations, services, and graces sovereignly given by God according to 1 Corinthians chapter 12. The supernatural gifts (charismata) are endowments distributed by the Holy Spirit. In the New Testament the purpose and mission of spiritual gifts was the edification (building up), exhortation (encouragement), and comforting (strengthening) the body of Christ, which is a dynamic of the prophetic function. Moreover, the dual Greek term that Mary Fairchild talks about in her article is translated in Scripture as "spiritual gifts," referring to spirituals or things of the spirit, according to 1 Corinthians 12:1.

Furthermore, in verse 4 of 1 Corinthians 12 it states that there are diversities of gifts—*charisma*, which is of the root word *charis,* meaning "grace," which we commonly use when we refer to a gifted person as being "charismatic." But in verse 5, we see that there are differences of administration, ministries, or services (*diakonia*), while in verse 6 it talks about the diversities of operation, activities, or in-workings (*energemata*), which reflects the innate nature of the supernatural gifts of the Spirit that God works in a believer. Furthermore, in verse 7 it reveals the term *manifestation* (*phanerosis*) of the Spirit that is endowed and delegated to each *one* individually for the overall benefit of *all* corporately in the church.

Generally speaking, the gifts of the Spirit are God-given abilities, ministry offices, and manifestations that empower the Spirit-filled believer to bless, assist, and strengthen others while the fruit of the Spirit and the nine gifts of the Spirit assist the believer personally with his or her Christian walk. These gifts, offices, and manifestations of the Holy Spirit are diverse and should promote unity, joy, peace, and order within the body of Christ. To learn more on spiritual gifts, ascension ministry gifts (offices) and their function, read the following passages of Scripture: Romans 12:6–8; 1 Corinthians 12:4–11, 28–31; 1 Peter 4:10.

EPHESIANS 4:11–13; 1 CORINTHIANS 12:28
—THE ASCENSION GIFTS OF THE SON
(Fivefold Officials Given to the Church to
Facilitate and Equip the Body of Christ)

Ephesians 4:8, 11–13 (ESV) says, "When he ascended on high he led a host of captives and he gave gifts to men....And he gave the apostles, the prophets, the evangelists, the shepherds and teachers, to equip the saints for the work of ministry, for building up of the body of Christ, until we all attain to the unity of the faith and of the knowledge of the Son of God, to mature manhood, to the measure of the stature of the fullness of Christ."

This passage of Scripture involves Jesus setting the captives free, and in doing so, giving gifts to men. In other words, Jesus gifted the church with headship ministries, and began to reveal the names and titles of those gifted headship ministries. What are those ascension headship gifts that Jesus gave? The Bible says that He gave the apostles, prophets, evangelists, pastors (shepherds), and teachers. Simply, the gifts that Jesus presented were actually gifted people who had a sovereign calling from birth to be an apostle, prophet, evangelist, pastor (shepherd), or teacher. We must understand that the Holy Spirit is God's gift through Christ to the Christian believers both personally and collectively. The Holy Spirit works together with the Father and the Son to fulfill God's eternal purposes. God is the giver of the gifts, not man. Some people may identify and call these headship ministries ministry gifts, post-ascension-gift ministries, the fivefold ministry offices, or the five-folders of the church. We must understand that they are the extension of Jesus Christ's ministry. They are the five headship ministries of Christ, who is the Head of His church.

These are not considered "body" gifts of Christ, but rather the governmental ascension headship gifts. We must be clear not to mix them with gifts of the Holy Spirit but identify them as ascension gifts of Jesus Christ. We see that Jesus ascended and gave His mantle and leadership grace to men for the benefit of the body of Christ. Jesus gave these headship gifts to the church for a divine purpose.

Moreover, these headship ascension gifts have specific callings, graces, measures of rule, functions, abilities, and roles, but are not limited to them depending on assignment and activities. Whatever name you choose to classify them, we must understand that they are vital to the foundational structure, growth, health, and building process. Furthermore, these fivefold ministry offices are not just gifts to men but are called and chosen of the Lord before the foundation of the world to serve, disclose, and declare the overall purpose of God in the earth through the Spirit-filled believer.

The hand of God is upon those of you who have been sovereignly handpicked before you entered your mother's womb to facilitate the work of God in your generation. I believe that God has not designated nor has He designed the fivefold officers to function separately or independently, but rather interdependently. They work interchangeably and as a team. The synergy of teamwork will promote a clear plumb line that does not hinder, stifle, or block the power of God from flowing effectively. The headship gifts needs the body, and vice versa. In the twenty-first century church we need the hand of God directing, leading, guiding, challenging, covering, and protecting us. Speaking of the hand of God, we can see that God's hand represents power, authority, permission, and His sovereignty. Jesus is right now seated at the right hand of His Father.

In other words, the fivefold ministry is symbolic of God's hand, the five fingers represented in the church. The apostolic, prophetic, evangelistic, pastoral, and teaching ministries are parts of God's government in the church that release the kingdom power. The Father has placed Jesus as the Head of His church and all things concerning His church. In other words, Jesus has His hand directly involved in the building of the *ecclesia* (called out ones) called the church. Understanding the supernatural gifts of the Holy Spirit will allow you to know God's order and fivefold officers in the church, as He has set some as apostles, some prophets, some evangelists, some pastors, and some teachers. God is a God of order and not confusion. There is no big "I" and little "you" in the kingdom of God and in His church.

With any structure, government, kingdom, or system, there has to be an order and flow chart of how things function, operate, and flow so that there is clarity of purpose. All fivefold ministers or officers are called to govern, gather, protect, guard, prophesy, guide, build, encourage, comfort, direct, and bless the body of Christ. I remember Dr. Bill Hamon, founder of Christian International, who is considered one of the pioneers and fathers of the prophetic restoration movement, came to my local assembly and taught on the fivefold ministry and their purpose. But what was interesting about his teaching was that he showed the prophetic leaders and ministers at the conference an illustration of a human hand that I never forgot. He related the hand to the "hand of God," which describes the governmental position, function, and placement of the fivefold ministry officers in the church: apostle, prophet, evangelist, pastor, and teacher.

First Peter 5:5-6 (ESV) says, "Clothe yourselves, all of you, with humility toward one another, for God opposes the proud but gives grace to the humble. Humble yourselves, therefore, under the mighty hand of God so that at the proper time he may exalt you."

We can see in verse 6 of the above scripture that humility brings promotion. It is divine wisdom for a person to be covered under the protective hand of God. When a person submits to the order of God and relates in love with others in the body of Christ, whether in the kingdom or not, God will give them provision and favor. Those who are rebellious and will not submit to the order of God or to those whom He places in authority are running the risk of being unprotected and open to demonic influences and unwarranted attacks. If you are a fivefold minister or believer and you know that there is a greater cause burning within you to do greater works for the Lord, but feel like you have fallen out of agreement with Him, then the time is now to make a decision and repent so that you come under the protective covering of God and those in headship position in the body of Christ. We need the hand of the Lord working in our lives like never before. Below I have identified in simple form the headship government ministry gifts of Jesus Christ by relating them to a five-fingered hand:

1. **The Apostle = Thumb**: The thumb of the hand represents the apostle's ministry, which, like the thumb, is considered the strongest and positioned strategically to bring support to the whole. An apostle can start, plant, and strengthen new and existing churches, ministries, and people, while at

the same time representing teamwork. They have an ability to interact, touch, bring together, relate, reach, and impact others if they need to. Jesus being the foundation and Head of His church, an apostle has the grace throughout their ministry to operate in various and even all dimensions of the ministry gifts, but not at the same time. The Greek word *apostolos*, from which we derive the word *apostle*, literally means "one who is sent forth."[40] Apostles, like those with the other headship gifts, are sent by God by way of the Holy Spirit. They are commissioned special messengers, delegates, envoys, and ambassadors representing the king and His kingdom.

Moreover, the apostle, like the thumb, has been designed by the strength of their calling to take hold of something, whether it is a new vision, dream, plan, blueprint, project, etc., and gather others around them to bring what God puts in their heart to full maturation. One of an apostle's primary focuses is bringing order, transforming, building, impacting, fathering, covering, teaching, preaching, and demonstrating the kingdom of God in the people they meet. Can you image the church without modern-day apostles? I liken it to a hand missing a thumb, and how ineffective the hand can be without the thumb, which is the base of the hand. The apostolic ministry is vital and important to Christ and His eternal church. The thumb can touch every finger on the hand; so does an apostle who should be in covenant relationship and submission to others under their leadership or in the body of Christ at large.

2. **The Prophet = Forefinger/Index Finger**: The index or pointer finger refers to the prophet, who is called to point the way to God, the way back to God, and the way a believer should walk in God. In other words, the pointer finger represents the special anointing and call of the prophet to receive revelation and insight, and the ability to

---

40   Conner, 139. See also Blue Letter Bible, s.v. "apostolos," www.blueletterbible. org/lang/lexicon/Lexicon.cfm?strongs=G652 (accessed June 5, 2013).

confirm people's destinies. The prophet's ministry can also confirm, bring clarity, and point out sin or areas of error while at the same time ordaining, identifying, establishing, activating, and speaking into something. Like the forefinger, the prophetic nature of the prophet is the ability through their tremendous gift, call and office to prophesy with authority, power, strength, love, and clarity.

The forefinger is next to the thumb, and both the prophet and apostle are foundational ministries that need each other, especially because the apostle plants by the Spirit and the prophet can water (build) what the apostle establishes. The prophet needs the apostle and vice versa. The prophet and the apostle have a working relationship. They together have a close-knit relationship in the hand ministry of the body of Christ. The forefinger, which represents the prophet's ministry, also illustrates the realm of authority and grace through their gift and office to minister prophetically, which outlines the nature of prophecy—a dual function and dimension in foretelling (prediction of future) and forth-telling (speaking forth).

The prophet is also the mouthpiece of God, and no ministry office has the grace and the authority to prophesy like a prophet can. I am not saying that others cannot prophesy, but they are limited to edification, exhortation, and comfort. Can you imagine the hand without the index finger to point you in the right direction and show you the way? We are not to replace the function of the Holy Spirit who has been sent to assist and guide us with prophets. But prophets today are just as vital to the hand as any other finger. We need to know what God is doing and saying to us in the earth today. We need the ministry of modern-day prophets in our midst.

The New Testament Greek word for prophecy is *propheteuo*, which means "to foretell events, divine, speak under inspiration, exercise the prophetic office; to proclaim a divine revelation, prophesy, to foretell the future; to speak forth by divine inspiration; to break forth under sudden impulse in lofty discourse or in praise of the divine counsels."[41] This Greek word *propheteuo* is translated "prophesy." (See Matthew 15:7; Luke 1:67; Acts 2:17–18, 21:9; and 1 Corinthians 14:1, 3–5.)

3. **The Evangelist = Middle Finger**: The middle finger is the longest, most visible and extended finger on the hand. It represents the ministry gift of an evangelist. The middle finger, like the evangelist, can reach, touch, and extend further than the rest. The evangelistic ministries are notable for their mass revivals, worldwide crusades, and mission trips that are held in large settings and last for long periods of time. The middle finger is the longest or largest finger on the hand, and the evangelist has a grace and passion to evangelize the world. They can move in tremendous gifts of the Holy Spirit that release revival fires that ignite in the hearts of unbelievers. The evangelistic ministries have a heart to win multiple souls for Christ. One of the primary objectives is being a witness for Christ; bring healing, miracle and redemption to the lost.

An evangelist loves going out and not being confined to the four-walled church. Their commission is in the "Great Commission," to disciple whole nations, which should be all of the headship and Christian believers' objective and agenda. The anointing on an evangelist is a gift to draw, win, gather, convince, persuade, and encourage. In addition, they work with the local church to bring new converts into the local assembly to get them discipled, trained, equipped, and deployed (commissioned) by the Holy Spirit to win others to Christ.

The evangelists are called to bring the gospel, or good news. There are three words related to the ministry of an evangelist, all of which come from a similar root word in the Greek: *euaggelizo,* meaning "to announce good news or glad tidings (SC 2097)," *euaggelion,* "the gospel or the

---

41   Conner, 154. See also Blue Letter Bible, s.v. "prophēteuō," www
.blueletterbible.org/lang/lexicon/Lexicon.cfm?strongs=G4395 (accessed June 5,
2013).

good message (SC 2098)," and *euanggelistes,* "a preacher
or messenger of good news (SC 2099)."[42] We can see that
an evangelist is clearly one called to herald the gospel of
Jesus Christ and a preacher or messenger of the word they
deliver, which brings glad tidings. Can you picture the hand
without the middle finger? The evangelistic ministry is so
vital to the church of Jesus Christ today. Without the evangelist, who will bring the harvest into the kingdom? We
need evangelists more today than ever before. There are
those who think evangelism is not necessary, but I believe
it is just as important to the fivefold ministry as the prophet
and apostle foundationally set in the church.

4. **The Pastor** = **Ring Finger**: The ring finger represents the
ministry of the pastor. This finger is the one on which the
wedding ring is placed. The pastor is the shepherd of the
Lord's people. The pastor is graced with the ability and
anointing to labor with the people. He or she is married
to the people, in covenant relationship with them to feed,
clean, correct, bless, and love them more than any other. A
pastor is so committed to those God has entrusted them
with that he will leave the rest to go after the one who has
left or broken covenant.

The ring finger is symbolic and a representation of
a long-term relationship and true accountability. It's a
working relationship between a pastor and their local saints.
A pastor will lay down his life for his own, just a husband
will give his life for his wife as Christ did for the church
and for His people. Apostles and prophets will come and go,
as they travel extensively, but a true shepherd is committed
to the house of God and bound to it as he brings balance,
productivity, maturity in the new believers, and spiritual
nourishment.

---

42   Conner, 170. See also Blue Letter Bible, s.v. "euaggelistēs," www
.blueletterbible.org/lang/lexicon/Lexicon.cfm?strongs=G2099; s.v. "euaggelizō,"
www.blueletterbible.org/lang/lexicon/Lexicon.cfm?strongs=G2097;
s.v. "euaggelizō," www.blueletterbible.org/lang/lexicon/Lexicon.
cfm?strongs=G2097(accessed June 5, 2013).

Moreover, the pastor is called to protect, guide, oversee, defend, rule, supervise, feed, tend to, watch, manage, assist, walk alongside, give spiritual counsel, and stand with their local saints no matter what. A pastor may seem overprotective at times only because in their heart of hearts is a holy jealousy that comes from God and causes them to love unconditionally and protect the Lord's inheritance.

Their local church is like the ring finger with a beautiful ring on it; it's a reminder of the vow and love that they committed to. Whether sick or in good health, through ups and downs, difficulties and victories, a pastor is always there and knows when to put his own agenda aside for the sole purpose of pleasing God and being a great representation of Christ as the Good Shepherd. A pastor is patient, not overbearing, considerate, courteous, transparent, a teacher, and very relational. In other words, a true pastor is social, approachable, a good listener, understanding, compassionate, fair, balanced, fatherly, has great interpersonal skills, and is a lover of God and His people.

Furthermore, as the apostles and prophets are the most misunderstood and rejected, the pastoral ministry is much needed today in the church. Most people have in one way or another encountered, known, or visited a church that was primarily governed by a pastor, lead pastor, senior pastor, or the like; whether they married you, baptized you, Christened or dedicated your newborn child, counseled you, or even pastored you. It is vital that we have good moral and ethical pastors loving us as Christ loves His church. Note that I said *pastors*, plural, not one authoritative individual who is not submitted to others. I cannot imagine the body of Christ without pastors/elders and governing overseers tending to the house of God. The New Testament Greek word for pastor is *poimen* (SC 4166), which means "a shepherd" (literally or figuratively).[43]

---

43   Conner, 176. See also Blue Letter Bible, s.v. "poimēn," www.blueletterbible.org/lang/lexicon/Lexicon.cfm?strongs=G4166 (accessed June 5, 2013).

5. The Teacher = Pinky Finger: The little finger on the hand represents the ministry of the teacher. It is the smallest finger on the hand and is able to reach the small areas of things that the other fingers may overlook. Even though the pinky finger is the smallest, it doesn't mean that the teacher's office is insignificant among the other fivefold ministry officers and in the body of Christ. Usually the pastor and teacher are interchangeable and is a share ministry.

A pastor and teacher don't always share ministry, but together they are vital to the practicality and implementation of the principles of God's Word. One of the gifts and anointing of teachers is that they are sticklers to attention to detail, precision, and accuracy, and are able to research, to dig out; reach the cracks and crevices of things. Like the pinky finger, a teacher can fit into tight spaces to reach and illuminate the dark (hidden) areas of the Word of God, while at the same time bringing balance to the body of Christ through fundamental teaching. Their approach is very practical, didactic, revelatory, and prophetic, teaching the Word with clarity that will produce stability, maturation, application, accountability, and responsibility. The ministry of the teacher brings foundational balance to the body of Christ as the pinky finger does to the hand.

A teacher is not limited to just teaching, but can operate as well in any other spiritual gifts. Furthermore, they can be prophetic, evangelistic, apostolic, and pastoral in their delivery and style of teaching that bring results. I believe that ministry gift of the teacher is so vital and needed for church growth, spiritual growth, discipleship, training, equipping, and empowering. Teachers are solely dedicated to revealing and discovering the truth of God's Word without violating the original intent of the Word of God. They build people on the Word of God, line upon line, precept upon precept. We need the teacher mantle, gift, anointing, and ministry in this hour. I do not know where I would be if someone hadn't taken the time to teach me and labor with me to make sure I understood what I was taught.

The New Testament Greek word for teacher is *didasko* (SC 1321), which means "to learn or to teach." There is another Greek word, *didaktikos* (SC 1317), which means "instructive ('didactic')" translated, "apt to teach."[44]

1 Corinthians 12:8–10, 28—The Nine Supernatural Gifts of the Spirit

Word of Wisdom

The gift of word of wisdom is a supernatural ability by the Holy Spirit to ascertain the divine purpose for accomplishing the Lord's objective and will in any given situation and the "how" to fulfill it in a strategic way. It is the ability to rightly apply knowledge and discernment in one's own life and in the lives of others who seek counsel, while the wisdom of God works interactively in this gift. Moreover, it is also the divine perception of God and knowing His divine direction for something in particular, and appropriate spiritual intuition in solving a major and/or unexpected problem or crisis. This gift works effectively in "what to do" types of circumstances and a supernatural knowing of how to handle things in a godly manner. It is a divine insight into the mind, counsel, and truth of God's Word. In this gift there is an ability to execute sound judgment with patience. When I think about the gift of word of wisdom it is "What would Jesus do?" in a situation mindset.

This particular gift is one of my strongest gifts because God has given me a special grace and gift to help senior leaders, other prophets, and those who are in need of the counsel of the Lord. Prophets and Christian believers can operate in this gift of the Spirit. Prophets especially should be able to minister in the wisdom of God. I have witnessed what the word of wisdom gift can do in a person's life; it has brought much clarity, protection, many warnings, and provision.

---

44   Conner, 187. See also Blue Letter Bible, s.v. "didaskalos," www
.blueletterbible.org/lang/lexicon/Lexicon.cfm?strongs=G1320; s.v. "didaktos,"
www.blueletterbible.org/lang/lexicon/Lexicon.cfm?strongs=G1318; s.v.
"didaskō," www.blueletterbible.org/lang/lexicon/Lexicon.cfm?strongs=G1321; s.v.
"didaktikos," www.blueletterbible.org/lang/lexicon/Lexicon.cfm?strongs=G1317
(accessed June 5, 2013).

Word of Knowledge

The gift of word of knowledge is a supernatural ability to contain revelation of God's eternal plan, will, and agenda. It is the ability to utilize moral wisdom for righteous living and establishing godly relationships. In this gift, there is a supernatural possession to know specific facts, information, and revelation about a person, place, thing, or situation that may have happened presently or in the past. This divine knowing is initiated and given by the Holy Spirit without the assistance of any human resources, but primarily by divine help. In other words, it's an ability by the Spirit to know what you know without actually seeing the evidence or even having prior encounters with a person, situation, place, etc. Furthermore, this gift can also refer to the knowledge of God, things pertaining to things possessed by God, as it relates to the Word of God. This unique gift implies a depth and greater capacity to understand the communicated works of the Lord. I have seen this gift, which is considered a prophetic revelatory gift, in operation in prophets.

In other words, prophets have the prophetic insight to know things in the spirit that others may know but have not shared that information with anyone. God has given me the ability through my prophetic gift to know things that may have happened in someone's past, or that is currently occurring, and He would couple the gift of wisdom to give them godly wisdom, direction, instructions, and time to make a decision pertaining to their future and destiny in God. Jesus operated in the gift when speaking to the Samaritan woman at the well, Nathan at the fig tree, and knowing that Judas was going to betray Him.

Discerning of Spirits

The gift of discerning of spirits is a supernatural power that allows a believer to detect the realm of spiritual activities and their spirits. One of the dynamics and elements of this powerful gift is the Holy Spirit innate ability to perceive, identify, verify, discern, and distinguish between truth and error, spirituality and carnality, angelic and demonic, prophetic and new age/psychic, and the Holy Spirit work or the human spirit/flesh at work. Remarkably, this gift of the Holy Spirit can sense demonic and angelic presence and the power of spiritual insight through supernatural revelation into the schemes, tricks, traps, devices, plans, and purposes of the adversary and his demonic arsenal.

This gift also has the ability to identify specific sicknesses or diseases with the help of the other gifts of wisdom and knowledge working interchangeably. We must understand that other gifts can overlap and mix with each other to fulfill God's overall purpose. Jesus was also able, through this gift, to perceive men's thoughts and motivations. The Word of God can sharpen one's ability in this particular gift. The Bible says the Word of the Lord is sharper then any two-edged sword and pierces down to the bone and marrow, and is the discerner of the heart. The Word of God increases any Holy Spirit gift through the believer.

Faith

The gift of faith is a supernatural ability to contend against unbelief, doubt, anxiety, fear, and uneasiness. This gift gives a believer the ability to trust and believe in God without a shadow of doubt in their heart. In addition, this type of faith given by the Holy Spirit is considered saving faith or the measure of faith that is given to all Spirit-filled believers, but this is faith that is able to meet the demands head-on without any inner reservation. This type of faith is not a gift that every believer has or can just ignorantly utilize, but it comes with an inner conviction and holy discontentment to fulfill the high calling of the Lord.

Moreover, a believer that operates in this type of gift has the supernatural faith allotted to them by the Lord to believe Him for the miracles, and also obtain miracles in his or her own life. Apostles, prophets, evangelists, and intercessors are more prone to operate in this type of faith that is required to demonstrate the kingdom of God that will result in change. I have seen believers more in this gifting even though they may not be called to a fivefold ministry office. We so desperately need the gift of faith to be operative in our lives, and to relate with people of tremendous faith.

Prophets, apostles, and evangelists more often have to move in this type of gift to prophesy, work miracles, heal the sick, win the harvest of souls, and believe God for financial resources. This faith gift has the supernatural potential to meet adverse situations, circumstances, and problems head-on while at the same time trusting in the promises of God's Word. Have you ever needed a miracle or something immediately and didn't know how you were going to receive it, but as you read the Word of God, heard a preached message, or overheard someone give a testimony something began to quicken your spirit and all of a sudden all that doubt, fear, unbelief, worry, and distrust that you once had went straight out the window? It was the gift of faith stirring on the inside of you.

The Bible says in Hebrews 11:1 (NKJV) that "now faith is the substance of things hoped for, the evidence of things not seen." We must move beyond the simple gift of faith into a realm or dimension of faith that moves mountains. The Bible also says that faith comes by hearing and hearing by the Word of God. Prophetically God wants to fine-tune our ability to hear and grow in faith through His Word. When you look at your physical ears, they kind of look like a baby embryo; so that being said, when we hear the Word of God, that faith is summoned, and in the Spirit our faith will mature to trust in His Word because faith comes only by hearing the Word of God. So if you want to grow and move in faith, keep hearing and hearing and hearing God's prophetic promises over your life, and you will mature and fulfill that call.

Healing

The gift(s) of healing refers to supernatural healing without any human assistance or guidance. Also, notice that it is called the *gifts* of healing, which is plural. So in other words, there is no one particular way of healing a condition, but through this gift a believer is able to identify one or more areas they are able to flow in without any help from others. This gift is creative in itself, but in some cases, depending on the severity of the sickness or condition, there may be some Spirit-led divine applications of natural directives, implementations, and medical means treating different types of situations. Every sickness may be rare and different and would need special attention when this gift is active. I flow very heavily in the gifts of healing, and God gives me a word of knowledge or divine information about a person's condition, along with the gift of wisdom and discerning of spirits also working together. I am able to identify the condition, see what demonic spirits of infirmity or disease are at work in their body, and with godly wisdom I am able to walk them through their healing and deliverance with simple instructions.

For example, I was in a meeting once and God revealed to me that there was a person that was having problems walking and had this condition for a very long time and God wanted to heal them. So this woman came walking up to the altar in a walker as my brother and I were ministering healing and prophecy. She was disabled and was in need of not only healing but a total miracle. As we saw her condition, there came upon us a supernatural faith to see her made whole, and my hands began to burn. We both laid our hands on her and commanded her body to align itself to the original design and order of God, and she fell out under the power of God. Suddenly she arose and was not in need of her walker. God totally healed her. She began to run around the church screaming, "Thank You, Jesus" while weeping because the Lord healed her from a lifelong condition she'd had since she was a little girl. The gift of healing was at work along with the gifts of faith and miracles. Prophets can move in the gift of healing, as we see many times throughout the Bible Jesus and others operating in healings.

Working of Miracles

The gift of working of miracles or the miraculous is a supernatural enablement to intervene and superimpose any earthly and evil powers or forces. This type of gift is superior in nature because it transcends beyond natural laws to fulfill God's eternal purposes. As I stated before, each gift of the Holy Spirit is not limited to one specific function, but can work closely if need be with other gifts of the Spirit. It is not hard to see the manifestation of just one gift at work in a believer's life, but typically you will witness several of them working closely knit together. The only hard part is identifying these gifts' manifestations if they are working together. That is why I am simply bringing some clarity to this gift's function.

This unique gift works closely with the gift of faith and gifts of healing so that in turn it brings authority and power over sickness, death, the devil, and the binding forces of our day. Jesus is the Miracle Worker. The majority of Jesus' apostolic ministry was prayer, working of miracles, deliverance, healings, casting out demon-possessed individuals, raising the dead, providing supernatural resources, food, fathering, and being about Daddy God's business. Jesus was anointed by the Spirit of God to do what He was able to do. He needed the enablement, endowment, and empowerment of the Spirit to operate on a high realm. This type of gift is vital to the church and world. Can you imagine the church if more people around the world were equipped, trained, and sent to work miracles in marketplaces, workplaces, cities, communities, regions, and every realm of society? I have witnessed five-year-olds move in the gifts of miracles. God wants to use and activate this gift in greater way.

Prophecy

The gift of prophecy is a supernatural gift of proclamation and declaration in a known tongue. I define this gift as the God-inspired ability to speak forth in a known tongue as the Holy Spirit gives them utterance according to 1 Corinthians 12:10). The gift of prophecy is a gift that speaks something by the Spirit and not by human intellect. The prophet of God is the mouthpiece or spokesman of God, through whom inspired words of the Lord are uttered. They speak as God's representatives in the earth, but Christian believers can prophesy who may not be called or stationed in that ministry office. There are several biblical references of people who had the gift of prophecy, one being Philip's four daughters, who were not prophetesses but were able to prophesy. (See Acts 21:8–14, 9.) I believe that the gift of prophecy and the ministry office of the prophet are now more received today in the twenty-first century then in past centuries. God loves to speak to and through His people.

The Bible says in 2 Peter 1:21 that holy men of God spoke as they were moved of the Holy Spirit. Prophets were holy men that spoke by the Holy Spirit. The word of the Lord through a holy believer is like fresh water springing forth to bring refreshing. It is God's idea that you prophesy and speak whether you are a beginner or not. The gift of prophecy via the Holy Spirit is only limited to exhortation (stir up), edification (to build up), comfort (to bind up), and I will go so far as to say to bring holy conviction (to open up) for the sole purpose of blessing and upgrading the saints. The gift of prophecy reveals the heart, intention, motive, and counsel of the Lord to individuals and the body of Christ at large. The prophecy has two functions, as I stated before—foretelling and forth-telling. God will get His point across one way or another. Prophecy released in the church brings confirmation, affirmation, and makes strong His word. It also discloses what He is going to do in a particular time, season, and even generation.

Diverse Kinds of Tongues

The gift of diverse or different kinds of tongues is a supernatural utterance spoken in an unknown language or tongue. In other words, the speaker of the diverse kinds of tongues does not understand what they are uttering forth because it is Holy Spirit-inspired. It's an inspired communication by the Spirit. It also serves as the divine evidence and sign of the baptism of the Holy Ghost. Tongues are a sign to unbelievers and, like the gift of prophecy, is a sign to believers. In other words, when the gift of tongues is at work in a believer, usually it will get unbelievers' attention; I have seen unbelievers question what was happening. I even had an unbeliever ask me if I was crazy, but after I was done this unbeliever eventually became a believer in Christ. The supernatural gift can be also interpreted so that the entire body of Christ is strengthened, encouraged and built up.

Tongues are also used to stir a believer up in their most holy faith in God. I love speaking in diverse tongues because it builds me up to prophesy as well as operate in any other gifts of the Spirit. I utilize the gift of different kinds of tongues to get myself out of the realm of the flesh and move instantly into the spiritual realm. Speaking in tongues takes you into the spiritual realm. We should make it a habit to pray, sing, worship, and even read in tongues. I have made speaking in different kinds of tongues a part of my prayer life. As a youth, after receiving the baptism of the Spirit, I would pray and sing in the Spirit for hours.

I can recall many times growing up in the prophetic that while I was asleep, my peers heard me speaking in tongues. I am reminded of Paul the apostle, who prayed in the Spirit or tongues and worshipped in tongues as well. In other words, he spoke in a known tongue and also in an unknown tongue. There have been times when I sang the song of the Lord in the gift of tongues unto the Lord, and someone would come and tell me that I blessed them, and they knew what I was saying; God prophesied through me in an unknown language. This gift is prevalent among Pentecostal believers. We should not be limited to being with the Spirit, but go beyond that and prophesy and work miracles.

Interpretation of Tongues

The gift of interpretation of tongues is the supernatural ability to disclose and make known in a known tongue the meaning of the unknown tongue that was uttered. We must not confuse the interpretation of tongues or the one who possesses the gift with one who is a translator of a language, because the interpreter never understands the tongue they are interpreting; rather, by supernatural faith they proclaim and reveal by divine revelation the meaning. This gift is exercised in the body of Christ in an unusual, miraculous way that is viewed as a supernatural phenomenon.

The gift of interpretation of tongues usually follows the gift of tongues if there are no prophets who can just prophesy in public the word of the Lord or interpreters present. I can remember a time when I was stretched by faith to operate in this Holy Spirit interpretation gift. Ironically, I had been asking the Lord in prayer to give me this particular gift, and one Sunday morning, the Spirit of God took over a meeting and His glory filled the room. Those in attendance began to speak in tongues for most of the service, then suddenly I felt in my spirit a supernatural faith to interpret what was released. Of course, I had no clue what everyone was saying, but no one stood up to acknowledge that they had a prophecy or word of the Lord, so I volunteered and spoke by faith what I sensed God was saying through the gifts of tongues that were corporately spoken. The people were amazed, blessed, edified, and some were even weeping because God spoke through me and confirmed His plan to some of them who were present. In this gift, a Spirit-filled believer is not interpreting and operating through their own mind or intellect, but having the mind of Christ to share His heart.

Romans 12:3–8: The Motivational Gifts of the Father

Prophecy

We can see that in this particular category prophecy is once again mentioned. We can see that the Father views prophets, prophecy, and the prophetic ministry as an important aspect to the body of Christ. The motivational gift serves its purpose to reveal Christ, and prophecy has a major role in the church, which is characterized in a general sense as a whole to influence the world around us. Prophecy spoken through a man or woman of God who walks in humility, good godly character, and integrity can bring transformation to whole nations, cities, territories, and churches. Romans 12:3–8 really outlines the purpose, motivation, and reason for serving God with your spiritual gifts. Verse 6 says that those who prophesy should use it to the grace that is given to them and also minister prophetically to the proportion of their faith. I always say that your car can only go but so far as your gas tank allows. So in other words, a person can only prophesy to the measure of their faith. I have seen people prophesy outside their grace or measure of faith and wreck themselves before they got started.

The Bible says that we should grow in grace. That means to me that we can grow in the anointing and gift in our lives. If we are faithful over the few things that are given to us, then we can become mature rulers over much. Prophecy in general is vital to the overall makeup of the church, as well as the other gifts. The Bible also says to whom much is given much is required. God knows how much we can take because He knows His children better than we know ourselves. Those operating in the motivational gift to prophesy will speak with divine insight to the strategies and spiritual DNA of heaven and see to it that it comes to pass in the earth. Those who possess this motivational gift of prophecy or to prophesy will not waver or compromise themselves for the sake of population or worldly fame but become worthy, valuable assets to the kingdom of God and His victorious church. The Father utilizes this motivational prophetic gift as what I call the "eyes" (to see) and "ears" (to hear) of the body of Christ.

Ministry

Ministry is not for the faint at heart but those who are going to endure until the end. Ministry is not for the purpose of becoming wealthy and to lord over people, but it is primarily to serve, love, help, and minister to meet the needs of others. Jesus said that He did not come to be served but to serve. Whatever capacity of ministry we function in, we must never forget that we are servants first and leaders second. When Philip inquired about who will be least or greatest in the kingdom, Jesus' response to his question was that those who want to be great must be the servant or slave of all first. In other words, humility is greatness! I remember my twin brother, Naim, sharing with me that his boss would always say, "Naim, how can I serve you? We work for *you!*" I thought that statement was profound. That being said, ministry is working for others. It's our service to help others become better, which is the Father's motive and should be ours as well.

Prophets are especially called to serve God and His people, and operate in the ministry of helps. That's right; I said the ministry of helps. How can a person lead if they never helped another lead? The Bible says in Amos 3:7 (NKJV, emphasis added), "Surely the Lord GOD does nothing, unless He reveals His secrets to his *servants* the prophets." We can see that in this scripture the prophets were called servants first before they were called prophets. In other words, prophets and prophetic believers are servants of God first before they are leaders in their sphere of influence, activity, or work. The office of deacon is also an ordained ministry in the local church and is an important part of the upkeep and maintenance of the work of the Lord. This type of gift of the Father, generally speaking, represents spiritually the "hands" in the body of Christ. We need more laborers in the kingdom who don't have feeble hands and legs.

Teaching

This motivational gift of the Father is necessary in the building of the Word of God in the body, because teaching is the foundational aspect of the church. The teaching ability can explain and reveal truths of God's Word for the overall benefit of the church. We must be studious and devoted to the Word of God. I believe prophets and prophetic people should be teachers (equippers) of the Word and reproduce themselves in others. A prophetic minister should teach on the prophetic, prayer, intercession, worship, praise, drama, the arts, and the gifts of the Spirit. We need sound doctrine presented to the body of Christ so that there is Spirit illumination that provides a safeguard against erroneous teaching and the Gnostics teacher who comes with human philosophies and knowledge.

We need the knowledge of God released in the church to upgrade the saints to present truth. Teaching ministry is different from prophetic ministry, but both in their own right are needed. The teaching element brings clarity to the divine truth and makes it simple and applicable to fulfill. Moreover, teachers in particular are lovers of the Word and they are committed to studying, just as prophets and believers should be lovers of the Word of God and maintain a consistent study life. The Bible says to study to show thyself approved. We must understand that the teaching dynamic authenticates what the teacher has spent hours trying to research and discover. This type of gift is considered the "mind" to the body of Christ. The Bible says that we are to have the mind of Christ; we are able to think like Him.

Giving

This motivation gift of giving is a truly a supernatural gift that carries with it the spirit of generosity. A person with this gift feels a burden, call, and Spirit-leading to give to a specific cause, work, vision, ministry, person, project, and purpose. The Father is the Master Giver because He has given to us His own begotten Son. The Bible says that we are more blessed to give than to receive. I realize that at crucial times in my life, God would touch a person's heart to sow into my life. Usually it would be exactly or more than what I was in need of.

The gift of giving is a God-given gift, and this person isn't just limited to giving monies, per se, but also resources. This individual becomes a kingdom investor and plants seeds that reap a bountiful harvest. Moreover, the gift of giving is a supernatural giving that meets the need or needs of others. The gift of giving is a strong gift that is needed in the body of Christ. These people give out of their hearts and do not give with any ulterior motives, agendas, and objectives. People who operate in this gift usually do it without anyone knowing and in private. They are blessed to be a blessing. Moreover, prophets should be givers not only in prophecy, counsel, and directing people to God and back to God, but also able to prophetically help others to invest their resources and money wisely.

I have come to find out that we cannot judge a book by its cover. When I was in desperate need of a financial breakthrough and resources for kingdom projects, God would send me someone like the widow woman in the Bible who had something for herself and her child, but gave her last to feed the prophet Elijah; then he asked her what she needed, and God did it for her. Remember, when you help someone else in need, God will supply all of your needs. God sent the prophet Elijah to someone who needed a miracle, and he needed to survive and eat and she fed him, and God multiplied her resources and banking account.

Whenever the widow needed something, the barrel was always supernaturally full. God would send me people that didn't look like they had anything for face value, but they would bless my life, even though they were obedient to God and gave me their last. It moved me to do something for them and I knew that there was power in my mouth as a prophet. So I would ask them what they needed or what they wanted me to pray for, and supernaturally God would move on their request on the behalf of me prophesying and praying it into being.

The spirit of generosity is connected to the spirit of liberality. God will never make a stingy, selfish, and prideful person wealthy because He resists them and gives grace to the humble. God gives the power to get wealth. But there are those who may not be on the frontline of ministry like the fivefold officers but they are called to support them with their resources and even to help underwrite their vision financially. Those with the gift of giving minister by giving of their own resources to those who may not have any. (See 2 Corinthians 1:12; 8:2; 9:11–13.) This kind of gift is what is considered the "arms" of the body of Christ, technically speaking, because they supply financial and economic support through their personal resources.

Exhortation

I like this type of gift of exhortation because it is one of the prophetic functions. Everyone in the body of Christ needs a little encouragement now and then. This gift is a building gift that in the broader sense can comfort, console, advise, instruct or entreat. (See Acts 4:36; Hebrews 10:25.) The exhortation or encouragement gift is like the "mouth" of the body of Christ that's sole purpose is to call aside believers to God and make an appeal to them while motivating them to do better and remain diligent to the purposes of God in their lives. Like the prophetic ministry this exhortation gift become the reinforcement of God in a believer's life to keep on pressing forward and become a champion in the faith.

Administration/Leadership

In the body of Christ we need organization, which is key to the order and structure of things. There are those who are called and gifted with the skill set to make things happen decently and in order. God is raising up those who can carry out assignments with diligence, perseverance, and excellence. Moreover, it will take Holy Spirit-filled individuals with the gifts to model, supervise, organize, and develop a game plan and strategy for success in the body of Christ.

Leadership is the model and foundation that keeps things in their right perspective, place, and position. I do understand that everyone may not have a call or passion to administrate but all are called in one way or another to assist the leadership in its vision to see continuity, productivity, maturity, and synergy in the work of God. Those with the gift to administrate come up with a long-term goal and objective and see to it that it reaches its deadlines. Moreover, those who possess the gift of leadership, administration, or government are usually those who are standing on the front and alongside the leadership team to facilitate the overall vision and gather others to partner with it. I call this type of gift of leadership a "head" to the body of Christ. We know that Jesus is the Head of His church but He uses individuals in His church who reflect and represent Him as models. Prophets are called as one of the fivefold headship leaders to the church of Jesus Christ. They are called to administer and exemplify great ethical, moral integrity and godly character that will promote longevity.

Mercy

The gift of mercy is imperative to have in the body of Christ. There are those who are gifted with the ability to show mercy. I believe that it's not just a gift but a matter of a person's character and ability to forgive, forget, and not hold grudges. People with this type of mercy gift love to relate with others by demonstrating love, respect, honesty, empathy, compassion, fairness, and courtesy. Moreover, those with this gift are exceptionally nice, kind, generous, and unbiased, and treat people with dignity and honor. They can share in one's suffering and pain to bring joy, peace, and encouragement in spite of what they had to encounter. We need believers in the body of Christ who have a heart to forgive and not judge, because we are not the judge—Christ is the Judge.

We are to bring cheerfulness and motivation to the body of Christ. Many have already been judged, condemned, and rejected by others in the world for making a decision to stand for Christ. In addition, we need the mercy ministry as well for those unbelievers who are coming into the kingdom. New believers do not need anyone scrutinizing them and looking at them with an eye of suspicion. The Bible says, "Blessed are the merciful, for they shall obtain mercy" (Matt. 5:7, NKJV). In other words, we must be ministers of mercy so that we ourselves will receive mercy. There is no reason not to give mercy, because there will come a time in your life that you will want someone to favor you. This mercy gift is what I call the "heart" of the body of Christ.

DIVERSITY OF THE SUPERNATURAL GIFTS OF THE HOLY SPIRIT

Having come to an understanding of the nature of spiritual gifts, it is good to find exactly what gifts have been given. In the New Testament, only the apostle Paul mentions them by name. He gives us five such lists. All the lists are different, so it is necessary to look at them all together. The gifts are found in Romans 12:6–8 (seven), 1 Corinthians 12:8–10 (nine), 1 Corinthians 12:28 (eight), 1 Corinthians

12:29–30 (seven), and Ephesians 4:11 (five). Subtracting those repeated gifts brings the total to nineteen. The following chart below shows them all as they are listed in these New Testament passages:

Romans 12:6–8	1 Corinthians 12:29–30	1 Corinthians 12:8–10	Ephesians 4:11	1 Corinthians 12:28
prophecy	apostles	word of wisdom	apostles	apostles
ministry	prophecy	word of knowledge	prophets	prophets
teaching	teaching	faith	evangelists	teachers
exhortation	miracles	healing	pastors and teachers	miracles
giving	healing	miracles		healings
ruling	tongues	prophecy		helping
showing mercy	interpreting tongues	discerning of spirits		governing
		kinds of tongues		diverse tongues
		interpreting tongues		

First Corinthians 12:28 (KJV) is the key list in that it mentions the gifts in order of importance: "And God hath set some in the church, first apostles, secondarily prophets, thirdly teachers, after that miracles, then gifts of healing, helps, governments, diversities of tongues." Since it is obvious that some of the gifts toward the bottom of the list (such as healing and miracles) were in operation before the gifts higher in the list (such as apostles)—apostles being first in rank, then prophets second in rank, and teachers third in rank—this must indicate the order of importance and not just the order in which they were given to the church by Christ.

In the list of the gifts of the Holy Spirit there is some overlapping or mixture in the gifts. It may suggest that there are no two spiritual gifts listed that are exactly the same, though it would be difficult to find any real difference between some of their function since they correlate with each other. In other words, it would be difficult to display and differentiate between the gift of helps and the gift of showing mercy. Both have the same focus: ministry (service) for others. We have the same problem differentiating between ruling and governing, which can be difficult to separate without studying the terms.

Even if exact identity is not intended, there is still mixture in the gifts of the Holy Spirit. This is the case, for instance, regarding the gifts of the word of wisdom, word of knowledge, exhortation, teaching, helps, and service. Likewise, the gifts of healing may not be as broad as the gift of miracles, but the similarity is obvious and clear.

UNDERSTANDING THE SUPERNATURAL GIFTS OF THE HOLY SPIRIT

It is my desire that we understand the gifts of the Holy Spirit, which will help the believer to maximize their full potential in the Lord. We must first understand the nature of these gifts and what 1 Corinthians 12 reveals. I will not discuss the in-depth meaning of each one, but pull out the simple terms biblically.

What is the biblical term *spiritual*?

> Now concerning spiritual gifts, brethren, I would not have you ignorant.
>
> —1 CORINTHIANS 12:1, KJV

We can see that the apostle Paul was teaching the Corinthian church things that were related to the subject of spiritual gifts, and they were not to be ignorant concerning them. The King James Version uses the term *spiritual*, which is a Greek word, *pneumatikon*, describing the things of the spirit, belonging to the spirit, or controlled by the spirit.[45] In other words, spiritual gifts are properties and endowments by the Spirit of God, and the church in the first century needed to understand them for clarity. It was Paul's apos-

---

45   The King James Study Bible (previously published as The Liberty Annotated Study Bible as The Annotated Study Bible, King James Version) © 1988 by Liberty University, "Pneumatikon" term word for "spiritual" is found in the reference of 1 Corinthians 12:1 on page 1781. See also Blue Letter Bible, s.v. "pneumatikos," www.blueletterbible.org/lang/lexicon/Lexicon.cfm?strongs=G4152 (accessed June 4, 2013).

tolic heart to bring clarity to things concerning the spirit, which are the spiritual gifts of God. This church was known for their ability to minister in the prophetic and in the gift of tongues but didn't know how to operate in them. We must understand the foundational and fundamental principle concerning how spiritual gifts work through us. I believe that we must get a better understanding of what pertains to God and function appropriately. I have seen people prophesy and minister in their gift but had no clue about the roles, functions, biblical definition, and purpose of the things that belong to the Spirit of God.

What is the biblical term *gifts*?

> Now there are diversities of gifts, but the same Spirit.
>
> —1 Corinthians 12:4, kjv

In this passage of Scripture we see that there are diversities of gifts in the church and they all are from the same Spirit. In other words, when you look at your physical body, there are different members on your body that make up the whole, but it's still one body or person. So even though there are different kinds of gifts in the body it is still one body and spirit working through it. The word *gifts* here is translated in Greek *charisma*, from the root word *charis*, from which we get the word grace (Rom. 12:6; 1 Cor. 12:4, 9, 28, 30–31; 1 Pet. 4:10).[46] So to clarify what the apostle Paul was saying, there are different gifts or graces in the body of Christ but the same Spirit. God has given various grace gifts to the body by His Spirit.

When we observe a gifted person, we usually refer to them as being very "charismatic." A person that has a lot of charisma is a person who is gifted and has a particular grace to do what they do. The Holy Spirit's gifts are the God graces that are distributed to those whom He chooses to give them to. The things belonging to the Spirit are the different God gifts or graces given to the body for the purpose that the whole body of Christ will profit from them. I believe

---

46   Blue Letter Bible, s.v. "charis," www.blueletterbible.org/lang/lexicon
.cfm?strongs=G5485; s.v. "charisma," www.blueletterbible.org/lang/lexicon/
Lexicon.cfm?strongs=G5486 (accessed June 4, 2013).

that spiritual gifts are "charismatic" because they are considered gifts of grace.

Prophets are deemed charismatic in their prophesying, teaching, training, prayers, worship, singing, etc. I have always been very charismatic in my personality because it had the ability to get people's attention. There are those who are gifted in a particular area of ministry but lack the godly character to sustain momentum and longevity in ministry. Regardless how gifted a person may be, we should never measure a person's gift, grace, or calling over character. Godly character and integrity enriches our spiritual gift. I have witnessed young prophetic ministers try to flow in the gifts but lack good character, mostly because there is a lack of true accountability, transparency, relationship, fathering, nurturing, and foundational biblical principles established in their lives.

The Bible says that gifts and calls come without repentance. In other words, gifts and callings of the Lord came with you when you were created by the Lord. A person doesn't have to work for it or receive by merit. The call of God on a person's life comes without repentance. You don't have to repent to receive it; it was born with you. I have heard and witnessed some young leaders say that they are anointed and it doesn't matter what they do or say, "I am anointed regardless." That type of statement and mentality is dangerous and self-deception.

We should never get to the point that we think we are anointed, called, and graced to do and say whatever we feel because God called us. A wise pastor said to me, "Hakeem, make sure that your character matches the level of your anointing and you will go far in God." I keep that in the forefront of my mind as I travel across the country ministering in the prophetic and healing ministry. The point I am trying to make is that the people of the Corinthian church were so gifted that they lacked apostolic order and structure. They became so caught up in their ability to move in the Spirit while speaking in tongues and prophesying that they became arrogant, prideful, and self-centered. This gifted church needed the apostolic alignment that came to them through their apostle and apostolic father, Paul. It was Paul's corrective approach that brought spiritual alignment, clarity, and unity in the functionality of the Holy Spirit gifts.

What is the biblical term *administration*?

First Corinthians 12:5 (KJV) says, "And there are differences of administrations, but the same Lord."

In this passage of Scripture we see that in the church there are also differences of administration, or in other translations it would be the word *ministries*. The apostle Paul shares that there are different types of ministry services or administrations but the same Spirit working in and through the body of saints. There are those who can administer in different capacities and render their service in their gift. As there are differences of administration or ministries they are provided by the Spirit to serve. According to the Holman Illustrated Bible Dictionary, states the King James Version of 1 Corinthians 12:5 speaks of differences of administrations are translated in the Greek *diakonia* (service).[47] We are all called to serve each other for the building up of the body of Christ. The Greek word for *diakonia* means a service or ministry to the people. In addition, the King James Version translates this word as ministry, ministration, ministering, serving, relief, office, service, administration, do service and to minister which we also get the word deacon from.

What is the biblical term *operations*?

> And here are diversities of operations, but it is the same God which worketh all in all.
>
> —1 Corinthians 12:6, KJV

The apostle Paul goes on to say that there are diversities of operations but the same Lord which worketh them all in all. In the King James Version the term that Paul calls "operation" is another word called "activities." We can see that it is the Lord that also gives various operations or activities in the body of Christ and that He works them all in all. In other words, God works through Holy Spirit-filled believers this diversity of activities. I love that the Lord works them all and in all so that the activities of the Holy Spirit are initiated by the Lord and not by the individual. The believers cooperate with the Spirit of the Lord to accomplish His purpose. God grants to those

---

47 Conner, 124. See also *Holman Illustrated Bible Dictionary*, s.v. "diakonia."

He has designated in His body the ability to carry out the work of the ministry. Jesus stated that He was sent to work the work that the Father sent Him to accomplish, and we are to do the same. These "workings" in 1 Corinthians 12:6 are translated in Greek *energeia,* from which we get our English word *energy.*[48] Like the energizer bunny, the Holy Spirit enables the believer to keep going and going and going in the Spirit. We have the faith to work the work of God.

What is the biblical term *manifestation?*

First Corinthians 12:7 (KJV) says, "But the manifestation of the Spirit is given to every man to profit withal."

Finally we see that the apostle Paul states that the manifestation of the Spirit is given to every man to profit all. In other words, we are to benefit from the manifestation of God's Spirit present among us through each other. As he makes clear the various spiritual gifts, ministries, administrations, operations, or working of the Spirit through the body of believers, Paul states that the manifestation of them is the evidence of the Lord's activities. When we see the visible manifestations of the Spirit among us, then we believers know that it's the Lord's working and expressing Himself through the many-membered body of Christ. Paul felt the need to explain thoroughly the different spiritual gifts, ministries, and operations so that everyone in the Corinthian church would help each other build the church of Jesus Christ and others would profit from it.

We must be clear that the Holy Spirit bestows the gifts sovereignly to whomever He wills as the occasion recommends and demands. I love seeing people manifest the gifts of the Spirit; in other words, prophets prophesying by the power of God, apostles working miracles, evangelists winning the lost and bringing restoration, teachers explaining and expounding, pastors committed to the flock and other spiritual gifts on display brings great joy, unity, love, and strength. The gifts of the Spirit are, to me, exhibited for others to see God and be encouraged. When a prophet ministers in the prophetic gift it brings encouragement, exhortation, and comfort to the body of Christ at large.

---

48   Blue Letter Bible, s.v. "energeia," www.blueletterbible.org/lang/lexicon/ Lexicon/cfm?strongs=G1753 (accessed June 4, 2013).

A prophet is displaying the manifestation of the Spirit when he or she is prophesying. In other words, when they speak, they are speaking and moved by the Spirit of God. They are releasing the word of the Lord by the inspiration and working of the Spirit. The diversity and manifestations of the Spirit is the direct expression of God through the believer. Just as we have different personalities, character, gifts, etc., this uniqueness in the body of Christ expresses the multifaceted dimensions of how the Lord wants to display Himself through His corporate and local body. The word *manifestation* is translated in Greek "*phanerosis,*" which means to display or make visible.[49]

Gift(s) of the Holy Spirit and Gift of the Spirit

I have already given a brief description of what the nine gifts of the Holy Spirit are, but I have found that there are those who simply make the mistake of confusing the gifts of the Holy Spirit with the gift of the Spirit. There is a difference. The gift(s) of the Holy Spirit are manifested in nine expressions of the Holy Spirit outlined in 1 Corinthians 12:6–10: the word of wisdom, knowledge, discerning of spirits, gifts of healing, working of miracles, faith, prophecy, diversities of tongues, and interpretation of tongues. Meanwhile, the gift (singular) of the Spirit is not the gifts (plural) of the Holy Spirit. The gifts of the Holy Spirit are the supernatural abilities endowed by the Spirit to equip believers for ministry service (see 1 Cor. 12:1–31), but the gift of the Holy Spirit is referring to the Holy Spirit Himself that a person receives at salvation. The Holy Spirit is the Promise sent by our Lord Jesus Christ. Acts 2:38 (NKJV, emphasis added) says, "Then Peter said to them, 'Repent, and let every one of you be baptized in the name of Jesus Christ for the remission of sins; and you shall receive the *gift* of the Holy Spirit.'" It is clear that Peter was not referring to the *gifts* of the Holy Spirit, but the *gift* of the Holy Spirit.

Gifts of the Spirit and Fruit of the Spirit

I will not try to beat a dead horse by going over the gifts of the Spirit again, but I would like to make a clear biblical distinction between the gifts of the Holy Spirit and the fruit of the Holy Spirit.

---

49   Blue Letter Bible, s.v. "phanerōsis," www.blueletterbible.org/lang/lexicon/ Lexicon.cfm?strongs=G5321 (accessed June 4, 2013).

The fruit of the Holy Spirit can be found in the Book of Galatians chapter 5. Note that I said the fruit (singular) and not the fruits (plural) of the Spirit. I have heard believers call it "fruits of the Holy Spirit," which is incorrect even though there are nine characteristics of the Spirit expressed. We must understand that there are nine gifts of the Spirit and nine different characterized expressions of the Holy Spirit that should be visible in the life of the Christian believer and especially those who are called to the headship ministries outlined in Ephesians 4:11–13.

We must not confuse gifts of the Spirit with the fruit of the Spirit. To give an illustration, there is one fruit that is cut in nine pieces, and each believer can manifest that nature of the Spirit in their Christian walk. It is the Lord's desire that we walk in the Spirit so that we will not fulfill the lust of the flesh. We must pursue to manifest the whole fruit of the Spirit in our lives. So we know that there is one fruit of the Spirit divided into nine pieces, not nine different type fruits that one would see in a cornucopia. In Galatians 5:22–23 (NKJV, emphasis added) it says, "But the *fruit* of the Spirit is love, joy, peace, long-suffering, kindness, goodness, faithfulness, gentleness, self-control. Against such there is no law." The above passage of Scripture speaks of the different gifts of the Spirit. Nowhere in Galatians chapter 5 does it talk about the gifts of the Holy Spirit, but the godly character that all believers should walk in, and that is in the Spirit.

Spiritual Gifts and Natural Talents

This is an interesting topic in regards to the difference between a natural gift or talent and a spiritual one. The title of this book speaks of what we were born and created to accomplish in the earth for the Lord. Even though I speak on the subject of prophecy, prophets, prophetic ministry, and the spiritual gifts of God, we must keep in mind that we all were born with a natural gift, and even given spiritual gifts that may be dormant within us until we receive salvation and the infilling of the Spirit that activates it. I believe we all were born with a natural ability and talent to do what many others are not able to do. I am reminded of Michael Jordan, one of the greatest basketball players of our time, who is exceptionally gifted and talented in the area of basketball. He is in a different class all by himself among the rest, while on the other hand another basketball player in the NBA may not be as gifted or great as Michael Jordan. My point is that Michael was gifted and may even have been called to dominate in the area of the basketball, while the other player may be called to basketball as well, but not called to excel in it like Michael. Why? Because there is only one Michael Jordan.

Furthermore, there are those who look up to the legend and try to become like him because he set a standard that seems impossible to achieve. We must understand that when we were born, we were born with gifts and talents. It is our responsibility to discover what they are and fulfill them. But when born again by the Spirit, we are then given spiritual gifts, both natural, referring to talents, and supernatural (spiritual). Natural talent may be someone who can sing or dance, or any other natural talent without any prior training. In other words, a person's natural talent will come naturally. I believe a person can develop and master his or her natural ability to become greater.

Galatians 1:15–16 (NKJV) says, "But when it pleased God, who separated me from my mother's womb and called me through His grace, to reveal His Son in me, that I might preach Him among the Gentiles, I did not immediately confer with flesh and blood." We can see that Paul was separated from his mother's womb and called by the grace of God to preach Christ to the Gentiles. This confirms that he was born with a specific calling and called through the grace of God, which was his apostolic mission to the Gentile people. Paul had a spiritual gift from the Lord, which was the call of an apostle sent with a message of Christ to preach. Paul had the innate gift to preach in his mother's womb, but it didn't manifest until later on in his apostolic calling. Moreover, Paul evidently was wired with the tools, natural talents, and gifts at birth but he needed the empowerment and infilling of the Holy Spirit to cause his gifts to become spiritual. For example, if a college professor by profession in the secular realm has a natural teaching gift and suddenly receives the gift of the Spirit, now his teaching ability becomes empowered and takes on a supernatural ability beyond his own ability.

A college professor and a fivefold ministry teacher function in similar ways, but there is a difference, because one is natural and the other is supernatural. I have a natural talent to sing, but when I received the Holy Spirit in my life, my singing ability became Holy Spirit-anointed and brings results. I have witnessed people make their natural talents and gifts a calling. We should never confuse our natural gifts with the call of God on our lives. I know that I am called to be a prophet, but that doesn't mean that I was called to be a singer on *American Idol*. As a prophet I can use my singing ability to sing the song of the Lord in worship and to bless the body of Christ.

These people have not come into what God has called them to do. I believe one's natural gifts can accompany and assist in one's calling, but it's our job to know for a fact what we were destined to become in the earth. I knew from a very young age that God called me to minister for Him, but I was unsure in what capacity until I received many encounters with God and through the prophetic ministry. I believe the prophetic ministry is vital to the body of Christ because prophets can identify different gifts and callings in a person. There is nothing wrong with allowing the Holy Spirit to speak to you personally about your spiritual calling and gift, but prophets and apostles are uniquely gifted to identify, recognize, set, ordain, establish, activate, and release you into your God-given destiny.

Prophets and prophetic ministry is a ministry that should be utilized in the church today. We must understand contemporary prophets and prophecy to comprehend God's idea of this building gift to the church.

Chapter Eleven

PROPHETS AND PROPHECY

*He who receives a prophet in the name of a prophet shall receive
a prophet's reward. And he who receives righteous man in the
name of a righteous man shall receive a righteous man's reward.*
—Matthew 10:41, nkjv

A prophet of God is simply an inspired spokesman, a prophetic ambassador sent to speak on behalf of God to the
people. In the Old Testament we see that prophets were sent
by God as His divine messengers to declare and proclaim a "thus
saith the Lord" to the children of Israel and surrounding nations.
Moreover, we see Jesus, a prophet as well, making mention of sending
the people prophets and apostles (Luke 11:49). Prophets are sent by
the Lord. They have an apostolic dimension and ambassadorial function, because the word "sent" in Luke 11:49 comes from the word
apostolized.[50]

The prophets were *apostolized* (sent) to the people.[51] Prophets are
also set governmentally by God in the church in second ranking. (See
1 Corinthians 12:28.) Prophets and apostles are mentioned together
as a team in the Book of Ephesians 2:20; 3:5; and 4:11. The primary
function of a prophet who stands in that office is their remarkable
relationship and communion with their Lord and King. A prophet's desire and passion is knowing God's original plan, purpose, will,
and intention while cooperating with the Father to execute what is

---

50   Blue Letter Bible, s.v. "apostolos," www.blueletterbible.org/lang/lexicon/
Lexicon.cfm?strongs=G652 (accessed June 4, 2013).
51   John Eckhardt, *Dictionary of the Apostolic, second edition* (Olympia Fields,
IL: Crusaders Ministries, 2005), 276.

on His heart and mind. Prophets do instruct, teach, equip, train, lead, empower, correct, encourage, deliver, heal, and navigate God's people through His word, into right relationship with Him, and in righteous living.

A source of discontentment for a true prophet of God is heresy, doctrinal error, erroneous teachings, idolatry, apostasy, hypocrisy, and misrepresentation of the Lord and His eternal Word. Prophets cannot stand unrighteousness, injustices, and perversion of any sort. There is a holy indignation and discontentment that causes them to judge these areas and bring them under the ruler of the King, Jesus. In addition, a prophet has an innate ability to discern and judge spirits of divination, witchcraft, deception, error, and the motives and intents of one's heart, especially false prophets and prophecies.

PROPHETS MUST BE ACTIVATED
IN THE LOCAL CHURCH

I believe that it is imperative and vital to have prophets presently active or activated in the church. A church that operates in error and sin is typically a sign that there are no true prophets plugged into the local assembly. As it was important in the early church that prophets and prophecy be the culture, it should be the culture of today's church as well. Without prophets and the prophetic dimension within the local church, it can be boring, rigid, religious, ceremonial, and un-kingdom-like. We need prophets today speaking because God still speaks. To say there are not prophets today is to say that God the Father, God the Son, and God the Holy Spirit have stopped speaking today. Prophets are one of the foundations of the church that Christ has built along with apostles. We need them, as well as the rest of the five ministry gifts.

I like what John Loren Sandford said about hospitality for prophets in his book *Elijah Among Us*:

> People in the Bible time knew God would bless through His prophets. The people may not have wanted to be around when God spoke warnings and scolded through His prophets publicly, but they always wanted His prophets to be with them privately, in their homes. There were two major reasons for this. First they

knew this: "He who receives a prophet in a name of a prophet shall receive a prophet's reward" (Matthew 10:41). They knew if they did anything good for a prophet, the prophet became duty-bound to bless them. Second, Galatians 6:7 says what all had known for centuries, "Whatever a man sows, this he will also reap." The people knew if they did a good deed they would reap good from it.

Thus, they fully understood what Jesus meant when He said, "Do not store up for yourselves treasures on earth, where moth and rust destroy, and where thieves break in and steal. But store up for yourselves treasures in heaven, where neither moth nor rust destroys, and where thieves do not break in or steal" (Matthew 6:19–20). They knew the only way to lay up treasures that would not perish was to do good deeds. God's laws are incorruptible and infallible. If they helped a man of God, they knew they would receive their reward (Matthew 10:42).[52]

However, true prophets are sometimes not received, honored, embraced, or respected, and are reluctant to be accountable to senior leadership due to misunderstanding and so often rejection of them. We see during the Old Testament where prophets were used instrumentally to prophesy against false prophets, wicked kings, and a rebellious nation.

OLD TESTAMENT PROPHETS

There are those in the twenty-first century who believe that they are to be like the Old Testament prophets in their generation. During my prophetic career I have heard good prophecies and I have heard very bad ones, which will come with the territory. This doesn't mean that the person was not a genuine prophetic minister, but it may be due to the understanding of the new covenant role of the prophets in the church. Don't get me wrong, there are those who prophesy and are not called to the ministry office of the prophet; but my point is that we must understand the difference.

Simply, there are two primary differences between the old and new covenant prophets. First, the Old Testament prophets were used

---

52 John Loren Sandford, *Elijah Among Us* (Ada, MI: Chosen Books, 2002), 63.

of the Lord for direction, counsel, God's will, mind, and provision, because the Spirit was not accessible at that time for all flesh. On the other hand, there is no New Testament record of a prophet in the new covenant being used to dictate a believer's life by guiding them as the Old Testament prophets like Moses, Aaron, Samuel, Elijah, Elisha, and others did. These Old Testament prophets were used in the ministry of guidance. They were God's spokesmen, and so His New Testament prophets were as well. During those Old Testament times man did not have direct access to the Lord through Christ but through earthly mediators and priests.

Secondly, the Old Testament prophets were tremendously inspired of the Lord to write the infallible Scriptures and prophesy what was scribed. In the New Testament there is no record of a new covenant prophet ever writing the infallible Word of God and prophesying what he had written. Even today there is no prophet or an apostle adding to the Word of God. Not to say that prophets and apostles do not write books, articles, and songs today; but they don't write the Scriptures.

The prophets of old had to wait for the Lord to speak to them and come upon them. If a prophet came out prematurely with a presumptuous word, then they were labeled a false prophet and in some cases publicly stoned to death for the word not coming through. I truly thank God for His grace and truth today as a new covenant believer. Can you image if someone gave a prophetic word that was off, and his punishment was death? I believe we would not have a lot of people prophesying. But thank God for His love and saving grace. As the Old Testament was written primarily by prophets and the New Testament was written by apostles, there is no biblical reference that the New Testament prophets wrote the infallible word.

Furthermore, the New Testament prophets' direction, guidance, and word come from the Word of God, the indwelling presence of the Holy Spirit, and confirmation through other prophets in the church; while the Old Testament prophets, as I stated, didn't have the Spirit or even the Word because they had to wait on the Lord to download His will and mind. Hosea, Isaiah, Joel, Jeremiah, Amos, Ezekiel and other minor and major prophets were gifted to write the infallible Scriptures. What is the difference between a major prophet and minor one? Well, my understanding is that it had nothing to do with how great they were, but was measured by their level of influence and how extensive their book was. For example, if a prophet writes a 300-page book on the prophetic and another prophet writes only 150 pages, which is larger? Well, the 300-page one is, of course— but this doesn't mean the content in the 300-page book is more powerful than the 150-page one. I have read some profound books that were only twenty to fifty pages, while some larger ones lack true substance on the topic or subject.

Moreover, in Israel's history in the Old Testament the prophetic ministry was the only ministry beside the judges that was instrumental in the overall plan of God for His people. These men and women were holy prophets of God, while at the same time proclaiming His word, and were the prophetic symbol of God's voice to Israel. When the people saw the prophets coming in the Old Testament, there were two things that came to their mind: judgment or liberation.

In the Old Testament the prophets were also called or known as:

- The prophets (Hosea 12:10)

- Seers (1 Sam. 9:9; 2 Sam. 24:11; Amos 7:12; 2 Chron. 33:18; Isa. 29:10)

- Man of God (1 Sam. 9:6; 1 Kings 12:22)

- Holy men (2 Pet. 1:21)

- Servants (Hag. 2:23)

- Messengers of God (Isa. 42:19)

- The interpreters (Isa. 43:27, NRSV)

We can also see a similarity between the Old and New Testament prophets, because some Old Testament prophets were women. There are denominations today that do not believe in women preaching or having an influence and call from the Lord to ministry, which is not the Spirit of God. The Lord will use whomever He wants to use. If there were women oracles of the Lord in the Old Testament, then God is still going to use women today and in any generation.

The Bible says in the New Testament that in the last days He will pour out His Spirit on all flesh, which included "sons and daughters," servants and "handmaids" according to Acts 2:17–22, which was a prophecy spoken by the prophet Joel. (See Joel 2:28–32.)

In the Old Testament, women were divinely inspired of the Lord in their generation. These women of God were called *prophetesses*. The Old Testament prophetess is basically referring to a female prophet of God. Some Old Testament female prophets include:

- **Deborah,** who was a prophetic judge, a mother in Israel who led the song of the Lord in combat with Barak (Judg. 4:4).

- **Anna,** who was a prophetic prayer warrior, intercessor, and mother in Zion who committed her life to fasting and prayers in the temple at the age of eighty-four; she came from the tribe of Asher and the priests gave her was given residence in the temple by the priests (Luke 2:36–38).

- **Miriam,** who was Moses' older sibling, sung the prophetic song of the Lord and used the art of prophetic dance (Exod. 15:20).

- **Prophet Isaiah's wife,** who shared in the prophetic team ministry with her husband at times (Isa. 8:3).

- **Huldah,** who was used of God to prophesy and teach the Word of the Lord in Jerusalem (2 Kings 22:12–20; 2 Chron. 34:22).

- **Noadiah,** who was a false prophetess during the season of restoration from enslavement in Babylon (Neh. 6:14).

In the New Testament there were false prophets, including the famous personality who claimed to be a prophetess:

- **Jezebel,** who is the only so-called prophetess that the New Testament reveals as being labeled a prophetess. This false prophet was notorious for perverting and teaching false doctrine as a prophetess and teacher (Rev. 2:20).

- **Philip** the evangelist had four daughters who were not called to the ministry office of the prophet or called prophetesses, but, interestingly enough, they prophesied by the Spirit of God (Acts 21:7–9).

God is pouring out His Spirit upon all flesh regardless of age, nationality, gender, profession, etc. The Holy Spirit is readily available to be received and to speak. More in the Old Testament, the prophets had close-knit relationships with kings just like new covenant prophets should be in direct relationship with apostles and senior leaders of a local church. A prophet doesn't have authority uncovered, unaccountable, and in direct relationship with others to bring balance and reinforcement to their ministry.

In the Old Testament, as I stated, men approached God through another person, such as a priest, but primarily it was done through the prophets. We see today in the twenty-first century church people going to God through their pastor or leader. While there is nothing wrong with receiving wisdom, counsel, and confirmation, the Holy Spirit has been sent to guide us and lead the believer into all truth. The Bible says there is safety in a multitude of advisors, but we cannot replace the Holy Spirit with prophets, pastors, or anyone else.

Moreover, the kings in the Old Testament truly benefited from the prophetic ministry of the prophets:

- **David** had Gad the seer and Nathan the prophet (2 Sam. 12; 24:11).

- **Ahab** related with prophets Elijah and Elisha (1 Kings 17:1; 19:16).

- **Saul and David** both received the prophetic ministry of Samuel (1 Sam. 9–10, 16).

- **Solomon** benefited from Nathan, who was called to his daddy as well (1 Kings 1:38).

- **Rehoboam** consulted with Shemaiah the prophet (1 Kings 12:21–22).

As we can see, the prophetic ministry is not only important to the body of Christ, but God also sent them to kings. Jeremiah was sent to kings and nations to prophesy words of judgment to prophetically reform that nation and bring hope. New Testament prophets worked hand in hand with pastors and especially apostles sent by the Holy Spirit through the church. In the apostolic age in the first century, prophets were still used to declare the word of the Lord to His people and remind them of the new covenant and the Lord's promise of the Holy Spirit. We are in the days of Elijah where we are going to see great waves of miracles, healing, and prophetic revival that will change generations. The slogan of my ministry, Hakeem Collins International, is "Reform nations to change generations." It's about the next generation. God is going to use the prophetic anointing and prophetic creativity to birth something unprecedented, unpredicted, and unconventional in this season of restoration. You were born to prophesy and be successful.

Prophecy Is a Divine Ministry from the Lord

As I stated before, prophets and prophecy are God's idea for His glorious church. Throughout the Old and New Testaments we see that the prophetic dimension and ministry is emphasized more than any other, with the exception of the apostolic/apostles ministry. In my own life I have been touched and revolutionized by the power of prophecy. There have been times when I was at my lowest and felt misunderstood by those I trusted, but suddenly I would receive an e-mail, text message, or an inbox message from someone sharing a testimony that a prophecy I gave them has jump-started their life and they are actually seeing the Word of God unfold and come to pass.

At the moment of feeling unwanted and isolated, the Lord would send several people who had been blessed by the prophetic ministry to encourage me to keep advancing the King and His kingdom. When I read countless messages from different people, most of whom I don't remember, because I have ministered to thousands personally throughout my short life, these testimonies that flood my e-mail and social media sites are godly reminders that I was born to do this.

Interestingly, I have found that when someone finds out that I am a prophet, the first thing they do is ask me for a prophetic word. I have seen people chase me down for a prophetic word and not let me leave their presence until they received one. In addition, there have been times where I have been asked to give personal, individual prophecies to a meeting of about 150 people, which I can do by the grace on my life, but it is time-consuming and draining at times.

The point that I am trying to make is that there is an increasing demand for the prophetic ministry. Can you imagine what Jesus felt like when He was ministering in the power of God?

Team ministry is so needed today in the body of Christ. My brother and I travel a lot across the country ministering as a prophetic teaching and preaching team. The Bible says one can send a thousand to flight and two can chase ten thousand. The power of team ministry will cut down on a lot of time and eliminate haughtiness, pride, the appearance of a one-man show, and selfishness. Prophetic ministers, along with the rest of the fivefold, are God's equippers and enablers to get the saints ready for their own personal ministry or call by the Holy Spirit. We are in the days of the saints taking hold of the kingdom and advancing it for God's glory. Prophecy is a sign to the believer, but I believe that prophecy will also be used to convict the hearts of the unbelievers.

Cecil M. Robeck Jr. states "Prophecy appears to be given with an existential value in mind. It is given through a specific individual, to a specific individual or group of individuals, at a specific place, and within a specific time frame. Within that context it may be said to have a specific message with specific value."[53] I like what he shared, that the prophetic brings value to a specific person regardless of where you are. As I stated before, that prophetic word will find you! God values you so much that He has a "tailor-made" prophetic word that will fit your life.

Moreover, Wayne Arden Grudem observes: "Prophecy, then, is superior to the other gifts because the revelation on which it depends allows it to be suited to the specific needs of the moment, needs

---

53   Cecil M. Robeck, Jr., "Problems in the Contemporary Use of the Gift of Prophecy" (an unpublished paper given at the Society for Pentecostal Studies, November 14, 1980), 13.

which may only be known to God."[54] We see the importance of this divine gift to the body of Christ.

The Bible says in 2 Timothy 3:16 (NKJV), "All Scripture is given by inspiration of God, and is profitable for doctrine, for reproof, for correction, for instruction in righteousness." We can see that the Word of God is given by the inspiration of God. Prophecy outside of the Word of God is not sufficient enough to build on, but prophecy within the parameters of the Holy Scriptures can be confirmed and supported. Just as the Word of God is inspired and given by the Lord, so likewise when God-inspired prophecy comes forth through holy men of God. Second Peter 1:20–21 (NKJV) says, "…knowing this first, that no prophecy of Scripture is of any private interpretation, for prophecy never came by the will of man, but holy men of God spoke as they were moved by the Holy Spirit." It is interesting to me that no prophecy of Scripture is of any private interpretation. In other words, a prophet's vision, dream, or heavenly encounter is not their own vision, dream, or encounter, but is inspired by God; they spoke as they were moved by the Spirit to speak. The guidelines for the prophecy should never overextend the inspired one of God and should never be replaced by prophecy.

Therefore, there is no biblical prophecy that was ever produced merely because a man or woman wanted to prophesy (by the will of man). The prophetic in Scripture was given only by God through men, who "spoke" as they were carried along or moved by the Holy Spirit. The Holy Spirit was the active, revelatory agent working within the Old Testament prophets and through their lives and circumstances as they prophesied. This is a key verse for the doctrine of Scripture, indicating that Scripture is inspired by the Holy Spirit, but at the same time men spoke God's words, using their own personalities, knowledge, background, definition, and style. "They were carried along" implies that the inspiration of Scripture was invisibly directed by the Holy Spirit, though without overriding the personalities of the human authors or the prophets and teachers.

Therefore, Scripture is fully the Word of God, even though it

---

54   Wayne A. Grudem, The Gift of Prophecy (Wheaton, IL: Crossway Books, 2000), 128.

is recorded in the words of men. The exact way in which this was accomplished remains a divine mystery and not a private interpretation. What is true of Old Testament prophecy is true of all Scripture (see 2 Tim. 3:16). The only parameter and true guideline for the prophetic is found in the Word of God. We must understand and never make the mistake to overemphasize inspired prophecy (*rhema*) only over the inspired word of God (*logos*). In other words, a rhema prophetic word should never replace the logos written Word of God. That is why 1 Corinthians 13:9 states, "We know in part and we prophesy in part."

The prophetic word comes from God in part and the revelation may come later as well in part. The revelation can be accurate through a prophecy but the interpretation can be totally off track. That's why we must wait on God for the interpretation and just prophesy according to the proportion of our faith and allow Him to give us the interpretation, because revelation can come in bits and pieces. This is why team ministry is important for the purpose of understanding what is being revealed by the Spirit through other people working together to get the full picture. We must understand that in the prophetic function there are three elements that may come forth through three or several different people:

1. Revelation

2. Interpretation

3. Application

People shouldn't solely look to prophecy as the only guidance. We should admonish believers to have a recorder, write their personal prophecies down and share them later with other people for clarity and understanding. Prophecy to me is like an onion that has multiple layers that need to be unfolded with time to understand the fullness of what is being said. Second Peter 1:19 (ESV) says, "And we have something more sure, the prophetic word, to which you will do well to pay attention as to a lamp shining in a dark place, until the day dawns and the morning star rises in your hearts." The Word of God is a more sure word of prophecy, a lamp that shines in dark places that brings guidance and direction.

The prophetic comes to confirm the will, mind, and purpose of God that is already revealed through Scripture. I have seen people tell me what their prophecy outlined but they were not able to judge through the Scriptures to see if it was valid enough to walk out. I also have been in meetings where they focused on prophecy only and not on teaching the Word of God. This is dangerous and has the potential to create a culture of prophetic "junkies" and "babies" who would rather hear a prophetic word than preached Word of God. We know that prophecy is an important part of the ministry of the Holy Spirit, but if we idolize it we run the risk of being deceived. The prophetic ministry was an important part of the first century, and it is just as important today in the twenty-first century. The ministry of the Holy Spirit will inspire you to minister in the prophetic realm if you yield to His leading.

The Purpose and Importance
of the Gift of Prophecy

I thank my God always concerning you for the grace of God which was given to you by Christ Jesus, that you were enriched in everything by Him in all utterance and all knowledge, even as the testimony of Christ was confirmed in you, so that you come short in no gift, eagerly waiting for the revelation of our Lord Jesus Christ.

—1 Corinthians 1:4–7, nkjv

I love this passage of Scripture because the apostle Paul was open and transparent about his heart toward his spiritual children in the Corinthian church. He shared that he thanked God always concerning the grace the Lord had given to them by enriching them in everything in all utterance and all knowledge. The word *enriched* stood out to me and I looked it up. The Merriam-Webster Dictionary defines the word *enrich* as "to make rich or richer, to add to or improve with additions and to add beauty to." What were they commended for? They were commended that they were enriched in everything by the Lord in all utterance. It is the Lord's desire that we are enriched in the prophetic utterances of the Lord. Prophets and prophetic people are to make themselves rich in the prophetic dimension.

In other words, we are to upgrade and become wealthy in operating in the spiritual gifts, especially prophecy. No one is impoverished in the kingdom of God, but we all can do our best to become prophetically enriched or to improve. I have come to the realization that in the prophetic ministry I can always find room to grow, advance, learn, and improve. I will go so far as to say that the prophetic is important to the church of Jesus Christ because it builds up the corporate body and adds beauty. Prophecy can add and make one richer in his or her faith in God and bring about personal improvement. In the vocal gifts of the Holy Spirit, which are prophecy, diversities of tongues, and interpretation of tongues, prophecy is more superior because of its long-term impact and the effect it can bring about. The only reason that prophecy is relevantly important is because it is a ministry that constructs or builds up.

I believe God uses the prophetic because it brings life, restoration, reconstruction, reconciliation, improvement, enrichment, confirmation, strength, deliverance, healing, miracles, breakthroughs, upgrade, change, revival, and reformation. In the Book of Ezekiel, chapter 37, the Lord wanted to bring spiritual and economic renewal to Israel, so He used a prophet to do so. God took Ezekiel up in a vision and showed him a picture of His people scattered, defeated, brittle, and hopeless. Even though God judged them because of their hardness of heart, He wanted to restore a remnant of them and bring restoration. So the hand of the Lord came upon Ezekiel the prophet and the Lord showed him a valley of dry bones. In verse 5, God asked him a question in regards to the present condition of His people: "Can these bones live?" So Ezekiel answered and said, "Lord, You know." Then God told Ezekiel to prophesy to those dry bones and speak to them specifically to hear the word of the Lord.

As Ezekiel continued to prophesy to the bones in a creative way, he began to witness a supernatural metamorphosis take place as the bones, ligament, joints, sinew, skin, flesh, and things on the body were restored. But once fully restored, the only that the bones were missing was life. So again Ezekiel prophesied and commanded that the four winds would come and breathe into these bones. Suddenly the breath of life came into them, and they stood upon their feet and became an exceedingly great army (read Ezekiel 37:1–14).

This is a powerful illustration of the restoration power of the prophetic. I believe that this story is a picture of the church coming into the kingdom and becoming a kingdom family-army of the Lord. Jesus prophesied that He will send the Promise of the Father, and when the church was birthed in the Book of Acts, it was a "spiritual awakening" that took place in the Upper Room prayer meeting. (See Acts 1:4–12; 2:1.) We are the remnant of the Lord that has been chosen to survive.

THE BIBLICAL DEFINITION OF
ENCOURAGEMENT AND EXHORTATION

As I stated before about the biblical foundation of prophecy, the basic function and boundaries of the gift of prophecy or gift of prophesying in particular are limited to exhortation, edification, and comfort, according to 1 Corinthians 12:10. The two words that stand out to me in regards to the gift of prophecy are encouragement and exhortation.

In Dr. Ralph F. Wilson's article "Understanding the Gift of Prophecy: II. The Purpose of Prophecy Today," he writes: "Exhortation to obedience and service as well as encouragement and comfort from the Spirit to those experiencing pain and trouble are one aspect of the Spirit's building up of the church through prophecy."[55]

I searched in depth in regards to the Hebrew meaning of the words *exhortation* and *encouragement* and how they were used in the Old Testament. In the Young's Analytical Concordance to the Bible the translated Hebrew word for encourage is *chazag* which means "to be, become strong, to strengthen self and harden."

First Samuel 30:6 (NKJV) says, "Now David was greatly distressed, for the people spoke of stoning him, because the soul of all the people was grieved, every man for his sons and his daughters. But David strengthened himself in the LORD his God."

---

55   Ralph F. Wilson, "Understanding the Gift of Prophecy II. The Purpose of Prophecy Today," Joyful Heart Renewal Ministries, http://www.joyfulheart .com/scholar/purp-pro.htm (accessed August 6, 2013). Copyright © 1985-2013, Ralph F. Wilson. <pastor@joyfulheart.com> All rights reserved.

We can see that David was distressed at this point because the people, who were grieved themselves, wanted to kill him. The thing I like most about David is that he was able to make himself strong again in the Lord his God. The Bible doesn't go into detail about how he did it, but because I know that David was a worshipper, prophetic and a lover of God, he, in my opinion, must have sung the song of the Lord, or even prophesied to himself. Whatever method he used to encourage himself, it worked. There have been times where I had to look myself in the mirror and speak the promises of the Lord again over my life. The prophetic word can make a person become strong, harden, and to be; the word of the Lord grants you the ability and permission to be.

According to the Young's Analytical Concordance to the Bible, the word *exhort* is translated in four unique Hebrew words: *paraineo*, which means to exhort and recommend; *parakaleo* means to call near to or for; *protrepo* means to turn forward and propel; and *paraklesis*, which means a calling near or for.[56] We can see that the exhortation is means to encourage. In his book *Dictionary of the Apostolic*, page 124, Apostle John Eckhardt states that "New churches need apostolic exhortation. Churches that suffer persecution also need apostolic exhortation. Apostles bring great encouragement to believers and churches. This encouragement will strengthen local churches and motivate them in areas where they are weak." I truly believe that this gift of exhortation, as I stated before, is necessary for seasoned and new believers. Not only apostles encourage the church, but prophets alongside them, to bring tremendous strength to that local assembly.

Jesus said in John 14:16, 26 (NKJV), "And I will pray the Father, and He will give you another Helper, that He may abide with you forever....But when the Helper, the Holy Spirit, whom the Father will

---

56   Strong's Greek Concordance, s.v. "parakletos," 3875, http://biblesuite
.com/greek/3875.htm (accessed July 12, 2013). See also the *NAS Exhaustive
Concordance of the Bible with Hebrew-Aramaic and Greek Dictionaries*,
Copyright © 1981, 1998 by The Lockman Foundation; New Spirit-Filled Life Bible,
©2002 by Thomas Nelson, Inc and the Holy Bible New King James Version ©1982
by Thomas Nelson, Inc. Definition of parakletos is found on page 1472, located
in the "Word Wealth" Index section, Strong# 3875., *Dictionary of the Apostolic,
Revised, 2nd Edition*, ©2005 by John Eckhardt, page 124, published and produced
by Crusaders Ministries.

send in My name, He will teach you all things, and bring to your remembrance all things that I said to you." It is clear that Jesus is sharing that He will send the Helper, which is the Spirit of truth. The word Helper is the Holy Spirit, who is called the Comforter as well. The Greek translated word for helper is *parakletos,* made up of *para,* which means "beside," and *kaleo,* which means "to call," hence, "called to one's side" (SC 3875). The Holy Spirit is considered the *parakletos* who would, by function, be called to our side. He is sent by the Father to be with the believer and to help, assist, comfort, and encourage us.

REVELATION OF THE GIFT OF PROPHECY

First Corinthians 2:9–12 (NKJV) says:

> But as it is written, "Eye has not seen, nor ear heard, Nor have entered into the heart of man the things which God has prepared for those who love Him." But God has revealed them to us through His Spirit. For the Spirit searches all things, yes, the deep things of God. For what man knows the things of a man except the spirit of the man which is in him? Even so no one knows the things of God except the Spirit of God. Now we have received, not the spirit of the world, but the Spirit who is from God, that we might know the things that have been freely given to us by God.

Cecil Robeck observes and shares emphatically that, "Revelation is the particular characteristic of prophecy which sets it off from preaching and teaching. Indeed, one of the primary ways the Spirit builds up the church is by means of prophecy's revelation. Although the gift of prophecy has a great breadth, we should not imagine that its primary purpose is the setting forth of doctrine, even though 'instruction' was part of its original function (1 Corinthians 14:19). Rather, the gift of prophecy was a revelation from God with a word for the particular moment."[57]

In other words, anything revealed that comes through the gift of prophecy, spirit of prophecy, or through the prophet's ministry office should be disclosed and revealed through the Spirit of God who knows the things of the spirit and the heart of man.

---

57   Robeck, 13.

In this passage of Scripture, three key things on the human body stand out: eye, ear, and heart. When prophets and prophetic people move in the realm of the Spirit, God reveals them through the Spirit and uses our spiritual senses to communicate what the Spirit of God is saying. Only God knows the heart of man.

The Spirit has the capacity to search all things, even the deeper things of the Spirit. We must minister by the Spirit and not by the means of human intellect. I have received prophetic words from people who already knew me, and because they were familiar they prophesied a word that seemed like it was by the wisdom of God, but was really human wisdom and knowledge.

Those who are prophets and prophetic minister the deep things of God. God wants us to receive His divine plan, will, and hidden wisdom. There are things of the Spirit that our eyes, ears, and heart have not encountered. The Bible says that no one knows the things of the Spirit but the Spirit. The prophetic gift and spirit knows the spirit of a man. We see in verse 10 of 1 Corinthians 2 that God has revealed things to the apostles through His Spirit. The two necessary elements to know are that the things of the Spirit are God's revelation disclosed to man by the Spirit, and God requires man to give a spiritual response to that revelation that was given. (See 2:14–3:4.)

Therefore, a person knows his or her own inner thoughts and mind, so that the mind of God is known only by God's Spirit. When the prophetic is in operation, Jesus Christ is revealed. In other words, when I prophesy and reveal things about the person I am ministering to, God is revealing His mind, will, and intentions to them. The interesting part of the prophetic at work is that the hearer begins to see, hear, and sense in their heart the Spirit of God revealing His purpose to them. Their eyes, ears, and heart is being touched by the Spirit of God. Have you received a prophetic word so deep that you could not believe it was given? In your inner thoughts you knew that what was spoken was directly from the Lord, and only He would have revealed that.

As I stated earlier, the Spirit of God searches the depths of our very being. The prophetic gift is a vocal gift given by the Holy Spirit, but it also reveals the heart of man and releases the wisdom, counsel, and revelation knowledge of God's Word. The Spirit of God interprets Himself. The Spirit knows the things of the Spirit, so when the prophets and apostles receive their message it is divine revelation given by the Spirit of Christ. In verse 9, the apostle Paul begins to reveal man's inability to understand the deep things of God because they were operating in man's wisdom and not the mystery of God, which is His wisdom.

The Holy Spirit will by His inspiration reveal spiritual things and deeper realm of His Spirit to the spirit of man. We can see that the Spirit search all things like someone who thoroughly investigate or gather all of their facts and findings to solve a case. The Spirit inquires by investigating, tracking and studying by close examination the deep predetermined purpose, plan and destiny for each person's situation. The prophetic word reveal things from the Spirit that man may have not known because only God knows and reveal to whomever He chooses.

The word *reveal* comes from the Greek word *apokalypto*, which means to uncover, unveil or disclose.[58] The prophetic word or revelation can uncover, unveil, or disclose God's plans through three basic spiritual senses: the eyes, the ears, and the heart to comprehend. God wants to open up our ear gates, eye gates, and heart of hearts to reveal His intentions for our lives. In other words, God opens up our ears to hear what the Spirit is saying in the Spirit, opens our eyes to perceive, see, and understand from God's perspective, and also our hearts so that, through the spirit of love and compassion, we can feel with spiritual sensitivity what He feels.

Our spiritual vision can be opened by the Lord, and through the dynamic of prophecy Christ is revealed to the hearer.

Biblical prophets were known to have seen the visions of God. They would get taken up in the spirit and see things that they could not have initiated on their own. The Spirit of God transcends their natural vision and takes them in the heavenly vision. The ministry of prophecy should always be aiming to build up the body of Christ through faith in their Lord by disclosing and revealing what the Spirit released by the vision of the Lord. The Spirit of Christ has a vision for

---

58   Blue Letter Bible, s.v. "apokalyptō," www.blueletterbible.org/lang/lexicon/ Lexicon.cfm?strongs=G601 (accessed July 12, 2013).

His church and we must articulate it and implement it in the earth for His glory. In 2 Kings 6:17, Elisha prayed and inquired of the Lord to open up the *eyes* of the young man who was serving him.

> And Elisha prayed, and said, "LORD, I pray, open his eyes that he may see." Then the LORD opened the eyes of the young man, and he saw. And behold, the mountain was full of horses and chariots of fire all around Elisha.
>
> —2 KINGS 6:17, NKJV

We can see that the prophetic anointing and ministry can open up the spiritual eyes of those who are blind in deception or error, and in need of clarity of vision. The prophet Elisha prayed and the Lord granted his request. Next, the young man saw a part of the heaven army around about Elisha; it was time for spiritual warfare. God opened up the eyes of the servant so that he could see what Elisha already knew in the Spirit. There were more with them than there were against them. Elisha did not ask the Lord to show the young lad a miracle, because he was probably used to the miracle ministry of Elisha, but he asked the Lord to show his servant another realm or dimension in the Spirit. God will open our spiritual sight so that we will see into another realm with faith and assurance. We can see that the prophetic brought hope when Elisha's servant thought that they were outnumbered when their enemies were pursuing them. The prophetic gift brings hope.

The Bible says in Revelation 2:7, *"He who has an ear, let him hear what the Spirit says to the churches."* God wants to open up our spiritual ears that we may hear what the Spirit is saying to us. Just like the eyes can be opened, the Bible says that God can awaken our ears as well to hear the voice of Jesus.

> The Lord GOD has given Me the tongue of the learned, that I should know how to speak a word in season to him who is weary. He awakens Me morning by morning, He awakens My ear to hear as the learned. "The Lord GOD has opened My ear; And I was not rebellious, nor did I turn away."
>
> —ISAIAH 50:4–5, NKJV

In this above passage of Scripture we can see that the Lord has given Isaiah the prophet the tongue of the learned, which is the prophetic ability and skill to effectively deliver the message. God gives prophets the ability to interpret by the Spirit God's original mind, intent, purpose, and plan to those they are called to. God became the spiritual alarm clock that awakened their ears to hear. Not only does He awaken them daily, but He also teaches them by giving them the tongue of the wise or learned. Prophets are not to be rebellious and an island to themselves, but they are to be submitted to God and His Word, and linked to the local body of believers. Prophets and prophetic people are submitted to the Lord and do it out of obedience to God's strategy. (See Matthew 26:39.)

Lastly, we need our spiritual hearts to be opened—a listening heart. An interesting scripture that I love mediating on is the one that talks about King Solomon inquiring of the Lord to grant unto him a discerning heart:

> So give Your servant an understanding mind and a hearing heart
> to judge Your people, that I may discern between good and bad.
> For who is able to judge and rule this Your great people?
> —1 Kings 3:9, amp

King Solomon wanted an understanding mind and hearing heart to judge God's people, along with—as a young king who didn't have much experience ruling a kingdom—the ability to distinguish between good and evil. Prophets and prophetic people must have a heart that listens to the leading of God Spirit. God judges the inner thoughts of man and He also gives us by the Spirit the ability to discern and perceive, understand and recognize a person's motives and agendas. Solomon needed the wisdom of God to rule. In addition, it was wise of him to ask the Lord for wisdom and nothing materialistic. Because he asked for a heart to hear and to comprehend, the Lord blessed him tremendously with riches. An obedient servant, minister, and leader must seek the Lord for understanding and an open heart that will hear His voice in any situation in life.

THE MOUTHPIECE OF GOD

The prophets were mouthpieces of God speaking His word to their world, society, and generation regarding either past, present, or future truths. They were men of inspired utterance. Today God is raising up divine oracles and people who will prophesy as the Lord commands. I am not teaching people to be a prophesier or to just prophesy but to discern the voice of God to prophesy by the Spirit. Jesus said His sheep know His voice "and a stranger will they not follow" (John 10:4–5, KJV). There are many voices and frequencies in the realm of the spirit, but a prophet knows the Creator's voice and can tune into heaven's frequencies and transmit His mind, will, and divine purpose for humanity when needed.

In Barbara Wentroble's book *Fighting for Your Prophetic Promises*, she talks about growing in the gift of prophecy to the office of the prophet. She talks about a little girl who grows into such a beautiful woman. Although this baby girl goes through life struggles and goes through growth and development like we all do, through all of the processes of life the parents of the baby girl watch as she finally stands as a beautiful bride on her wedding day. Apostle Barbara Wentroble compares that life process and maturation to that of the gift of prophecy and the office of a prophet. She says, "Growing from the gift of prophecy to the office of prophet happens the same way. A prophet, once called, is not formed in a day. A prophet must fight to be faithful to the tasks that will prepare him for his calling from God. First, however, must come the anointing for the office. It is God who calls prophets and not any individual or organization."[59]

GIFT OF PROPHECY IN THE LOCAL CHURCH

The prophetic ministry in the early church was expressed and utilized for the purpose of establishing the voice of the Lord. As I mentioned before, prophecy, prophets, and the ministry gift of prophesying was God's idea and not man's. If it was God's idea in the Old and New Testaments, then it is a concept and culture that we as believers should embrace. As I researched the Scriptures in writing this book,

---

59 Barbara Wentroble, *Fighting for Your Prophetic Promises* (Ada, MI: Chosen Books, 2011), 131.

I found some appealing discoveries of the important role that New Covenant prophets were established by the Lord. This what I have found in regards to the ministry in the New Testament:

- Prophets were established and set by God governmentally in the NT church along with apostle and teachers (1 Cor. 12:28–29).

- Prophets are ranked second in order in the NT church by God (1 Cor. 12:29).

- Prophets are one out of four "headship" ascension-gift ministries given by Christ to His church as His extension (Eph. 4:11).

- Prophets can operate and flow in the spirit of prophecy (Rev. 19:10).

- Prophets have a resident ministry gift of prophecy in them (1 Cor. 14:3, 31; 12:28).

- Prophets are called, generally speaking, to 1) Equip, train, and mature the saints; 2) Activate, ordain, recognize, and assist the saints into their ministries; and 3) Edify, build up, and strengthen the church of Jesus Christ (Eph. 4:9–16).

- Prophets were tremendously used to confirm, set, affirm, and ordain mature leaders in the church, just like in Antioch when Paul and Barnabas were released as apostles (Acts 13:1–4).

- Prophets move in the ministry of consolation, encouragement, exhortation, and strength (Acts 15:22).

- Prophets can foretell through divine prediction what is to come to warn the people, as Agabus did in regards to the famine that happened (Acts 11:27–30; Acts 21:8–14).

- Prophets, along with the apostles, are foundational ministries in the NT church (Eph. 2:20–22; 3:5).

- Prophets have a special warfare mentality and confrontational grace to contend against false doctrine, prophets, and teachers who are like wolves in sheep's clothing (2 Thess. 2:11–12; Rev. 13; Matt. 24:11, 24).

- Prophets, along with apostles, possess by their call, mantle, office, and gift the spiritual ability and insight into God's divine plan, revelation, purpose, and heart concerning His church (Eph. 3:1–5).

As we take into consideration the role of the prophets and prophetic gift in the New Testament we can clearly see its importance and relevance in the early church and today. I believe it is a cutting-edge ministry that is in need *today* in the church and in the world. There are churches and leaders today that still refuse to embrace the prophetic ministry of the prophet in their church. A church without the voice of the Lord speaking is like a desert in need of water. The Bible says the church is built on the foundation laid by the apostles and prophets according to Ephesians 2:19–22.

New Covenant Prophets

The New Testament church made mention of prophets that were sent, used, and operated in the early church. Below is a list of the prophets identified:

- Agabus was a reputable prophet of God (Acts 11:28; 21:10–11).

- Judas and Silas were considered prophets (Acts 15:32).

- Ananias was sent as a prophet to Saul, who later became the great apostle Paul (Acts 9:1–15; 22:10–15).

- Prophets stationed in Tyre (Acts 21:4).

- Prophets sent from the city of Jerusalem (Acts 11:27).

- Prophets were in the midst of the displaced churches (2 Pet. 2:1–2; 1 John 4:1–3).

- Prophets and teachers were a part of the leadership team at Antioch (Acts 13:1–4).

- Prophets at Corinth (1 Cor. 14:27, 29; 12:28–29).

- Prophets were in Ephesus (Eph. 4:9–11).

- Prophetess Anna, an eighty-four-year-old woman of God who served in the temple (Luke 2:36–38).

- Jezebel, a self-appointed and self-acclaimed prophetess (Rev. 2:20).

- False prophets at Crete (Titus 1:10–13).

MIXING THE GIFT OF PROPHECY WITH THE OFFICE OF THE PROPHET

There is a difference between the gift and office of something. A person's gift (charisma) is something that a person can operate in with little or no effort because that's what they do. It is their gift. On the other hand, a person who stands or holds a particular office carries a greater responsibility than is required of a person flowing in a specific gift. I have come across people in ministry who mix the gift of prophecy with the office of the prophetic because they really don't know the difference. Also, because they believe that a person who prophesies is a prophet automatically. The gift of prophecy is found in the Book of 1 Corinthians 12:10, Romans 12:6, and Acts 2:18.

The gift of prophecy is a spiritual gift to utter things by the Spirit. It is a gift, not an office. Moreover, the gift of prophecy is simply the God-given ability to speak forth by the Spirit supernatural things that pertain to things of the Spirit in a known tongue that is communicated to a specific situation or person. The office of the prophet is mentioned in Ephesians 4:11 and 1 Corinthians 12:28–29. The office of the prophet is a headship leadership position called, sent, set, and stationed in the church for the sole purpose of equipping, perfecting, training, and making the saints fully ready and qualified for ministry service.

In addition, the office is a seat of the prophet's authority and power. The prophet flows and operates from that place by God's authority. The power of their prophetic office is recalibrated through the prophetic mantle. They are God's special messengers and His mouthpieces. Moreover, a prophet's office is who they are, and that was predetermined before they were born. A person operating in a gift is what they do, but a prophetic officer is who they are. It is the Lord who set them in their office and not anyone else. The local church is called to establish, confirm, and recognize the call of the prophet on someone's life and utilize them for the upbuilding of the body of Christ. The gift of prophecy is limited to exhortation, encouragement, and comfort, while someone who functions in the office of prophet has a greater level of authority, power, and release from God, because God set them there.

The prophetic office carries much weight in the prophetic realm when it comes to the hearing and speaking as "oracles of God." When a prophet prophesies, prays, and engages in prophetic acts of warfare, he carries in his mantle a supernatural ability to create, root out, pull down, destroy, overthrow, build, plant, and call things into divine alignment. (See Jeremiah 1:9–10.) The office of the prophet is the highest level in the prophetic realm. Throughout the Old Testament, when God wanted to get things done He used the prophets to do it. God also reveals His secrets to His servants, the prophets (Amos 3:7). We need prophets and seers operating in their office in the local assembly to combat and address false prophets, teachers, doctrine, and demonic behaviors, patterns, systems, and strategies.

Chapter Twelve

FALSE PROPHETS AND PROPHECY

But the prophet who speaks a word presumptuously in My
name which I have not commanded him to speak, or which he
speaks in the name of other gods, that prophet shall die.' You
may say in your heart, 'How will we know the word which the
Lord has not spoken?' When a prophet speaks in the name of
the Lord, if the thing does not come about or come true, that
is the thing which the Lord has not spoken. The prophet has
spoken it presumptuously; you shall not be afraid of him.
—Deuteronomy 18:20–22, nas

A S THE LORD is raising up new covenant-type prophetic models today in the church, the adversary is also. Just as there were true prophets in the early church, there were false ones in disguise. In Deuteronomy 19:20–22, it reveals the nature of a presumed word that God has not given. The Lord was very serious addressing false prophecy and prophets in the days of Moses. The Lord was telling Moses that He would raise up a prophet like him from among the people and He will put His word in His mouth. Jesus was that prophet that God was referring to because this type of prophetic representative will speak what God puts in His mouth.

True prophets only speak what God commands them to speak. God went on to say that the prophet who presumes to speak a word in My name, which He has not commanded for them to speak, or speak in the name of another god, then that prophet will die. Obviously, the Lord's punishment for releasing presumptuous words in His name or any other god's name will be to serve the death penalty.

The Old Testament prophetic guidelines were very severe and shouldn't have been taken lightly. In verses 21 and 22, the Lord gives the outline on how to determine if the word was from Him or from that prophet. He says that if a word spoken in His name that He did not say doesn't come to pass, that prophet spoke presumptuously and the people should not fear him. The Lord said that the prophecy was presumptuously spoken, and the people should not receive that prophet. This is interesting because I have received and even released a presumptuous word before through my prophetic ministry. I have had people come to me about a situation and immaturely I gave them what I wanted to see happen to them out of good intention and motive, but it wasn't God plan.

Due to the fact that I released that word in the prophetic authority that I had, I figured that God would honor my request because I ministered it in accordance to His word; but the Lord said it wasn't what He revealed to me by His Spirit, but what I already knew in regards to the Scriptures about a situation. As prophets and prophetic people we must not prophesy out of the personal need of someone who comes to us for a prophetic word or counsel. We must seek the Lord in everything we do and release what God says, no matter what. Some people are not open to receive what God reveals to them.

I recall a time when I was in a choir meeting and the leader wanted me to pray that God would supernaturally heal his mother, but in my spirit (inner knowing by the Spirit) the Lord revealed to me that she would not live to the end of the year. It would have been devastating to this leader if I had told him what God revealed to me by the Spirit. With wisdom I just prayed that God would comfort his heart and that he would be able to endure the season to come, and that the Lord's will be done. His mother passed away in December of that year, and it was one of the most trying times of his adult life. Can you imagine what would have happened if I prophesied that God was going to heal her completely, decreeing healing scriptures over her life? Most likely I would have been labeled a false prophet because what I released presumptuously wasn't what God had spoken.

We must understand that God's will always supersedes our will. My point is that even though a genuine prophet missed it in a prophecy doesn't mean that he or she is a false prophet, technically. I have hit and missed many times in the prophetic ministry while others may not have known it because in my Spirit I knew it because we sometime value or look at people on the outer appearance and not the heart. God doesn't look at the outward but in the inward.

The Merriam Webster's Dictionary defines the word *presumption* as "a presumptuous attitude or conduct, and attitude or belief dictated by probability."[60] God doesn't want us to prophesy out of our own presumptuous attitude and beliefs that are dictated by probability, but Holy Spirit-inspired utterance of assurance. Prophets don't prophesy out of presumptuous probability, but confirm the supernatural acts of God performing His Word in a person's life that brings impossibility into being. Let me be clear on what a false prophet is; a false prophet is simply a person who turns you away from the true and living God.

John the Apostle wrote in 1 John 4:1–3 (NKJV):

Beloved, do not believe every spirit, but test the spirits, whether they are of God; because many false prophets have gone out into the world. By this you know the Spirit of God: Every spirit that confesses that Jesus Christ has come in the flesh is of God, and every spirit that does not confess that Jesus Christ has come in the flesh is not of God. And this is the spirit of the Antichrist, which you have heard was coming, and is now already in the world.

First John 4:1 tells us to "try" or "test the spirits." This mandate is for our protection. The way to test a false prophet was by his or her teachings, not by what they would actually say. In Deuteronomy 13, God says a word can actually come to pass, but that He is testing you to determine whether you love the Lord. That is powerful to know, that a word can come to pass so the Lord can test a person.

In the Old and New Testament there were instances where false prophetic ministry posed a threat to the upbuilding of the church and would come to devour the flock. There are Bible guidelines and tests by which all prophets, apostles, teachers, and other ministry gifts have to show proof of authenticity. There were examples, instances, evidences, and warnings in both the Old and New Testaments against false prophets. Throughout the Word of God there are countless passages that warn of false prophets and to beware of them. We must

---

60 *Merriam-Webster's Dictionary and Thesaurus*, s.v "presumption."

understand that Satan hates the prophets and apostles, so in turn he will gather up false prophets, apostles, and teachers to deceive the people.

Below I have provided for your own study some biblical principles for testing the ministry of the prophet and prophecy:

- Testing of the three spirits that can be at work in the prophetic utterances is the *Holy* Spirit, *human* spirit and *demonic* spirit (John 4:1–3; Ezek. 13:1–6; Jer. 23:17, 26–32).

- Testing of the teaching or doctrine that a prophet shares (1 John 4:1–6; 1 Tim. 4:1–3; Isaiah 8:18–20; Matt. 24:11; Mark 13:22; Rev. 16:13–14).

- Testing of the fruit in that prophet (Matt. 7:15–23; Rev. 2:20; Rom. 6:16–22).

- Testing of prophetic fulfillment of the prophecy they release (Deut. 18:19–22).

- Testing of their ministry call to the people to bring them back to the Lord and cause people to repent and serve God (Heb. 12:17–14).

- Testing if the prophet covets, especially a lover of money (Mic. 3:11; 2 Pet. 2:1–3).

- Testing if the prophet initiates worship or turns people away to worship of the deities (Deut. 13:1–5; Matt. 24:11, 24; 2 Thess. 4:1–3; Isa. 8:18–20).

- Testing prophecy function that promotes and is limited to edify, exhort, and comfort (1 Cor. 14:4).

- Testing prophecy that advocates freedom or bondage (Rom. 8:15).

- Testing prophecy that generates life (2 Cor. 3:6).

- Testing prophecy that brings glory to Christ Jesus (John 16:13–14).

- Testing prophecy that challenges obedience to God (Deut. 13:1–5).

- Testing that aligns, confirms, and agrees with the inspired Holy Scriptures (2 Tim. 3:16).

- Testing prophecy that bears witness to the Spirit in the born-again believer (1 John 2:27).

There is an interesting scripture in Ezekiel 13:2–3 that says, "Son of man, prophesy against the prophets of Israel who prophesy, and say to those who prophesy out of their own heart, 'Hear the word of the LORD!' Thus says the Lord GOD: 'Woe to the foolish prophets, who follow their own spirit and have seen nothing!'" God says one can actually say they are hearing from the Lord, but it really is their own spirit.

Moreover, in the Corinthian church there was a limit to those who could prophesy. The prophets were to minister one by one, in turn, while each of the others judged the word. The Bible says that the spirit of the prophet is subject to the prophet. So that being said, prophecy must be judged by others. Prophets are not the only ones to judge each other; it the responsibility of the believer to judge the word as well. We are not to judge the prophet, because he or she is not perfect, but we are to judge the word and the spirit of the word.

Let two or three prophets speak, and let the others judge.
—1 CORINTHIANS 14:29, NKJV

The apostle Paul wanted to bring order to the prophetic release and presbytery. I love to see prophets flowing together as a team. As a prophetic leader on the prophetic team at my local church, I usually go first to release a word. But sometimes when I am not the lead, what happens is the other prophet with me will begin to prophesy and I usually get the same things that the lead received from the Lord, which confirms that we are in tune to the voice of the Lord. Prophets recognized and used in the local church will eliminate a lot of false teaching, idolatry, pride, error, perversion, division, greed, and false prophets. I believe prophets serve as the watchmen along with the senior leader when it comes to discerning the spiritual climate or temperature in the house. That is why I cannot express enough the importance of prophecy in the church; we should not despise its capabilities.

Dr. Bill Hamon, in his book *Prophets, Pitfalls & Principles: God's Prophetic People Today*, talked about what he calls the "Ten M's" for ministry that will assist believers and leaders in determining a prophetic minister's true or false statuses. The "Ten M's" for ministry by Bishop Hamon is a good checks and balances for seasoned and emerging leaders below which one can study on their own with biblical references:

1. **Manhood** (Gen. 1:26–27; Rom. 8:29; Heb. 2:6,10)

2. **Ministry** (2 Cor. 6:3; Matt. 7:15–21; Deut. 18:22)

3. **Message** (Eph. 4:15; 1 Tim. 4:2; Mark 16:20)

4. **Maturity** (James 3:17; Gal. 5:22; 1 Cor. 13)

5. **Marriage** (1 Tim. 3:2,5; 1 Pet. 3:1,7)

6. **Methods** (Titus 1:16; Rom. 1:18; 3:7–8)

7. **Manners** (Titus 1:7; 3:1–2; Eph. 4:29; 5:4)

8. **Money** (1 Tim. 3:6, AMP; 1 Tim. 6:5–17)

9. **Morality** (1 Cor. 6:9–18; Eph. 5:3; Matt. 5:28)

10. **Motive** (Matt. 6:1; 1 Cor. 16:15; Prov. 16:2; 1 Cor. 13:1–3)[61]

DO NOT DESPISE TO PROPHESY!

Do not quench (suppress or subdue) the Holy Spirit; Do not spurn the gifts and utterances of the prophets [do not depreciate prophetic revelations nor despise inspired instruction or exhortation or warning]. But test and prove all things [until you can recognize] what is good; [to that] hold fast.

—1 THESSALONIANS 5:19–20, AMP

---

61 Bill Hamon, *Prophets, Pitfalls, and Principles* (Shippensburg, PA: Destiny Image Publishers, 1991), 66.

Within the context of this passage of Scripture we see that we are not to quench, suppress, or subdue the Holy Spirit. In addition it also says not to spurn the gifts and utterance of the prophets. It is important to know that the Holy Spirit wants to have free access and permission to flow through you. There are those who will keep Him bottled up and never experience the refreshing that comes. God wants to speak to us and through us. The Holy Spirit is gentle as a dove and will not make us do something that we don't feel comfortable doing. He will use someone who wants to be used. Furthermore, in the Scriptures it says we are not to depreciate prophetic revelations and despise inspired instruction that comes to exhort and warn. Prophets and prophetic people are people of revelation. The gifts and prophetic utterance from the prophets should not be taken lightly, but seriously.

Prophets are instrumental in their ability to bring correction, order, balance, and strength. When we as a church don't welcome prophets, then we are despising inspired instruction, directives, warnings, and wisdom of God. The word *despise* in Merriam Webster's Dictionary means "to look down on with contempt or aversion, detest, to regard as negligible, worthless or distasteful." The prophetic revelation and word that comes from the Spirit through His prophets should not be looked down upon, viewed as worthless or distasteful. The word of the Lord should be honored and respected; it is God who is speaking it. I believe that we should test all things that are released through prophetic utterance, because there are three spirits that can be in operation: the Holy Spirit, human spirit, and satanic spirits.

Moreover, we are admonished in the Word not to spurn the gifts and utterances by the prophets. We are to truly appreciate the ministry gift, anointing, and graces in the body of Christ and not reject them. The word *spurn* in Merriam Webster's Dictionary means "to kick away or trample on, to reject with disdain." This is very crucial when it comes to prophecy and prophets operating in the local church. God still speaks! He will do it through those who will allow Him to speak. We are not to kick away or trample on the prophetic pearls that are released from the throneroom of God. I believe that if we value our personal prophecies, then we should also value God's written Word so much more. People will only value what they love and hold dear to their hearts. God's Word is His bond. In addition, we must prove all things. God will not have you ignorant. We are to examine what is being uttered when it is released. It is our responsibly to, by the Spirit, discern and prove what we have heard is good and acceptable.

False Prophets Are Like Hungry Wolves

Matthew 7:15 (NKJV) says, "Beware of false prophets, who come to you in sheep's clothing, but inwardly they are ravenous wolves."

This is a strong warning from Jesus as He is informing His disciples about false prophets who come in one manner but inwardly they are ravenous wolves. Jesus, who is the Good Shepherd, understands that while there are true prophetic messengers, there are false ones as well. Wolves represent the false prophets. Jesus compares them to ravenous wolves dressed up in sheep's clothing. That is why we need the true prophets operating in the local church to identify and call out the wolves that come into the sheepfold camouflaged as innocent sheep. There are many false prophets among us today who come in pretending to be holy, righteous, humble, and meek, but their true nature is destructive, selfish, violent, and murderous.

We are to test these so-called prophets who come into the local church and prophesy but inwardly they are about getting your money, your members, your possessions, and whatever else they can take from you. These false prophets have ulterior motives and they will use their gift to deceive God's people. The Bible is clear that we are to examine those claiming to be prophets or who prophesy by their fruit—that is their lifestyle, character, teaching, influence, and spirit. A wolf is characterized for its boldness and fierceness of attack. One interesting thing about a wolf is that it can kill more than it can eat because blood gets it stirred up. Jesus as the Good Shepherd realizes that the wolf is the greatest enemy of the sheep. Even in the Old Testament false prophets were the enemy of God's people. They were known for bringing people under enslavement and bondage through deception.

JUDGING THE SUPERNATURAL
AND THE PROPHETIC GIFT

First Corinthians 2:14–15 (AMP) says:

> But the natural, nonspiritual man does not accept or welcome
> or admit into his heart the gifts and teachings and revelations
> of the Spirit of God, for they are folly (meaningless nonsense) to
> him; and he is incapable of knowing them [of progressively rec-
> ognizing, understanding, and becoming better acquainted with
> them] because they are spiritually discerned and estimated and
> appreciated. But the spiritual man tries all thing [he examines,
> investigates, inquires into, questions, and discerns all things], yet
> is himself to be put on trial and judged by no one [he can read
> the meaning of everything, but no one can properly discern or
> appraise or get an insight into him].

The Bible says that the natural, non-spiritual man does not accept
or welcome or even admit in their hearts the gifts and teaching
and revelation of the Spirit of God. To them it is meaningless and
basically nonsense. But the spiritual man examines, investigates,
and puts into question that which they discern. The spiritual man
must judge the supernatural and even those who speak prophetically. Prophets and prophetic people are to judge the supernatural
and make sure that the source is God. The Bible says that the Spirit
searches all things and even the deep things of God. It should be the
responsibility of the Christian believer to sharpen their discernment
of spiritual things.

SPIRITUAL FRUIT INSPECTOR

> You will know them by their fruits. Do men gather grapes from
> thornbushes or figs from thistles? Even so, every good tree bears
> good fruit, but a bad tree bears bad fruit.
>
> —MATTHEW 7:16–17

Jesus said in the above scripture that you should know people by
the fruit that they bear. Moreover, Jesus goes on to say later in the

chapter that a bad tree cannot produce good fruit, and vice versa. One of the ways that I have learned in the prophetic which gives me the ability to assess a situation is to watch. Whenever I am in a prophetic meeting, the Lord often instructs me to just pray and watch. Most of the time He gives me something regarding the particular church, conference, or meeting that I have been invited to. As I am watching, I am able to discern the atmosphere as well as make eye contact with people in the congregation. Then usually as I am scanning the room, God begins to give me words of knowledge in regards to a person's present condition, whether it is sickness, financial, marital, and economical or anything that they may be dealing with.

In addition, the Lord would give me the name of and specific facts about a person, and when it is time for me to minister and preach, I already know those whom I will call out to prophesy to. I have developed this gift of discerning of spirits and have asked the Lord to show me in the meetings what to do to bring divine breakthrough in a person's life. We are not just called to be spiritual fruit inspectors but to also cultivate the soil in people's lives by planting the Word of the Lord so that they can bring forth God fruit. Prophets are not to judge people, but they judge righteously. In John 7:24 (AMP) it says, "Be honest in your judgment and do not decide at a glance (superficially and by appearances); but judge fairly and righteously." So we can see that the believer can judge fairly and righteously.

No Room for Error!

As we come into the truth of God's Word and connect with others in ministry, there will be no room for error. The Bible says that the people err not knowing the Scriptures. Prophets and prophetic people must be lovers of God's Word and search the Scriptures with a noble heart and with all readiness to examine the Word or what is being taught by others, if what they say is true. I have been in healthy dialogue in regards to doctrine. Then there are those who will believe everything they hear without searching it out for themselves.

Then the brethren immediately sent Paul and Silas away by night to Berea. When they arrived, they went into the synagogue of the Jews. These were more fair-minded than those in Thessalonica, in that they received the word with all readiness, and searched the Scriptures daily to find out whether these things were so. There many of them believed, and also not a few of the Greeks, prominent women as well as men.

—ACTS 17:10–12, NKJV

Paul and Silas were ministering in Berea, and when they arrived there and taught in the synagogue of the Jews, they saw that the Jews in Berea were not closed-minded to the teachings they heard. They were open to receive and were able to search the Scriptures to examine whether what Paul and Silas were sharing was accurate. Prophets and prophetic people must have an open mind to fresh new things of the Spirit and search the Word of God for spiritual nuggets and truth. One thing that I like about the Bereans is that they received the Word with readiness and examined the Scriptures daily.

Prophets should study the Word of God daily like never before. There is nothing more frustrating than receiving a prophetic word from someone that doesn't know the Word. I have heard prophecy from people who included cartoon characters and their favorite movie in their prophecies. In other words, they have spent more time in front of the television than in the Word of God. I heard a wise man say one day, "what you put in, that will come also come out." When a prophet spends valuable time in prayer and in the Word of God, so much strength, authority, boldness, power, and confidence flow from them. They will not walk in error. Prophetic servants of God are submitted to the Word of God because the Word of God is the final authority. It should be the heartbeat of any believer of Christ to have burning hunger and desire to learn more.

As Spirit-filled believers, we must grow in the knowledge of our Lord Jesus Christ and become more like Him. People err because of a lack of knowing the Word of God. It is imperative and necessary for prophetic ministers to devote their time to prayer, fasting, worship, and the Word. In the twenty-first century we have access to far too much technology and information to be ignorant. God will not have you ignorant. An awesome Scripture that I mediate on a lot is Hebrews 4:11–13, which talks about how the Word of God discovers our condition. Even as I said that prophecy will find you out as it did when it came to Jeremiah. The Word of God is the discerner of the intents and motives of man's heart.

Hebrews 4:11–13 (NKJV) says:

Let us therefore be diligent to enter that rest, lest anyone fall according to the same example of disobedience. For the word of God is living and powerful, and sharper than any two-edged sword, piercing even to the division of soul and spirit, and of joints and marrow, and is a discerner of the thoughts and intents of the heart. And there is no creature hidden from His sight, but all things are naked and open to the eyes of Him to whom we must give account.

This is a remarkable scripture that characterizes the Word of God as living and powerful. The Word (logos) of God's written Word has life because it is from the Lord Himself; likewise with the spoken (rhema) word that comes forth prophetically. We must understand that there is nothing hidden to God of which He is ignorant. I have learned that as I increase my study of the Word of God and take time out to mediate on it, my life starts transforming. I would recommend that young prophets and those who desire to minister in the prophetic submit to churches that are strong in Word and in power.

Hebrews 4:11–13 outlines that God's Word is sharper than any two-edged sword, piercing even the division of soul and spirit, joints and marrow, and discerns the thoughts and intents of the heart. Only through God's Word can He give us the "prophetic advantage" or "prophetic edge" to judge, discern, and examine our lives before Him. The Lord wants to teach us to use the Word of God for our advantage, especially when there is spiritual warfare. The Bible says that the weapons of our warfare are not carnal but mighty through God. The Word of God is the sword (s-word) of the Spirit, according to Ephesians 6:17.

PROPHECIES BRING GLORY AND HONOR TO CHRIST

Revelation 19:20 says, "At this I fell at his feet to worship him. But he said to me, "Do not do it! I am a fellow servant with you and with your brothers who hold to the testimony of Jesus. Worship God! For the testimony of Jesus is the spirit of prophecy."

The spirit of prophecy is the testimony of Jesus Christ. When a Spirit-filled believer prophesies by the Spirit, it the Spirit of Christ that is being released. One's motivation for anything should always be God-centered and never self-centered. The wrong attitude and spirit when prophesying can release the wrong word and heart to someone. It will not be the Spirit of Christ but the human spirit at work. Jesus is the Spirit of prophecy and He gets the glory. The primary ministry of the Holy Spirit is to bring honor, esteem, reverence, praise, homage, and glory to Jesus. We must understand that any prophetic dream, vision, utterance, or gift should accomplish that intended purpose.

In 1 Corinthians 12:3 (NKJV) it says, *"Therefore I make know to you that no one speaking by the Spirit of God calls Jesus accursed, and no one can say that Jesus is Lord except by the Holy Spirit."* We can see that the principle here in this text is that Christ is to be glorified. Anyone speaking by the Spirit will not say that Jesus is accursed, because all manifestation of the Spirit will harmonize and be in alignment with the truth about Jesus. Jesus is the Prophet of all prophets and the primary assignment of the Spirit is to bring people under the lordship of Jesus and not ourselves. A prophecy that promotes self and self-glorification has to be judged appropriately in the local church.

We are to judge prophecy and not the prophet. We can test the prophet's spirit and motivation, but ultimately the prophetic word, if in error, will expose the prophet's spirit and intentions.

Prophets of Integrity

I believe in this hour that God is raising up men and women of integrity. Prophets especially must be vessels of honor, dignity, and integrity. There is nothing more frustrating than for someone to breach their word. That is why the Bible tells us not to make promises that we are not able to keep. The Bible says to let your answer be yes or no, and anything outside of that is not from God. Prophets and prophetic people should be people of great value not only when relating with others within the local church, but every day of their lives.

The word *integrity* in the Merriam Webster's Dictionary means "adherence to a code of value, soundness and completeness."[62] It is funny that there are prophets and leaders who require others to keep a standard that they themselves cannot fulfill. We are to be a people of soundness and completeness, and to adhere to the code of value that is outlined in the Word of God. I personally will not prophesy, teach, preach, and recommend someone to do something that I myself cannot honor. As prophetic leaders we must understand that we are held accountable to what we speak out of our mouths. False prophets are deceivers, liars, and con artists who lack moral, ethical, and spiritual integrity. That is why we are to test the spirit by the spirit to see if it is of God. Not every person prophesying in the name of Jesus who gives a "thus saith the Lord" is from Him.

Furthermore, Mark 13:22–23 (NKJV) says, "For false christs and false prophets will rise and show signs and wonders to deceive, if possible, even the elect. But take heed; see, I have told you all things beforehand." We see that Jesus is warning His disciples in the first century that there will be false so-called messiahs and prophets emerging showing signs and wonders to deceive people. That is why I advocate prophets in the local church for the purpose of allowing them to be the spiritual "anti-virus" or "spyware" that protect the church from damaging and deceiving information, data, doctrine, and agendas. I have been around young prophets who were impressed with another prophet's gift. They overlooked the obvious that was spilling out of their character and lifestyle. The young prophet was in awe that the other prophet could call out names, social security numbers, banking account information, and addresses; but God is not impressed with a person's gift, but their lifestyle, holy unto Him.

I always say that God is a God of His Word and operates in integrity. So if this prophet is calling out names and telephone numbers only for the purpose of getting your money and deceiving you with signs, wonders, and miracles, then you are already walking in error. We judge the spirit of the prophet and his words, which would allow us to discern if it's God, satanic, or the human spirit.

While in the workplace, one of my responsibilities in the banking industry is to be accurate to detail and distinguish between the

---

62   *Merriam-Webster's Dictionary and Thesaurus*, s.v. "integrity."

authentic or counterfeit monies. The difference between them is that they feel and look different. When someone has been around the truth a lot, it is easy to identity the false. Even in ministry a person can discern the false from the true because something doesn't feel, look, sound, or even smell right. Satan always tries to duplicate but, unlike God, he doesn't have the power to create. So Jesus was warning His disciples to beware of the false prophets and messiahs. Importantly, they will come with miraculous signs and wonders, but they are really deceivers. We can see that Elijah the prophet miraculously had to address and slay 450 prophets of Baal and 400 prophets of Asherah whom Jezebel supported on Mount Carmel (1 Kings 18:19–40).

The name Jezebel in Revelation 2:20 and 1 Kings 19:1 instantly signified evil for John's readers. King Ahab's wife, Jezebel, left a bitter taste in Israel (1 Kings 16:31; 21:25; 2 Kings 9:7–10, 22). After her passing, Jews avoided naming their own daughters Jezebel. In Revelation 2, a woman called Jezebel is teaching people to worship false gods and encouraging immorality. This wicked woman Jezebel was no follower or disciple of Christ but a false prophet leading people astray into apostasy. Yet the believers at Thyatira stood by witnessing and tolerating her teaching and promotion of sexual promiscuity in the name of religion. Whether Jezebel is an actual name or a nickname, this woman's wicked actions parallel Queen Jezebel's in 1 Kings 16 and 2 Kings 9.

THE CALLING BEGINS IN GOD

The Bible says that we know all things work together for good to those who love God, to those who are the called according to His purpose (Rom. 8:28). This shines light that whatever personal trial, tribulation, suffering, and hardship one may face, it all is working together to fulfill what God desires to fulfill in the lives of those who love Him and are called. We must understand that we have been called according to His purpose. The call originates with God and not in another person. Jeremiah was called, chosen, ordained, and set apart as a prophet in his mother's womb. Even the Bible says that God chose us before the foundation of the world, and that we should be holy and without blame before Him in love because He has pre-destined us to be adopted as sons by Jesus Christ (Eph. 1:4–5).

This is great news for the redeemed of the Lord. We have received the spirit of adoption as sons of the King. We have been predestined to be a kingdom people. Who we really are is found in Christ. So that being said, the prophetic call like Jeremiah's began in God, who knew you first. God doesn't want a prophet or Christian believer walking around looking for validation from man, but from Him alone. Once a person discovers his or her calling in God, that will release clarity of assignment, purpose, relationship, resources, and provision that is needed to fulfill it. The prophetic ministry can bring clarity of one's identity in God.

Prophecy Coming to Pass

As I mentioned before about prophets who presumed a word that God has not revealed, they were not to be received, and called presumptuous. One thing that I must say is that we cannot make a prophecy happen if it is not God's will. I have found people wasting valuable time in the realm of the spirit chasing after a call that wasn't there or looking for a prophecy to meet their needs or objectives. Consequently, the person will abort the true prophetic promise of God over their life because they refuse to cooperate with the Lord. I do believe in pursuing fulfilling the word of the Lord over your life and walking in total obedience. There are specific anointings that are available and active in the season that God requires them, so that what He spoke over you can be fulfilled in His timing. What I am saying is that certain words that we receive from the Lord are not for right now but for a divine time. Most prophecies are conditional and provisional. We must partner with heaven to fulfill the call of God on earth.

In his book *Developing Your Prophetic Gifting*, Graham Cooke states: "There are no unconditional personal prophecies. Personal prophecy refers to the possibility, not the inevitability. If your response is poor and full of unbelief or your lifestyle is one that continually grieves the Holy Spirit, you may not expect those prophecies to be fulfilled."[63]

I believe this is a sound and true statement. There are those who may argue that if God said it, then it will just happen; but I didn't agree, solely because it's called "personal prophecy." It is your word and it's up to you to do everything in your power to align with that word. Obedience is the key to fulfilling your personal prophecy. Moreover, when a prophecy is fulfilled in a person's life it is a sign that God is with that person. A lot of times in the body of Christ people get jealous, envious, or even covet someone else's gift because of a measure of success.

When a person walks out their prophecy, then God makes sure you succeed in it. Success and prosperity is connected to true prophetic ministries. The Bible says it like this, "... *have faith in the Lord your God and you will be upheld; have faith in his prophets and you will be successful,*" in 2 Chronicles 20:20. Having faith in God and in His prophets will release success. The prophet Samuel was one who had faith in His Lord and spoke what God said as a young prophet, and none of his words failed (1 Sam. 3:19, 20).

How many prophets are there today whose prophecies keep failing or falling? Are we honorable before the Lord? And are we prophesying our will or the Father's will? As Jesus was moved with compassion to heal those who needed a physician, we as kingdom believers should be moved by the Holy Spirit to prophesy what the Lord reveals to us. A prophet's calling will be recognized by the local church leadership. Samuel did not have to make claims that he was a prophet; the city knew. All Israel recognized his calling and accepted his ministry. A true prophet will be recognized by other believers.

FALSE PROPHETICS

If there arises among you a prophet or a dreamer of dreams, and he gives you a sign or a wonder, and the sign or wonder comes to pass, of which he spoke to you, saying, "Let us go after other gods"—which you have not known—"and let us serve them," you

---

63   Graham Cooke, *Developing Your Prophetic Gifting* (Grand Rapids, MI: Chosen Books, 2003), 110.

shall not listen to the words of that prophet or that dreamer of dreams, for the LORD your God is testing you to know whether you love the LORD your God with all your heart and with all your soul.

—DEUTERONOMY 13:1–3, NKJV

This passage of Scripture is profound and moving because the Lord was putting His servant leaders to the test when it came to discerning the motives of their hearts and loyalty to Him. The Bible says that God is a jealous God and a jealous lover (Deut. 4:24; Exod. 34:14). The Lord was informing His people not to follow after false prophets and dreamers of dreams. The Lord so totally abhors the worship of false gods that He commands any city in the midst of the Israelites that worships them will be wiped out (vv. 5, 9, 15).

Moreover, God was testing the hearts of His people by seeing if they would follow after other gods when they were influenced by false prophets and dreamers of dreams who performed miracles that came to pass. And if these false prophets told them to worship other gods the people were not in relationship with and did not know, then He instructed them not to listen. This is a picture of God's love for His people, seeing if they loved Him or any other god. False prophets lead you to other gods or things. We are not to receive them nor follow after them. We can also see that these prophets and dreamers of dreams were able to produce signs and wonders. Prophecy and dreams are normal means that God uses to communicate to His people, but both unique channels of communication can be misused, abused, and mishandled. True prophets have the authority and power of God to work miracles with signs and wonders; but false prophets, magicians, and the like can exercise such power as well. (See Exodus 7:10–12.)

Woe to them! For they have gone in the way of Cain, have run greedily in the error of Balaam for profit, and perished in the rebellion of Korah.

—JUDE 11, NKJV

Balaam is an example of a greedy prophet whose only agenda was not the agenda of the Lord, but his own self-gain for power, wealth, honor, and authority, which caused him to walk in error. Balaam was once a genuine prophetic voice. The prophecies that came forth from were keen and precise; Balaam's reputation for being accurate had reached the ears King Balak. King Balak, with itching ears, was drawn to Balaam and wanted to prostitute or merchandise his gift for a profit. Prophets are not for profits! Just like there are a lot of nonprofit churches and organizations, there are also a lot of non-*prophet* churches and organization. We need prophets in the midst of us today speaking the word of the Lord. The prophetic ministry is not for hire and there are lots of false prophets that are hirelings. We must understand that when the prophetic ministries are prostituted by pastors or senior leaders for the purpose of drawing a crowd, to raise their offering, or for entertainment, then they run the risk of walking in falsehood. I have seen churches despise prophecy and prophets; but if they see how the gift can change things, people will misuse it for all the wrong reasons.

Balaam compromised himself for profit, and because of that he ended up shorting his prophetic ministry and life. Balaam died as a soothsayer and false prophet (Josh. 13:22). It took a donkey to speak and stop a prophetic donkey (Balaam) from self-destructing. The donkey saw an angel, which prohibited him from moving forward. The nature of a donkey is stubbornness, rebellion, and resistance. Prophetic people should not be so selfish or stubborn in their own pursuit if God hasn't permitted them. I have been offered housing allowances, big honorariums, and positions in churches if only I did and said what the pastors told me to. But I have refused these offers because I have already been bought with a price through Christ Jesus, and I am God's prophet, not man's. God is not raising up rebellious prophets like Balaam, but obedient ones like Samuel.

Prophetic Integrity and Character Is Key

Graham Cook, a major prophetic voice, makes a good point in his book *Developing Your Prophetic Gifting* in regards to relationship prophecy and character. He states, "It is important that we allow others access into our relationships, marriage, sexuality, finances, parenting, how we run our home and our ministries, to speak into these areas of our lives. It is always the unshared areas of our life where Jesus is not Lord. The enemy is flying around our lives looking for a landing strip; relationship of openness and honesty will plough up any fertile ground where sin may grow."[64]

Character is one of the ways to test a person. There is a saying, "You can't judge a book by its cover," which is a true statement. We are to judge people by their fruit. Even though we can't judge a book by its cover, we can judge a book by the "table of contents" of a person's life. Prophets and prophetic people must be in vertical and horizontal spiritual relationship with others in the kingdom of God. I know some young ministers who are not in relationship with anyone and will not submit to a local church for relational and accountability purposes, but they will throw a baby tantrum if someone doesn't invite them in to minister. God is not raising up "lone rangers" today, but prophets and leaders who will submit mutually to each other in love. True accountability is not control but protection, honor, love, and liberty. Prophets must walk in a godly character and fruit of the Spirit. (See Galatians 5:22–23.)

Galatians 5:19–21 outlines the works of the flesh, which are:

- Adultery

- Fornication/sexuality immorality

- Uncleanness

- Lewdness

- Idolatry

- Sorcery/witchcraft

- Hatred

- Contentions/arguments

- Jealousy

- Outbursts of wrath/rage

- Selfish ambitions/pride

---

64 Cooke, 87.

- Dissension/disputes

- Heresies

- Envy

- Murders

- Drunkenness

- Revelries

These above are the works of the flesh that fights against the Spirit. In addition, we are to walk in the Spirit and not fulfill the lusts of the flesh. We need true, healthy, transparent relationships in the body of Christ that will bring restoration, reconciliation, and healing to a fallen believer in the kingdom. We must work out any soulish and fleshly areas that may manifest in our lives. If we have any of these enemies of the Spirit working in our lives then it will manifest through our character and even our ministry. Prophets must be clear from any areas of the flesh that will cause a backlash, retaliation, and sabotage to the advancement of the kingdom.

DISCERNING CORRECT BIBLICAL TEACHINGS

Beloved, do not believe every spirit, but test the spirits, whether they are of God; because many false prophets have gone out into the world. But this you know the Spirit of God: Every spirit that confesses that Jesus Christ has come in the flesh is of God, and every spirit that does not confess that Jesus Christ has come in the flesh is not of God. And this is the spirit of the Antichrist, which you have heard was coming, and is now already in the world.

—1 JOHN 4:1–3, NKJV

In the twenty-first century there are all types of weird, perverted, and demonic doctrines and new teaching that even some churches adopted in their church bylaws and constitutions. Some churches have secretly and publicly supported same-sex marriage and other behavior that is contrary to law of God. I remember being invited to speak at a church that believes in same-sex marriage, and of course

I declined the invitation. The pastor wanted an explanation, and I told him that I do not support inclusive teachings or any progressive church that advocates homosexuality. I went on to say that I only support what the Word of God supports. Prophets and prophetic people must discern what spirit is in operation in churches.

The antichrist spirit is a spirit, not an individual. The Bible said that this is a spirit of the antichrist. Any teaching, doctrine, lifestyle, etc., is considered an antichrist spirit. John was talking about discerning truth and error when it came to the things of God. He stated that every spirit that does not confess Jesus Christ has come in the flesh and is not of God, and he identified it as an antichrist spirit. Prophets, apostles, and Christian believers should not compromise their belief and standard of righteousness when it comes to the Word of God. I have been among different streams of the prophetic and I also have heard many strange teachings that didn't sound right. It was the Spirit of God and the discerning of spirits raising red flags in my spirit.

Discernment of Spirits

The gift of discerning is a vital gift that is needed to detect any diabolical presence at work. The early church was aware of false prophets, teachers, and witches that would try to hinder the apostolic mission. The apostle Paul and Silas encountered resistance in Philippi. Prophets and apostles will face many hindrances when advancing the King and His kingdom. We can see an example of Paul being annoyed and distressed by a demonic spirit at work in a slave girl in Acts 16:16–18 below:

> Once when we were going to the place of prayer, we were met by a slave girl who had a spirit by which she predicted the future. She earned a great deal of money for her owners by fortune telling. This girl followed Paul and the rest of us, shouting, "These men are servants of the Most High God, who are telling you the way to be saved." She kept this up for many days. Finally Paul became so troubled that he turned around and said to the spirit, "In the name of Jesus Christ I command you to come out of her!" At that moment the spirit left her.

We can see in the above passage of Scripture that when Paul and Silas went to prayer, a slave girl possessed with the spirit of divination met them. She followed them, crying out that they were the servants of the Most High God who proclaim to us the way of salvation. Note that the spirit did not confess Christ but said that they are servants of the Most High God. We must understand that demonic spirits knows that there is power in the name of Jesus and also they recognize the Most High God. The spirit of divination in the slave girl was following them to distract them. Have you ever purposed in your heart to do something, then you were distracted by something or someone? Have you decided in your heart to pray, read the Word, or go into worship, and your phone rang, a text message came through, or someone needed you?

I have encountered this a lot in my Christian walk. I am not saying that everything is demonic or a distraction, but that whenever you want to do something good, evil is always present. This slave girl was crying out the truth of who they were in God, but she had the wrong intentions of making public their godly identities. The Bible says that she did this for many days, following them, and Paul was annoyed in his spirit and discerned the spirit at work in her. So Paul, being irritated, turned and commanded that spirit to come out of her. Paul moved in a supernatural power that brought great deliverance to a fortune-teller. It is evident that Paul didn't cast the spirit of divination out of her on the first day that she followed him, but he was patient and probably was discerning the motives of this spirit.

WARNING SIGNS OF THE PROPHETIC

The Word of God gives us warning signs of the false and those who operate with the wrong spirit in this day and age. While testing and discerning demonic spirits, prophetic utterance, dreams, visions, false prophets and the like, we must maintain a godly poise and attitude at the same time. We are not called to run around looking for demons or false prophets, but we are to not be ignorant or naïve of their existence. On the other hand, we are to be very careful when it comes to the true prophets of God and not mock, misuse, take advantage of, abuse, disrespect, and shun them.

The Bible in 1 Chronicles 16:22 declares, *"Do not touch my chosen people, and do not hurt my prophets."* God's chosen people and prophetic leaders were the apple of His eye. We are to value God's Word, His prophets, and leaders that He has sovereignly called. Prophecy and utterance should be value. Our personal calling from the Lord should be first priority. We have to learn to honor and value each other and not think to ourselves that everyone has a demon or spirit. Sometime we can be cutting down with our words what God is building and we don't even know it. Prophecy is conditional; are you meeting the condition? Rejecting to come into compliance to God's Word or rejecting true prophets or despising prophecy can be lethal. An example of this is seen as follows.

> Now the king had put the officer on whose arm he leaned in charge of the gate, and the people trampled him in the gateway, and he died, just as the man of God had foretold when the king came down to his house. It happened as the man of God had said to the king: "About this time tomorrow, a seah of the finest flour will sell for a shekel and two seahs of barley for a shekel at the gate of Samaria." The officer had said to the man of God, "Look, even if the Lord should open the floodgates of the heavens, could this happen?" The man of God had replied, "You will see it with your own eyes, but you will not eat any of it!" And that is exactly what happened to him, for the people trampled him in the gateway, and he died.
>
> —2 Kings 7:17–20

> But Elisha said to him, "Was not my spirit with you when the man got down from his chariot to meet you? Is this the time to take money or to accept clothes—or olive groves and vineyards, or flocks and herds, or male and female slaves? Naaman's leprosy will cling to you and to your descendants forever." Then Gehazi went from Elisha's presence and his skin was leprous—it had become as white as snow.
>
> —2 Kings 5:26–27

> Then Jeremiah said to all the officials and all the people: "The Lord sent me to prophesy against this house and this city all the

things you have heard. Now reform your ways and your actions and obey the Lord your God. Then the Lord will relent and not bring the disaster he has pronounced against you. As for me, I am in your hands; do with me whatever you think is good and right. Be assured, however, that if you put me to death, you will bring the guilt of innocent blood on yourselves and on this city and on those who live in it, for in truth the Lord has sent me to you to speak all these words in your hearing."

—JEREMIAH 26:12–15

Whenever God brings forth a ministry, Satan will bring forth a counterfeit. In other words, before there is an authentic ministry, there are false ministries as well. That should not put us off but just make us careful. If we hear that counterfeit money is in circulation, we do not stop using money. We just become more careful. As the prophetic ministry grows, false prophets will become more prevalent. We should not reject prophecy but be vigilant. Church leaders should guard against false prophets. The best way to do this is to have a fully developed prophetic ministry in their local church. True prophets are the best antidote to combat false prophets.

An authentic prophet can admit that he may be untrue and therefore wrong in many areas. He knows that his protection from error is within the unity of our Lord's body. Conversely, the false prophet confuses his anointing with what he thinks in his soul, heart and mind, so that he thinks he cannot be wrong.[65]

THE MINISTRY GIFT OF PROPHECY IN THE SPIRIT VERSUS THE FLESH

Spirit	Flesh
Obedience	Rebellion
Honesty	Deception
Truthfulness	Lies
Virtue	Natural
Boldness	Timidity

---

65   John and Paula Sandford, *The Elijah Task* (Lake Mary, FL: Charisma House, 2006), 36.

Spirit	Flesh
Perseverance	Procrastination
Sincerity	Selfishness
Power	Charm
Meekness	Pridefulness
Longsuffering	Impatience
Peace	Discord
Faith	Fear
Temperance	Gluttony
Goodness	Evil
Joy	Dissention
Gentleness	Harshness

Chapter Thirteen

BIRTHED THROUGH ORDINATION

Do not neglect the gift that is in you, which was given to you
by prophecy with the laying on of the hands of the eldership.
—1 Timothy 4:14, NKJV

T IMOTHY WAS A young apostolic leader and elder of the Lord's
assembly. He was admonished and exhorted by Paul to stir
up the gift of God that was in him through the laying on of
his apostolic hand. Timothy came from a family who understood
having faith, which dwelt in his grandmother Lois and was therefore
passed down to his mother Eunice. What was in Timothy started
in his grandmother and mother. He needed to know that the apostolic calling of an apostle was resident within him. He had the moth-
erly impartation and natural upbringing in the Lord, but Timothy
needed apostolic fathering and impartation as well. This was to be
transferred through the laying on of Paul's hands and prophetic
words. Paul wanted Timothy to keep the fire burning by stirring up
the gift of God that was in him.

The calling of an apostle was in him, and he needed to use that
which was imparted by the laying on of hands for ministry purposes.
We know that he was considered a spiritual son to Paul, and Paul
fathered him in the faith and call of God. Paul did not specify the
actual gift of God that Timothy was reminded to stir up, but he used
the Greek word *charisma,* which suggests a distinct manifestation of
the Holy Spirit's bestowment upon Timothy through prayers, laying
on of hands, and prophecy. (See 1 Timothy 1:18; 4:14.)

This charisma gift was the apostolic ministry gift that was in Paul
and already in Timothy, although he needed it to be activated. It
was Timothy's responsibility to be a steward over that which was

imparted. This grace and spiritual equipment should be used for ministry reasons. This isn't just for those who are called to the five-fold ministry; this principle is for all believers. What is imparted by God and through godly leadership must be used for God's glory.

Timothy, through ordination and commission, received his apostolic birth certificate to function legally in the earth. This type of New Testament principle of ordination and commissioning transfers spiritual authority and power, and it is especially done through apostles and prophets of God. Apostles were used in the Book of Acts to ordain elders with the laying on of hands and fasting (Acts 14:23).

TIME OF RELEASE

Mark 3:14–15 (NKJV) says, "Then He appointed twelve, that they might be with Him and that He might send them out to preach, and to have power to heal sicknesses and to cast out demons." Jesus understood that principle of appointing and sending. He was not just one with authority, but He also delegated His authority to others. We see that His heart was to appoint those who would be with Him, so that He could send them out to have power to heal and cast out devils. Jesus had chosen twelve ordinary men to do great exploits in His name. He gave them authority and power.

When Jesus appointed the Twelve, He was making them into something. Moreover, Jesus gave them authority or power, which comes from the Greek word *exousia,* which is one of the four "power" words (*dunamis, exousia, ischus* and *kratos*). *Exousia,* pronounced (*ex-oo-see-ah*) means "the authority or right to act, ability, privilege, capacity, delegated authority."[66] Jesus had the *exousia* to forgive sin, heal the sick, and cast out demonic spirits. *Exousia* is the right to use *dunamis.* For example, a police officer has the *exousia* (authority which is signified in his badge or seal) to use his *dunamis* (weapon or gun).

Likewise, Christ Jesus gives His followers *exousia* to preach, teach, heal, and deliver through the Holy Spirit. Powerless believers and leaders become powerful when they discover the *exousia* (authority)

---

66   Blue Letter Bible, s.v. "exousia," www.blueletterbible.org/lang/lexicon/Lexicon.cfm?strongs=G1849 (accessed June 5, 2013).

resident in the name of Jesus and His blood that was shed. Timothy was given delegated authority and power through the Holy Spirit, which was done through the laying on of hands of Paul and prophecy.

Paul's heart, I believe, was like Jesus. He wanted those he related with in the faith to learn from him and then to go out in divine power to extend the work of the Lord. It's God's appointment, and it's up to us to know what is on our birth certificate for our own record. Knowing this information, like Isaiah and Jeremiah, is imperative in moving forward in the work of the Lord. Not knowing for what purpose or who, what, where, when, and why we were born is a sad thing, for we all have a purpose, destiny and high calling in the Lord.

These two prophets of God knew without a shadow of a doubt that their calling was connected to the purpose of them being conceived in the first place. We can also see a similar expression used in respect to Paul the Apostle in Galatians 1:15 when he said, "But when it pleased God, who set me apart from my mother's womb." The appointment and ordination to a specific work or call was done before he ever came into existence.

I have come into contact with people who pursue public ordination by men to ministry offices, but they lack the grace, integrity, anointing, character, and gifting to walk in such a holy call. It is also disheartening to see people seek man's approval instead of seeking the approval of God. Some people are very quick to say what man says and not reference what God has said about them. With that in mind, I wholeheartedly believe in public affirmation and prophetic commissioning through the local governing leadership team in a church. Ordinations and public recognition through the local eldership team is important in the earth realm to validate and confirm the will of the Lord in a person's life. I believe people should not pursue public ordination for selfish ambition and motivations if they have not encountered a personal relationship with the Holy Spirit.

A Ministry Birth Certificate

Prophetic ordination is like a birth certificate being given to a person who has been proven and recognized in a particular call. I have seen ordination of men and women who were called to a particular ministry office, but the candidate wanted to be ordained and recognized as something else, so the local church granted their request because they may have been the biggest tither in the church or they may have known this individual for many years. (It's just as counterfeit as the following. Say a person is born a male and the doctor determines, by thorough examination, that the baby is in fact a male. But still the mother says, "No, I wanted a girl," so she decides that it's a girl, and that's final. The mother also wants the doctor to put another gender on the birth certificate to say that it is girl, and the doctor foolishly does what the parent requested. Can you imagine?)

On the other hand, a public commissioning service serves as a vehicle to release people into their God-given calling, which causes them to maximize their godly potential with confidence and reinforcement. Even Jesus had to submit to the baptism by John the baptizer to fulfill all righteousness. While immersed in water the heavens opened up and the Spirit of the Lord descended down on Him like a dove. The voice of the Father affirmed and credentialed the identity of His Son publicly (Matt. 3:13–17).

A Divine Affirmation, Confirmation, and Commissioning

Jesus' public ordination was at the Jordan River and not in a church. We need divine affirmation by God through men and women called to the church to equip, train, impart, raise up, and send out mature saints via the Holy Spirit's timing to do the work of the ministry. The prophetic word is the birth certificate that identifies the purpose, will, and plan of God in your life.

To fulfill all righteousness in your own life and to walk in your prophetic fulfillment, ordination can establish you in the earth realm and release you fully into your spiritual careers. But it's not mandatory in regard to how God calls and releases a person into public service. God calls people and confirms them differently than others.

How do I know this? When the Lord created each of us, He fearfully and wonderfully detailed us and made us uniquely different. I have heard people say that they do not like the way they look because they may be overweight, too skinny, tall or short. Or they may be too light, dark, or they wish they had black, long hair, or wish they were another nationality. Whatever you may call a flaw or imperfection is the very thing that God created wonderfully, which makes you different. I do understand that people are born with birth defects and deformities. Although, just like the man in the Bible who was born blind with his disability that had nothing to do with his parents or from any sin of theirs that was passed down, sometimes God uses what we see as a disability for His glory through a miracle. Everything God creates brings Him glory (John 9:1–41).

We must know that we are called to bring God glory out of our lives and do what He has created us to do. We were born to fulfill God's will in the earth. In ministry we cannot say, "I do not want to be a prophet, but a pastor instead because it's better," or vice versa. One cannot pick and choose when they are going to be promoted and released into ministry by choosing an organization to ordain them or not.

Do It God's Way and Not Man's Way!

Sadly, I have witnessed young leaders in different types of denominations say, "You have to do it this way", "Do it that way," or "Do it our denomination's way"—and if you do not get ordained their way then they say it's not God's order and not an authentic ordination. I believe that it is prideful, sectarian, religious, systematic, and discriminatory to say that a person has to do things a certain religious way or man's way for God to approve it or not. God is not denominational, organizational, institutional, religious, or racist, but He is covenant relational, multidimensional, and sovereign. We must do things according to God's ways and not man's way.

God is spirit and not earthly, carnal, or fleshly. He does things His way. If God affirms you outside the church, like Jesus in the Jordan River, or at several meetings with prophets and apostolic leadership confirming the call through a network, fellowship, and organization, then let God, who is all-knowing, do what He does best.

The Lord will affirm you first as a faithful, pleasing son and daughter by saying, "This is my beloved in whom I am well pleased." Allow the fruit, anointing, and grace of the Holy Spirit on your life to speak for you. Only time will tell if one has been called to a particular office or not. There are people all over the world who have never been licensed, ordained, or credentialed by a religious organization, but heaven has validated them, affirming their calling with much fruit, signs, wonders, and the supernatural following them.

There are also remote places around the world where men and women are being raised up in obscurity and released by God into holy service. Many of these leaders in those nations have not had the opportunity to be identified, confirmed, and released in their calling by prophets and a prophetic presbytery of a local assembly, but they are doing tremendous work in the kingdom. So that being said, if God had called you and appointed you, know that you have been created and equipped with the necessary tools, intellect, ability, talent, and grace to fulfill it with or without a public ordination from men. Just know that you have been born to do this. We must understand that our birth is connected to our purpose. Jesus said for this purpose or reason was the Son of Man made manifest, that He may destroy the works of darkness.

Birthed into Something New

Jesus was born and sent on an assignment to destroy the works of sin and Satan. I can remember when I first got baptized in water in 1988. I was given a baptism certificate that gave public record of that historical day in my life. It was a public declaration and death of the old nature being and a birth into something new as a new creation. Even though I understood that the birth certificate was spiritual, it was a practice that was done publicly before the church so that my repentance and salvation were sincere and honest. Every time I think about the first time I was baptized it causes me to encounter the same anointing and new beginning.

Likewise, when a person receives a prophecy or receives prophetic ministry, it births a person into something new and unfamiliar. Ordinations with prophetic utterances can birth leaders as well as whole churches, ministries, and congregations into new realms, authority, dimension, and power. Some people have never encountered and are unfamiliar with the prophetic, prophets, baptism by the Spirit, ordinations, healing, miracles, gifts of the Spirit, deliverance, and laying-on of hands.

A public ordination, for example, can be a person being singled out several times in a meeting among other believers, whereby prophets and/or the leadership team can confirm your calling with the laying-on of hands and with prophetic utterances following. This has happened to me several times by the way of leaders who had no prior knowledge of who I was or any awareness of my ministerial background. But they were used by the Lord to identify the apostolic and prophetic call and grace on my life. They spontaneously laid their hands on me while in strong intercessory prayer and prophetic worship, and they imparted gifts into my life. Notice that I did not say that this was my local church, network, fellowship, or ministry that I was a part of, but it was God working through the local body of believers and prophetic presbytery confirming and releasing me into my calling. (See Acts 6:3, 6; 13:1–3; 14:21–23; and Titus 1:5.)

God Ordains the Ordinary to Become Extraordinary!

God is the God of the new. He will do something new and outside the human mind-set and religious paradigms. Ordination is a biblical function and should be practiced in the twenty-first-century church for releasing leaders into their callings and spiritual positions. Jesus Himself also ordained the original twelve apostles of the Lamb in Mark 3:14 and even sent out seventy other unnamed apostolic leaders to do what He has sent them to do.

When a person is being ordained they are receiving godly honor through the laying on of hands and with prophecy, at which time gifts can be transferred and imparted. (See 1 Timothy 4:14; 2 Timothy 1:16.) The words *ordain* and *ordination* come from the Latin word *ordinare,* which means "to arrange, to place in order or to appoint, to establish and put in order."[67] I like the Latin word *ordinare* because God uses "ordinary" people to do extraordinary things for His kingdom and for His eternal purposes.

---

67 *Merriam-Webster Dictionary Online,* s.v. "ordain," http://www.merriam
-webster.com/dictionary/ordained (accessed June 5, 2013). See also http://
en.wiktionary.org/wiki/ordinare.

For myself, in the Lord's timing, He used several local governing churches over the course of my life that I was not an active member of to set me apart, to place me in order, and to appoint me and establish me in the earth realm to the office of prophet. God had already done that before I was formed in my mother's womb. In addition, I never had to go tell the pastor of a local church what my calling was because the church was a prophetic church who believed in releasing and sending leaders. I believe apostles, prophets, and marketplace leaders should be identified and released into society to impact and transform it for the kingdom of God. Typically, your gift will always make room for you and bring you in the presence of those of great influence. Regardless, if people do not believe in modern-day prophets and apostles, just know that your gift has the ability to create doors of opportunity for you.

Growing in the Prophetic Starts at Home

Let's take a look at 1 Samuel 3:19–21, where it says, "And Samuel grew, and the LORD was with him, and did let none of his words fall to the ground. And all Israel from Dan even to Beersheba knew that Samuel was established to be a prophet of the LORD. And the LORD appeared again in Shiloh: for the LORD revealed himself to Samuel in Shiloh by the word of the LORD." This passage of Scripture is interesting to me because none of Samuel's prophecies fell to the ground, or failed to come to pass, because it was the Lord that did not allow them to fall. The prophet Samuel was flawless in the prophetic, which gained him attention and recognition of the public (the cities of Dan and Beersheba)—and not through an organization or network.

Again, nothing is wrong with the Antioch type of model for churches, organizations, and networks that release leaders into their holy call, but it's not limited to only these models and structures. The people of the cities recognized Samuel's gift and what he was born to be as a prophet. The Word said that all of Israel, from Dan to Beersheba, knew that he was an established prophet of God. God confirmed his calling at Shiloh several times, and then the public recognized and affirmed the prophetic call on his life.

People will notice something particular about you without you needing to find people to validate you. I am not speaking about being a lone ranger and an island while lacking mutual accountability; my point is that one must know who they are first, who created them, why they were born, and what they were born to be and do. In God's timing you will be established in your calling. Having a license or ordination paper still does not validate that someone has been called.

IF IT BARKS AND ACTS LIKE A DOG, IT'S A DOG

Even those who have been called and received an ordination certificate through the local church or network may not necessarily fully walk in their calling. It is all up to the individual to make their election and call sure. Have you ever heard the saying, "If it barks like a dog and walks like a dog, it's a dog"? A person can convince themselves all day long that they are a prophet or an apostle, but it's all in the calling and grace. So again, there is nothing wrong with cross-pollinating with others of like heart, mind, and vision, but to pursue them solely for the purpose of the organization and apostolic network to make you something is an identity fault.

Samuel the prophet had continued visitations of the Lord through God's revealed Word. In verse 21 of 1 Samuel 3, it says that the Lord again appeared at Shiloh, and He revealed Himself by the word of the Lord. Whenever a person encounters God personally, God always reveals Himself through His Word, and that is an element of the prophetic or prophecy. The Word of the Lord confirmed Samuel's prophetic ministry while he was a youth being trained and tutored as an assistant priest under the high priest Eli. Samuel did not have a clue regarding his prophetic destiny as a priest, judge, and prophet, but he was faithful in the presence of God at Shiloh, which is the place of encountering God. Shiloh is also a place of prayer, peace, tranquility, and calmness. It is where the ark of God was.

In your own personal Shiloh, where you have one-on-one devotion and intimacy with the Lord, God will appear to you and bring revelation of the calling on your life, and men will take notice of the anointing and grace on your life. So if you never receive a public ordination by a religious organization, just do what you have been called to do, and the public will recognize and validate what heaven has sanctioned.

Ordination is important in establishing government in the local church and for those who are emerging leaders called to impact nations, governments, systems, and territories as kingdom prophets and apostles. We need present and emerging leaders to be released in every generation in what they have been born to accomplish in the earth with the assistance of leaders to help them to get the spiritual and natural education needed to fulfill such a public service.

It is the Lord's will, according to Ephesians 4:11 and 1 Corinthians 12:28, for leaders to function in biblical offices, positions, and functions and not any extra manmade biblical terms such as *pope, chief apostle, archbishop, copastor, cell leader, first lady,* etc., which lack true biblical integrity, power, authority, and patterns.

PROPHECY BRINGS LIFE AND IDENTITY

My point and emphasis here is that prophecy can birth you into who you were originally called to be and solidify a person's identity. In other words, the prophetic ordination with prophets, apostles, and prophetic elders prophesying becomes a spiritual birth certificate for the candidate, just like when a person receives salvation and is regenerated by the Holy Spirit into a new creature in the kingdom. Jesus said that the words that He speaks are spirit life. The word of the Lord becomes the life seed and also a spiritual midwife to transition one into their destiny and purpose.

In 1 Corinthians 15:45 (NLT) we read, "The Scriptures tell us, 'The first man, Adam, became a living person.' But the last Adam—that is, Christ—is a life-giving Spirit." The word *spirit* in this passage of Scripture was referring to Christ as the life-giving spirit, coined by the apostle Paul when giving the expression of the reference to the last Adam (1 Cor. 15:45). The first Adam was made a living soul, while the last Adam, Jesus Christ, was made a "quickening spirit" or a "life-giving" spirit. In other words, the first Adam is of the earth or made from the dust, which makes him earthly, while the last Adam's origin is heaven, which makes Him spiritual. The contrast in this passage of Scripture is not so much an emphasis on the difference between the soul and the spirit as it is between "living" and "life-giving."

The first Adam was only limited to receiving spirit life by the very life source of life, by the only life-giver, and that is the Father who breathed (*ruach*) into his nostrils and he became a "living being." On the other hand the second Adam offers so much more than that, according to John 5:26. Therefore, the first Adam does not have the spiritual power, ability, and authority to impart spirit (*pneuma*) life.

We must understand that the principle of life is common with all men. Jesus made this clear in John 5:26 (KJV) by saying, "For as the Father hath life in himself, so has he given to the Son to have life in himself." We must understand that our spiritual bodies will be like Christ's. The first Adam was of the old creation, but those born of the spirit receive so much more as New Covenant believers—eternal life and the new creation that is given by the Spirit through the last Adam, who had a resurrected, glorious body.

The prophetic dimension, when released, begins to resurrect an individual's vision, purpose, dream, destiny, calling, and identity. God's Word is spirit (*pneuma*) life that brings spiritual vitality and productivity. That is the prophetic nature of God, who is life, and His word is spirit life. So when the prophetic is in operation, it becomes a womb in the spirit realm and causes people to be birthed into that which God has released out of His own mouth. God is a prophetic God and a prophetic Spirit as well, because everything created in the universe was conceived through words or through spoken words.

God's Word Is His Reputation and Authority

John 1:1–3 is a prime example of the power of God's spoken word expressed. The Lord can communicate and speak any language because He is the originator of communication, languages, and speech. The Word of God is just a powerful as Himself. God takes His Word spoken seriously, and we should as well when we hear Him speak to us. In Psalm 138:2 (NKJV) it says, "For You have magnified Your word above all Your name." According to Hebrew custom and culture the name of someone referred to his authority and reputation. Thus, the name of God refers to His power and reputation, just as the name of Jesus refers to His greatness, power, and distinguished reputation. That is why today we pray in the "name" of Jesus Christ, i.e., we pray according to His authority (John 15:16); we command through the power of spoken word, healing in the name of Jesus Christ (Acts 3:6); why devils must come out when believers use the name of Jesus Christ (Acts 16:18); and why water baptism was done in the name of Jesus Christ (Acts 10:48). God's name was His power and distinguished reputation, so a cultural knowing of this translation is, "God exalted His Word above all other things that are under His power and authority, even His authority itself."

When a prophetic word is spoken through a prophet or someone in godly authority, the person must understand the integrity of God's word when released. God's word is His authority, reputation, and integrity, which, when spoken, is sure to come to pass and fulfill what He has sent it to do as Creator, Father, and King of the universe.

PROPHECY ACCOMPLISHED

Take a look at one of my favorite Scriptures, which has strong emphasis on the prophetic nature and integrity of God. According to Isaiah 55:11 (GW), "My word, which comes from my mouth, is like the rain and snow. It will not come back to me without results. It will accomplish whatever I want and achieve whatever I send it to do." It is a unique function of the prophetic or prophecy that the word drops on us like rain or snow. When I use the term *prophecy*, I am simply referring to hearing the voice of God and speaking by the inspiration of the Holy Spirit. The inspiration and unction to prophesy can be described as raindrops coming upon a believer and a water fountain springing up from the inside of them when moved by the Spirit of God. Teaching and preaching are preplanned and prepared, but prophecy cannot be calculated. The prophetic unction and utterance must be stirred up and activated by faith in the Holy Spirit.

The Bible tells us that we are to, "Despise not prophesyings. Prove all things" (1 Thess. 5:20–21, KJV). When a prophecy is given, we are to test it and hold on to what is good in it. God's prophetic word over your life is tested and approved by God, and it shall not return to the Lord without accomplishing that which the Lord intends.

God has various ways of giving His word to people. In John 1:1–4 it says, "In the beginning was the Word, and the Word was with God, and the Word was God. He was with God in the beginning. Through him all things were made; without him nothing was made that has been made. In him was life, and that life was the light of all mankind." Jesus being the Word (the Greek term for "the word" being *logos*) and in relationship with the Father and solely involved in creating the universe and all things that were made. The word of the Lord that comes to a person is not just mere speech or language but a person being revealed and actively involved in a person's life through revelation, which is the light of men.

I believe the divine witnesses that we need from heaven are God the Father, God the Son, and God the Holy Spirit. They are very much involved in a person's prophetic affirmation, confirmation, and birthing process. When a person receives a word from the Lord to be a prophet, they are not just receiving divine self-expressions of Christ toward them, but they receive Jesus the prophet Himself, imparting His very own life, mind, will, plan, and purpose to them. The Scripture reads, "By the mouth of two or three witnesses shall every word be established" (2 Cor. 13:1, NKJV). So it's not just hearing a word only one time that makes you a prophet, apostle, or healing evangelist, but there must be other witnesses to confirm and make strong what you have been created to become. Not that you go around announcing who you are in God, but allow in God's timing confirmation to come through outside witnesses of your calling and mandate.

THE LOCAL ASSEMBLY BECOMES A TRAINING AND EQUIPPING CENTER

At my local church, Destiny Christian Church, I served as a leader on the prophetic team under Apostles Dale and LuAnne Mast in Dover, Delaware. Services at my church became one of many spiritual hubs and bases to sharpen my gift and serve in the prophetic to the body of Christ. This local expression and assembly was used of God to confirm and also affirm my calling, but it was done in God's timing publicly. Many local assemblies that I have served at and been a part of became springboards for myself and my twin brother, Naim, as we matured in the gift of God on our lives. I believe the local church becomes a spiritual womb or birthing place for ministry gifts to be exposed and cultivated.

The local church is the household of God where the saints gather together to worship God and to be baptized into the family of God. The local church becomes the spiritual womb and acts as the prenatal care unit for the gifts of God to be nourished and raised up before they are birthed out in full maturity, in the timing of the Lord. I can remember several times throughout my walk as a believer and a young prophetic minister being called out, hands laid on me, and prophesied to hundreds of times. I was encouraged and edified to walk in the power of the Lord and in that holy calling, but at the same time I never received a piece of paper of that affirmation and identification.

I did not understand why these ministries would never give me my credentials and ordination papers. It was due to wanting to have ownership and control over what a minister of the gospel should and should not do, but I realized that my credentials came from the Lord. In that, the Spirit of the Lord would confirm over and over the anointing of God that rested on my life. It was ironic to me that many great leaders would recognize the prophetic and apostolic call but did not want to be in relationship with me to develop and father me in the faith.

Through many years in the prophetic ministry, the Lord used my pastors, Apostles Dale and LuAnne Mast, to identify myself and my twin brother, Naim, and on February 19, 2012, we were ordained and recognized as prophets of God before our local congregation. Prior to this public ordination, my brother and I had received public recognition from many leaders who were not our pastors, although it's nothing like your own pastors and leaders who are prophets and apostles commissioning you into ministry.

I am thirty years old right now, writing my first book on the prophetic. I believe that the ordination has released the godly potential and eternal purposes of God for me to impact the world with the message of the kingdom.

OTHER PROPHECIES SHOULD ESTABLISH
AND CONFIRM ONE'S CALLING

I was given my prophetic birth right legally. Back in 2002—I was nineteen years old at the time—I had met Bob Jones of Statesville, North Carolina, who was a seer prophet. My brother and I received powerful prophetic words from him that we were going to be some of the new, emerging, major African-American prophetic voices who were to be a part of bringing a great harvest of 1 billion young people to the Lord. This prophecy that seer prophet Bob Jones received was a word from the Lord Jesus that he received when died in 1975 and came back to life. This powerful word Bob Jones received was that God was going to send him different prophets from different ethnicities who would be the next fire-starters on the East Coast, from the bottom of Florida up to Canada, in the shape of the number seven.

These new young prophets would evangelize a whole new generation of young people and win them to the Lord. He went on to say that God was going to cross-pollinate all the races together, and they would learn from each other. Collectively all the five new emerging prophets and apostles from different ethnicities would be a part of this end-time harvest of souls coming into the kingdom. The Lord informed Bob Jones that those who were in the prophecy were coming soon to meet him, and when they finally met him, he was happy because it was a fulfilled prophecy of the Lord.

He blessed us and taught us how to be "caught up," or in other words "raptured" up to sit on the lap of Papa, Father God. Bob Jones is considered our "spiritual prophetic papa." He was used instrumentally to recognize and ordain us as prophets. The unique part about the impartation, wisdom, and recognition that we received from him was that it was done in his own home in Statesville, North Caroline, with other well-known prophets present.

In addition, God allowed us to meet Kenneth and Brenda McDonald of North Carolina, who activated the gift of prophecy on the inside of us and released us to be all that God called us to be in the earth. This is just to name a few of many who were key leaders and who played a major role in our prophetic ministry office. Ordination in the local church is something life changing for the candidate, but it is a blessing of honor from the prophetic and apostolic presbytery of a local church.

David Cartledge states in his book *The Apostolic Revolution*:

Ordination is necessary to establish government of the local church and to release ministers at large. Ordination is not some empty ritual or rite of passage that elevates a person to a level of ministry. It is actually an impartation as much as recognition. All too often people have been ordained to ministry without the power that should accompany their call being released through the laying on of hands of apostles. The use of prophecy as a means of impartation will most often rest with apostles and prophets. It is difficult to measure the impact of such prophetic words in the moment of ordination, but it is obvious that many emerging ministries have been catapulted to another level of authority and faith through this type of impartation.[68]

Ordination and confirmation through such prophetic and apostolic leaders that do not confirm and identify the gift of God on your life by not giving you a record of that birthing and call is like a baby being born and not receiving the birth certificate confirming the sex, name, date, mother and father, and location of the birthing. It is also like a person graduating and not receiving their diploma or degree for finishing their education. I believe ordination and credentialing serves as public announcement that records your promotion in the spirit and recognizes in the earthly realm what heaven has ordained before the foundations of the world.

The ordination certificate should be your ministry birth certificate. That is not saying that you are a babe in Christ or in your Christian walk, but it's an identification for the person being recognized. This certificate has recorded in history the time, place, and the ministry leaders who participated in the ordination for accountability and provides full release to do what you have been designed and sent to do for Christ. Even in ancient times, whatever a king decreed and declared something, his words were written and recorded as law.

---

68   David Cartledge, *The Apostolic Revolution* (Chester Hill, Paraclete Institute, 2000).

Therefore, what God says about you and calls you is recorded and written and becomes law.

Through the Holy Spirit's enablement, a believer can operate and prophesy with the authority of God through the power of the spoken word that brings life. If the kingdom is within us, then we as kings have the power and authority to cause things to happen.

Chapter Fourteen

POWER OF THE SPOKEN WORD

Life and death are in the power of the tongue.
—Proverbs 18:21, NKJV

T HE PROPHETIC IS God's word, which is a seed that comes to us by faith in what He says. That word metaphorically impregnates us, which causes a person to nourish, water, feed and protect the word released. Once that word is received and believed, the person begins to go through many changes as the word of the Lord becomes them. Their lives begin to take shape from what God said. For example, if the prophetic word comes and says that God has called you to become something, then that seed will be planted in one's heart. Over time, through seasons of maturation and development, the person will become that which God has already spoken and prophesied.

The prophetic word brings clarity to a person's identity and overall purpose for their life. The individual has the responsibility and stewardship to cultivate that seed planted and to one day evolve into that which is released. We must understand that the person receiving the prophetic word may not look like or be what God said until that word is spoken and released by God Himself to the person hearing the word by faith.

PROPHETIC CREATIVITY

The Bible says, "So then faith comes by hearing, and hearing by the word of God" (Rom. 10:17, NKJV). So by faith the word is received and believed. The individual, like Jesus' mother, now will give birth to the Promise and the Redeemer of the world. Again, the prophetic word

223

is the seed, and we become the womb. The egg over time develops and births out what God has originally intended us to become.

The power of the spoken word of God is demonstrated in Genesis 1:3 when "God said, 'Let there be light,' and there was light." God is not asking you to become but is commanding that you become that what He says. So in other words, God prophesies, "Let there be Hakeem," and there was Hakeem. When the Lord speaks forth who we are, He speaks what He has already had in His mind, and He calls us by name. And with that, He attaches His eternal purpose in us.

Furthermore, we can see that light came forth out of hiding and operated in its assignment. That assignment was to bring light to a dark cosmos. When the Lord prophesies, He always will prophesy what is and not what something is going to be. In other words, when the Lord said, "Let there *be* light," light was already there or existed, but light needed to be affirmed, identified, and summoned by the word of the Lord. The prophetic word of the Lord does that when it comes to a person. The Lord will say that you are a prophet or you are a leader or you are this and that, even though you may not be fully walking in that call.

Moreover, when the Lord says, "Let there be," the spoken word of the Lord is powerful, because the word of the Lord is released to permit something to come forth. For example, when the Creator spoke and said, "Let there be light," the light responded to the prophetic word and became when it was called out of darkness. When the creative power of the spoken word was released by God, God said, "Let there *be* light." God was giving permission for light to be and to function in its God-given assignment. When the Lord calls you to something for Him and says to be what He has created you to be, you now have the permission and commission by the Father to be all you can be in the Earth. The power of the spoken word and prophecy can do that same to any situation. You can speak things into existence in your life by the spoken word and faith.

CREATING YOUR WORLD THROUGH PROPHECY

By faith we understand that the worlds were framed by the word of God, so that the things which are seen were not made of things which are visible.

—HEBREWS 11:3, NKJV

We understand by faith that God is creative power; through His word as Creator He causes the worlds, which are the ages, and gives reference to time being framed. The creative power of the spoken word of God can frame things in a person's life. Prophecy can frame any situation if God's wisdom, direction and strategy is applied. The word *framed, kataritzo,* means "to arrange, set in order, equip, adjust, complete what is missing, lacking and make fully ready, repair and prepare."[69] The prophetic function and power of the spoken word can repair a person's life, marriage, etc. In addition, it can adjust and bring wholeness and completion, therefore making and preparing a person for what God has next for them. The prophetic word becomes a spiritual picture frame or a window for one to see through and see a glimpse or picture of their prophetic future or destiny.

Everything that God creates is given an assignment and purpose for existing, just like the prophet Jeremiah, who was called to be a prophet. Prophets are called and sent to speak the counsel of the Lord to whomever the Lord sends him or her. I will go into detail in later chapters in regard to what is a prophet, prophecy, and the prophetic nature.

COME OUT OF OBSCURITY AND
BECOME WHAT GOD SAID

God called light out of hiding or obscurity and told light to come forth and to be, so there was light. Light heard the word of the Lord and came forth. We can see that when God said, "Let there be light," and there was light, God gave light its name and identity. It was the

---

69   See http://www.studylight.org/lex/grk/gwview.cgi?n=2675, StudyLight
.org (accessed July 12, 2013). See also Strong's #2675- New Spirit-Filled Life® Bible, Copyright © 2002 by Thomas Nelson, Inc., page 1741, "Word Wealth" Index Section.

light's responsibility to respond and be what the Creator called it. Likewise, when the Lord has called us and says, "Let you be," there is a time and season where you will become all that He has predestined you to be as long as you take ownership and stewardship of the will of the Lord in your life.

Everything in life has been created by a seed. We are the seed that was downloaded into our mother's womb. It's a seed of greatness and full of potential. An apple seed does not look like an apple yet, but it's only the seed. Therefore, that little seed has the capacity, potential, and DNA to be an apple in the fullness of time. That's why it is called an apple seed; just like Jeremiah, he was called a prophet, but before the Lord placed him in his mother's womb he was just a prophetic seed that was given an assignment and prophetic coding to be a prophet called to the nations. Whatever the Lord put inside of you is a seed of who you really were born to be. There is nothing in the universe that has not been created without a seed being planted. God releases his spiritual seed into the earth and from the earth. This is what you really are, a seed that will sprout forth or be birthed out.

Life Starts from a Seed

Galatians 3:29 (NKJV) reads, "And if you are Christ's, then you are Abraham's seed, and heirs according to the promise." We are heirs of the promise because we have been baptized into the spiritual family of Christ. Like any seed, life starts out as a seed and then forms and matures into that we are to become in Christ Jesus. The Bible says not to despise small beginnings. We must understand that everything in life has a beginning, and that small beginning is the seed. The seed is the beginning of who a person is really to become.

I am reminded of when a woman gets pregnant. In order for conception to take place there, of course, has to be sexual intercourse between a man and a woman. The man releases himself (seed, sperm) into the woman, and millions of sperm are racing down the female organs to reach the egg. But only one sperm out of millions makes it. The rest die. This is very profound to me, because you have made it out of millions of sperms and became the champion seed that made it to the finish line (egg), which became the beginning of your life.

The word of the Lord, spoken from the Father, is a seed of creation. The word is prophetic, because God's words do not fall to the ground but fall inside of us on the earth as a seed sown to bring forth that which He speaks. The prophetic word fathers (imparts) and mothers (nourishes) the seed sown into our lives, which in due season and maturation comes to pass.

I love the prophetic because it has brought understanding to certain situations and seasons that I could not comprehend in particular seasons of my life. I would receive many prophetic words about being a spiritual father and having spiritual sons and daughters in the faith, but I could not and didn't understand the prophecy, nor grasp it fully like Abraham. For me, I was in search of a spiritual father and had spiritual leaders who would show me the way, but I never knew that God was going to raise me up to be a father in the faith.

I could remember a prophet of God who spoke a prophetic word to me back in 2004 saying, "Son, you have been looking for spiritual parenting and fathering, but the Lord says that through trial and error you are the father that you have been looking for, for I have called you to be a spiritual father and model to the next generation. And I am your father, so as I father you, you will father others, says the Lord." I had many teachers, instructors in Christ, but not many fathers in the faith or in the calling that was on my life. We as believers are the seed of Abraham, being the descendants of Abraham.

The prophetic word or dream may seem too impossible to fulfill or too farfetched because of time, chronological age, or failures that we may have encountered through life that have caused us to walk in unbelief, doubt, and criticism. But those words or dreams are true if God speaks them to us. Regardless of how old Abraham and Sarah were, they were chosen to release and conceive a promised seed that would bless all the nations of the earth. It only takes one seed to release a harvest and just one prophetic word to release the promise.

In Genesis it talks about the Promised Seed, which was Christ, who was going to bruise the head of the serpent with His heel. In Eve, she carried the vindication and justice of the Promised Seed (Christ) who would defeat sin and death. All we need in life is a seed, which is the Word of God spoken in power. Genesis also talks about seed-time and harvest-time, which is the law that God has established. In every seed, there is a time of harvest and productivity. They work hand and hand. In other words, if you plant an oak tree seed, you are not going to expect a palm tree but an oak tree in the season of fullness. When prophecy comes forth in a person's life it's a seed of potential, and there will come a time for the seed to maximize its godly potential.

I have listed just a few powerful Scriptures in regard to the power of the spoken word:

A man shall be satisfied with good by the fruit of his mouth.
—PROVERBS 12:14, NKJV

Goodness comes by what you speak.

There is that speaketh like a piercing of a sword: but the tongue of the wise is health.
—PROVERBS 12:18

Health comes with those who use their words wisely.

He who guards his mouth keeps his life.
—PROVERBS 13:3, AMP

Life or death can be determined by what we declare.

The heart of the wise teacheth his mouth, and addeth learning to his lips."
—PROVERBS 16:23, KJV

God doesn't teach one mouth, but the heart of the wise man teaches their own mouth.

Death and life are in the power of the tongue: and they that love it shall eat the fruit of thereof.
—PROVERBS 18:21, KJV

Life and death is the creative power that a person's own tongue can bring to pass.

Death and life are in the power of the tongue, and they who indulge it shall eat the fruit of it [for death or life].

—Proverbs 18:21, amp

A man shall eat good by the fruit of his mouth.

—Proverbs 13:2, kjv

Good life and prosperity come by the spoken word.

A [self-confident] fool's mouth is his ruin, and his lips are the snare to himself.

—Proverbs 18:7, amp

Foolish and unwise people talk before they think and are ruined by their own words, which ensnares them and causes destruction. A wise man will think before he speaks.

Let the redeemed of the Lord say so, whom he hath redeemed from the hand of the enemy.

—Psalm 107:2, kjv

Salvation and redemption comes to those who know their God, and He will deliver them from the adversary.

Out of the abundance of the heart the mouth speaketh.

—Matthew 12:34, kjv

The mouth only speaks what's in it, whether good or evil.

And the tongue is a fire, a world of iniquity. The tongue is so set among our members that it defiles the whole body, and sets on fire the course of nature; and it is set on fire by hell.

—James 3:6, nkjv

The tongue is a small but powerful member and can change the direction of someone's destiny and course of life.

The power of the spoken word is creative and mighty. Jesus in Mark 11:23 (kjv) said to His disciples, "For verily I say unto you, that whosoever shall say unto this mountain, Be thou removed, and be cast into the sea; and shall not doubt in his heart, but shall believe that those things which he saith shall come to pass; he shall have whatsoever he saith."

This passage of Scripture is a principle that we must understand. Jesus was basically saying that if a person believes what they are speaking, then you can have it. In other words, if I can speak to an impossible situation like a mountain and tell it to relocate into the sea to be seen no more, then I can speak anything by the spoken word, and it will come to pass if I believe it. Jesus didn't say anything about praying to the mountain to move or interceding for the mountain to move; Jesus said simply to speak to the situation and it would happen. That's the absolute power of the spoken word.

Chapter Fifteen

BAPTIZED INTO THE FAMILY

*Now I say that the heir, as long as he is a child, does not differ at
all from a slave, though he is master of all, but is under guardians
and stewards until the time appointed by the father. Even so we,
when we were children, were in bondage under the elements of the
world. But when the fullness of the time had come, God sent forth
His Son, born of a woman, born under the law, to redeem those who
were under the law, that we might receive the adoption as sons. And
because you are sons, God has sent forth the Spirit of His Son into
your hearts, crying out, "Abba, Father!" Therefore you are no longer
a slave but a son, and if a son, then an heir of God through Christ.*
—GALATIANS 4:1–7

ANY PEOPLE WILL teach us many things, but who will
impart their very own lives into us? I believe there is a
spiritual company that certain people can identify themselves with; it's not an occult or sect but a particular spiritual apostolic and prophetic tribe or DNA that one can relate to in covenant.
God granted me the privilege and honor to relate to fathers and
mothers in the faith who I will not name for the lack of identity and
protection. I have been baptized into them and we have been baptized into one another.

To relate with these world leaders has added a strong grace and
identity in my calling. This type of apostolic, prophetic synergy and
parenting is what cross-pollination is. We must connect with different types of irons in the body of Christ for fine-tuning, sharpening, and accountability. The Bible says iron sharpens iron; in other
words, if you are a dull pencil and need sharpening, then it would be

wise for you to go to a pencil sharper to get your edge back and be sharp again.

Apostle John Eckhardt, who is an apostolic, pioneering voice of our day and my apostolic father, defines the term *cross-pollination* when he states:

> With the rise of many different apostolic networks, there can be a tendency to become isolated and exclusive. This can be avoided as apostles network with one another and cross-pollinate with their networks. Groups such as ICA (International Coalition of Apostles) formerly known as the NCA (National Coalition of Apostles) are bringing together different apostles to intermingle and raise the level of accountability between apostles. Different apostles and networks have different strengths and can help each other by cross-pollinating.[70]

THE POWER OF CROSS-POLLINATING

I believe this is an excellent definition of unity within the body of Christ. I believe it not only promotes unity, but also there is a mutual submission among other leading apostles. I believe cross-pollination is not just for apostles to relate, connect, love, and correct each other, but this should be for all believers in the kingdom. We are baptized by the Spirit of God, and we are citizens of the kingdom. We are all kings in the kingdom of God. The baptism into the family of God is our inheritance.

I have submitted my life, ministry gift, and doctrine to other seasoned men and women of God in the kingdom. I believe in accountability as a minister of the Lord. There are powerful apostles, prophets, and five-fold ministry leaders that I mutually respect and submit to for spiritual counsel, correction, guidance, spiritual covering, impartation, and love. These men and women have made tremendous spiritual deposits into me that were life changing. The prophetic words that they have released over my life set the course of my destiny. I am what I am because of who they are. I call them my family, and we have been immersed into each other. They have embraced me into their lives and vice versa.

---

70 Eckhardt, *Dictionary of the Apostolic, second edition*, 94–95.

We need each other in the body of Christ. We need to submit one to another in love. The awesome thing about those who I submit myself and ministry to is that they challenge me to grow and do what God has called me to do. In addition, they do not dwarf or stunt my growth in Christ but stretch me to go higher and impact my generation.

Importantly, above all, these men and women of God recognize the gift of God on my life and challenge me to go and to do what I have been born to do. We must be baptized into the family. I believe that we must be baptized into the family of God by the Holy Spirit's regenerative power and that prophets and kingdom believers must be plugged into a local church to operate in. Those who are planted in the house of the Lord will flourish. There is growth and development when a person's roots are connected to a body of other believers who share the same discontentment, passion, vision, ideas, concepts, belief systems, and burdens of the Lord as you do.

Baptized into Those You Serve and Follow

These leaders had to understand Moses' heart and spirit. It was a prophetic dimension and spirit that they operated in. Moses, being a prophet, judge, and shepherd, needed a leadership who would carry out specific assignments for the people as he spent time on the mountain receiving the Law and Commandments of the Lord. There were men that needed to be immersed and baptized into Moses' baptism.

We all can identify and relate with leaders and others who carry the same passion and discontentment as we do. We are immersed in the same culture, which should be a kingdom culture when relating to each other and in covenant with those leaders. I believe that when a person finds his or her spiritual company, whether it's in business, education, entertainment, government, the medical field, arts, or any other system, the person will connect with those who share the same field and craft.

Just like in the natural, a person is born into and shares his or her last name with family members for the purpose of identification. As it is in the natural, so it is in the Spirit. When a person is regenerated by the Spirit, they come into the kingdom. I believe locally there are leaders, ministries, churches, networks, and businesses in the marketplace and fellowships where people can be a part of and identify with the family that they have been baptized into. It's a culture that is represented, and if a church is earmarked with miracles, the prophetic, deliverance, healing, or wealth, then all that is a part of that specific culture. That family will have all things in common, because they all share in the revelation, breaking of bread, impartations, training, teaching, etc.

IMMERSED IN REVELATION KNOWLEDGE AND TRUTH

The Bible tells us of a time when Paul was meeting some people that needed to be brought into the present truth of the baptism of the Spirit. They were stuck in John's baptism. The people needed to come into something relevant and current to be effective in advancing the message of the kingdom in the first century. Paul the apostle, who was called to the Gentile world, had a responsibility to bring people into the new and baptize them in Christ's baptism of the Spirit and not John's baptism by water unto repentance.

Whenever we receive new revelation by the Spirit of God, we must be immersed into that truth and revelation so that it will shape our belief system, therefore allowing us to be consistent with what God is doing and saying. In other words, we should be immersed in the prophecies that we receive from the Lord, which cause to come into being that which the Lord said would happen. Being baptized into the family indicates that we are held accountable; are connected, relational, team players; and are submitted to one another in love.

We need kingdom ministry that will raise up, train, identify, and deploy Holy Spirit-filled, mature leaders into the world. I never had to go tell the pastor of a local church who I was or what I was called to do because I just did it. At the age of seven years old I was already prophesying and seeing things in the Spirit, having encounters with angels, and learning the voice of the Lord. I just could not identify or put a title to what I was already functioning in. It was the gift of God working on the inside of me. The gift was growing as I was growing. There was no one in my family that had these types of keen giftings and abilities. In addition, there was no one in my life that could train or mentor me in that call. I had to learn everything by the Holy Spirit in prayer, reading of the Word, fasting, and by faith as a child.

All of the prophetic encounters that my brother and I had were very rare and unique. We could not tell anyone about it, but only each other. We learned a tremendous amount and used to minister to each other in the prophetic in the days of our youth. My brother and I would prophesy and share words of warnings, wisdom, knowledge, and encouragement with strangers and anyone we came in contact with.

People would ask us how we knew the things that we knew about them. This was something that we were born with, and we learned later through many prophetic words by prophets that we were called to the prophetic ministry. This was a gift and grace given to us by the Lord. Others took notice of it very quickly because we seemed strange, particular, special, weird, and even crazy. The world labeled and named us strange, but our God called us His servant prophets.

A Person's Gift Will Become a Great Host for Them

We must understand that our gifts make room for us, and it will bring us in the presence of those with great influence (Prov. 18:16). It does not matter if people do not receive who you were born to be in the earth or if they do not believe in present-day prophets and apostles. The point that I am trying to make is that your gift creates rooms of opportunity for those who do believe and receive you. Know that in God's timing you will be established in your calling. Having a license or ordination paper still does not validate that someone has been called or is ready for full-time ministry. Even those who are called to ministry and have been ordained are not automatically validated or guaranteed that they will be successful and bear much fruit of that calling.

So again, there is nothing wrong with cross-pollinating with others of like heart, mind, calling, and vision, but to pursue them solely for the purposes of a religious organization making you something that you have not been born to be is what I call "identity default" and "identity crisis."

Consequently, when men try to look for man to make them something, not allowing God to make them who He has preordained, then that person is walking in an identity crisis. That person is a man-pleaser and seeker, not a God-pleaser and seeker. Usually one's calling, potential, and destiny can be confirmed and affirmed by seasoned leadership, but ultimately Jesus is the true Commissioner of His ambassadors.

The most dissatisfying indictment is to see people that are desiring and coveting something that God has not called them to be and searching out religious organizations to ordain them. There is a spirit of pride, idolatry, and perversion in operation when a person covets other people's gifts, callings, and natural possessions. We must understand that those being something that they have not been born, wired, and engineered by God to be may bring the judgment of God upon themselves.

Be on Guard and Protect Your Gift

The Gospel of Luke describes Jesus' warning to guard one's heart against covetousness when it says, "Take heed and beware of covetousness, for one's life does not consist in the abundance of the things he possesses" (Luke 12:15, NKJV). Jesus also describes the sins that defile a person as sins coming from untamed desires in the heart. The Book of James portrays covetous desire residing in the heart as being the internal source of temptation and sin. James the apostle goes on to describe how covetous desire leads to fighting and that lack of material possessions is caused by not asking God for them and by asking with wrong motives. He said, in essence, "You covet and cannot obtain, so you fight and quarrel."

It is imperative not to covet anything that God has not given you or ordained you to be. Usually those who do covet lack true identity in God and are operating in a spirit of self-deception. When a person does not really know what they have been born to be, it causes them to deny their God-given right to function properly in their call. It's like a man who was born a male and one day takes it upon himself to alter his physical appearance through major surgery to become a female. This is truly an act of perversion, rebellion, confusion, pride, and double-mindedness. The Bible says that we are fearfully and wonderfully created. God does not make any mistakes.

When He created you He said that you were very good. You have God's approval to be all that you desire you to be. You must know that there will never be another you born in the earth again. This statement is profound; when you were born, you were born an original, and when you die, you do not die being someone else or a copy. While you are still alive, maximize your full godly potential and be all that you were born to be. Do not allow others to make you compare yourself to others, because then you become what they say you are and not what God created you to be.

God is very much involved in every person's life from the very beginning, even at the beginning of conception. You are the spiritual offspring of the Lord, and He loves His children from the beginning of birth and from the time you were birthed out of the womb of your mother. Children are very special to God since they are a gift of God (Ps. 127:3). Because God is very much involved in every person's life from the beginning, this makes everyone special from the beginning.

CREATED FROM THE MIND OF GOD

Let's consider the Scripture below on the subject of being "born" and "created," which is very important to understand biblically and from a godly perspective. The passage of Scripture from which the title of this book is taken is Psalm 139. We are God's creation, as we read in the Psalms: "For You formed my inward parts; You covered me in my mother's womb" (Ps. 139:13, KJV). God made you for His divine purpose. He formed—"created"—what the text refers to as "inward parts." In Hebrew it means literally "kidneys."[71]

You may think that I am talking about what we usually think of as our own kidneys today, but rather it is our mind. This would be more in accordance with Jewish patterns of thought at the time David wrote this psalm. (See also Revelation 2:23.)

---

71   Blue Letter Bible, s.v. "kilyah," www.blueletterbible.org/lang/lexicon/Lexicon. cfm?strongs=H3629 (accessed June 4, 2013). See also the King James Study Bible (previously published as The Liberty Annotated Study Bible and as The Annotated Study Bible, King James Version; Copyright © 1988 Liberty University.) Reference to word "kidneys" is found in the *center-column index* references and notes, copyright © 1988 by Thomas Nelson, Inc. on page 863 of referencing Scripture of Psalm 7:9 KJV. In center-column reference to another meaning to the word "reins" means inner man or minds, Lit, "kidneys" in Hebrew thought.

Psalm 7:9 (KJV) says, "Oh let the wickedness of the wicked come to an end; but established the just; for their righteous God trieth the hearts and reins." In this passage of Scripture David was revealing that God tests one's heart and knows the inner man or mind. I am reminded of when God told Samuel the prophet that He doesn't see as man sees, because men see the outward appearance but God sees the heart of men (1 Sam. 17:7).

Understanding this will hopefully cause us to be responsible as good stewards. We will not use the body that God has given us in ways that would morally pollute it (1 Cor. 6:19). God wove you like a tapestry or like clay on the potter's wheel; each of us is a multi-complex creature (Exod. 26:36). All of our parts work together harmoniously; each part has a different function to accomplish and depends on the other parts (1 Cor. 12:14–18). God works with the skill that confounds man.

When God formed that initial human pair, He skillfully added mechanisms that would operate on the basis of natural law so that they would be able to re-create themselves. The Psalmist correctly identifies God as the Master Worker and Planner, who is the source of our origin and DNA.

God's Creative Masterpiece

God does not create a mistake and trash. He makes wonderful, creative works. God can turn all for good, for His glory, to make us more like His dear Son, Jesus. God spoke to Jeremiah through this observation when He told him to go and watch the potter at work in Jeremiah 18:1–5.

> This is the word that came to Jeremiah from the LORD: "Go down to the potter's house, and there I will give you my message." So I went down to the potter's house, and I saw him working at the wheel. But the pot he was shaping from the clay was marred in his hands; so the potter formed it into another pot, shaping it as seemed best to him. Then the word of the LORD came to me. He said, "Can I not do with you, Israel, as this potter does?" declares the LORD. "Like clay in the hand of the potter, so are you in my hand, Israel.

We must ask, Are we listening to God through our day and hearing Him as He speaks to us through the ordinary? God was trying to get Jeremiah to understand that He was the Potter and that Jeremiah's destiny, call, life and journey was in His hands, thereby showing him His creative nature. So, that being said, even if a person does not know what they have been born and created to do, that does not mean it's the end of the world or that they missed their calling. Just know that God is working things out on your behalf and will prepare you in due season for the work. A person does not need to covet another when he or she is secure in that which God has called them to do in their generation.

Remember that prophetic identity is traced back to your birth and even before you were born. Looking for affirmation from men can cause one to compromise or forfeit their own assignment. I have come into contact with people who had actually prayed to the Lord to make them something without asking the Lord what He has called them to be. Ministry idolatry, seeking to be something that you were not born to be by the Lord, is a sin. Ephesians and Colossians describe the sin of covetousness as a kind of idolatry and then also list this as sin, along with sexual immorality and impurity, which give rise to the wrath of God. I must say that if a person does not walk in and fulfill what God has originally ordained for their lives, they may walk under the judgment hand of the Lord.

Chapter Sixteen

JESUS BORN TO FULFILL PROPHECIES

So they said to him, "In Bethlehem of Judea, for thus it is
written by the prophet: 'But you, Bethlehem, in the land of
Judah, Are not the least among the rulers of Judah; For out of
you shall come a Ruler Who will shepherd My people Israel.'"
—Matthew 2:5–6, nkjv

W E CAN SEE that there were prophecies spoken before Jesus was ever conceived from His mother's womb. Herod and all of Jerusalem were troubled by just the announcement of His coming. Jesus was equipped and created to be King of not only the Jews but the King of all that believe on His name and receive Him into their lives.

Jesus did not have to have an earthly ordination through or anything physical to signify that he was born a King like earthly kings because His kingdom was not of this world. Jesus was born a King, and that spoke of His identity. When the Magi came with gifts, they came with gifts that they would give a king. They were not concerned about if He had a throne, kingdom, or people, but the sign in the heavens declared the prophetic fulfillment that a king had arrived. Jesus did not have to make an announcement like most religious people do that they are a prophet, apostle, or this and that; but instead He came meek and low-spirited. The Bible says, "Unto us a child is born, unto a son is given, and the government will be on His shoulders" (Isa. 9:6). This prophecy speaks of the coming King, ruler, and governor of God's people.

Jesus was birthed out of prophecy. The religious system and culture of His time were intimidated by Him because He not only demonstrated in word but also deed. Just the word that a governor and ruler would be born of the Jews shook the whole religious and civil system. During the first two years of Jesus' life, there were mass murders of young children under the age of two because Herod was angry that another king would emerge.

Just imagine the reaction of Satan and demons when they heard prophetically about your birthing. You must realize that when you and I were born, not only were you born a child of the Most High, but also we were given dominion (godly authority to rule in the earth). A believer must understand their true identity in God and know that when they were regenerated and baptized into the kingdom by the Spirit of God they became a king-priest.

Like Jesus, when you were born again in the spirit, all of hell was shaken. As a King Jesus exercised godly authority in the realm that He was given authority over. Jesus, being King, had to know His prophetic destiny and the will of His Father while growing up in life. He was not a novice in the things of God. Jesus fulfilled every prophecy spoken of Him.

Jesus, as King, knew how to conduct Himself as ambassador sent from the Father to redeem humanity back to the Father. Jesus came from His kingdom, which is an eternal, spiritual kingdom and not earthly. When we were born again, we were born into the kingdom. We have been translated or transferred from the kingdom of darkness into the kingdom of light (Col. 1:13). We have been born to rule. The kingdom is our inheritance. It is the Father's good pleasure to give us the kingdom. It's not an earthly, carnal, worldly kingdom but spiritual. Jesus knew how to operate in the kingdom, and a majority of His messages concerned the gospel of the kingdom.

You Were Not an Accident but Born on Purpose

The kingdom of God is within us. Jesus' birthing was not an accident, nor is your birthing an accident. You have been sent to the earth to fulfill something unprecedented for the Lord in your time and generation. Jesus was sent to the earth also to destroy the works of darkness, sin, hell, death, and the grave. That sounds like a king to me, one who came to conqueror sin and place all things under His feet.

Jesus fulfilled every prophetic word to the letter. The Bible says that every jot and tittle of that word would be fulfilled.

Jesus was the Promise of the Father. He was sent, and so are you. God had called you by name, and you were born to live so that in death others may live through you. You were born to leave your mark in society. You were born to change and shake the world. You were born to fulfill every prophetic promise of the Lord. Jesus is our perfect example.

My heart breaks when I hear people wanting to commit suicide. I know life has its circumstances and issues. Life can be hard at times. One may feel like it's the end of the world and wonder, What's the purpose for living? My answer to that question is that *you* are the purpose for living. Someone needs *you* to live. Just your very existence speaks volumes.

You were born to make a difference in your world. God said that you are the light of the world and the salt of the earth. That statement is very profound, because God is saying that the earth and the world need you and that your influence changes it. Jesus was not just born King, but He was God with us. Jesus' very own name, like Jeremiah, was prophetic. His name means "Savior"! He was the Savior of the world. His name is Christ, meaning "the Anointed One." Jesus was anointed of the Father and sent to redeem mankind back to right relationship with the Father. Even the religious leaders of Jesus' time were looking for a king and did not recognize that God was among them.

REJECTION BRINGS PROMOTION

Jesus, like many of us, has experienced being rejected and not received. Jesus was also the Stone that the builder rejected, but He became the chief Cornerstone. We must understand in our walk with the Lord that everyone is not going to celebrate, believe, or receive you. I believe prophetically that we need to experience some degree of rejection, because it causes us to look to the Lord. Rejection, I believe, causes a person to overcome being men-pleasers and a compromiser and causes confidence in their election of the Lord. Jesus was rejected by His very own people, and He didn't take His own life; therefore you have much to live for.

Out of rejection, Jesus became chief Cornerstone (Matt. 21:42–43; Acts 4:11; Eph. 2:20). He became what He was designed, created, and called to be. Jesus asked an important question to His disciples. He asked them, "Who do men say that I am?" and some of them said the prophet, some said John the Baptist. They were wrong, except Peter, who received revelation from the Father that Jesus was the Son of the living God. Jesus said to Peter that flesh and blood did not reveal that to him, but the Father in heaven. Peter got a revelation of Jesus' true identity as a Son of the Father. He was able to know Jesus' origin and prophetic identity.

THE ACTS OF GOD WORKING THROUGH YOU

Most people that you may come in contact with may never know who you are by revelation and relationship. They may know you by word of mouth that you are a prophet or etc. Your peers may never know what you have been born and created to do until they spend time with you and see God working through you. Some people will see the power of God working through you and still reject you, like those who saw God was with Jesus and still hardened their hearts.

But Jesus overcame temptation, rejection, and persecution by knowing His Father, His calling, purpose, identity, and prophetic assignment. Jesus operated, spoke, and lived like a King. Regardless of whether or not all people received Him to be their Messiah, Savior, Redeemer, and King, there was a remnant of believing Jews that followed Him.

The current population of the world is 7 billion people, and everyone was born and created by God to do something unique. That does not mean that everyone will fulfill their call, but you do not have to be that one.

Jesus' passion was to please the Father and finish His work. Jesus did not have to say that He was King. His prophecy declares it. Let your prophecy declare your coming and you coming into that prophecy. Have you heard the saying, "You are what you eat"? I believe it's true to a certain extent, but I would go on to say that you are your prophecy. Guard your prophecy and become that which the Lord has spoken over your life. Jesus was the prime example.

We can see in the Word of God during the life of Jesus that an angel of the Lord came to Jesus' mother, Mary, with a prophetic message, and the angel said to her, "You will conceive and give birth to a son, and you will name him Jesus." The prophecy of the birth of Jesus is found in Isaiah 7:14, which says, "Therefore the Lord himself will give you a sign. The virgin will conceive and give birth to a son, and will call him Immanuel." Jesus' name means "Savior" in Hebrew, *Immanuel*, which is interpreted as "God with us."

Jesus' calling was to save His people from the law of sin and death and redeem them back in right standing and fellowship with His Father. We can see specially that God knows us by name and knows every detail of our lives. It's important to know that one's calling has been outlined before they were ever conceived. Mary did not realize that she was birthing the Messiah, that what was conceived in her was of the Holy Spirit.

Supernatural Birth Through Prophecy

In the Gospel of Luke 1:26–37 there is a miraculous birthing that took place in Mary. Jesus was conceived in the womb of the Holy Spirit, and Mary's virgin body would be the natural conduit of what was done in the spirit. Jesus was born of the Holy Spirit and birthed naturally through Mary.

And in the sixth month the angel Gabriel was sent from God unto a city of Galilee, named Nazareth, To a virgin espoused to a man whose name was Joseph, of the house of David; and the virgin's name was Mary. And the angel came in unto her, and said, Hail, thou that art highly favoured, the Lord is with thee: blessed art thou among women. And when she saw him, she was troubled at his saying, and cast in her mind what manner of salutation this should be. And the angel said unto her, Fear not, Mary: for thou hast found favour with God. And, behold, thou shalt conceive in thy womb, and bring forth a son, and shalt call his name Jesus. He shall be great, and shall be called the Son of the Highest: and the Lord God shall give unto him the throne of his father David: And he shall reign over the house of Jacob for ever; and of his kingdom there shall be no end. Then said Mary unto the angel, How shall this be, seeing I know not a man? And the angel answered and said unto her, The Holy Ghost shall come upon thee, and the power of the Highest shall overshadow thee: therefore also that holy thing which shall be born of thee shall be called the Son of God. And, behold, thy cousin Elisabeth, she hath also conceived a son in her old age: and this is the sixth month with her, who was called barren. For with God nothing shall be impossible.

—Luke 1:26–37, kjv

An individual must know the purpose of their birthing and what God has called them to. Jesus' assignment in the earth and what He was born to do was connected to His name. He was to save His people. He was to be Immanuel to the people He was called to. He was born Jesus, Savior, to His people; that was the main purpose of His birthing.

Jesus' mother Mary received a prophetic word, which in due time came to pass with the birth of our Lord Jesus Christ. Everything spoken by the prophets and written in the Law was a type and shadow of the reality and prophetic fulfillment of Christ being birthed. Mary received a word from an angel with a prophetic message that would change her personal life but also that of humanity. Could you imagine Mary having angelic encounters and being chosen by the Lord to birth the Messiah and Savior? Mary was born to serve her purpose, to be the mother of Jesus, but in her womb, as a virgin, she would conceive a child born of the Holy Spirit.

Walking Out Personal Prophecies

The word of the Lord found her, and she had to receive the prophecy spiritually in her mind and soul before her natural womb and body would receive the seed that was imparted by the Holy Spirit. Joseph didn't understand the supernatural pregnancy, but it was in heaven's plan to fulfill all righteousness in the earth through Christ. Jesus fulfilled all prophecies that were spoken of Him to the letter. He was the fulfillment of prophecy. When we receive a word from the Lord it is our responsibility to war over our prophecies but also to walk in prophetic fulfillment. A person doesn't have to run around asking prophets for a word of the Lord. There are times where the word of

God will find you. People who run around looking for a prophecy all the time are mistaken and immature.

To receive a prophetic word from the Lord an individual must understand the severity of receiving one, because the person is now held accountable by God to fulfill it. I personally as a prophet do not look for, nor am I desperate for prophecy, because I know that we are judged by them if we do not obey. There is nothing wrong in asking for a prophetic word from seasoned, integral, and trained prophets who have a true word from God, but we must honor and respect them as well. We must honor them with prayers, intercession, and most importantly, financial seeds and blessing. A person is not paying for a prophecy, but they are honoring the man and woman of God for their time, gift, and ministry.

Jesus was not running all over Jerusalem looking for a prophetic word. He was more concerned about fulfilling the prophecies that were prophesied concerning Him and the current status of the world. When we focus on kingdom things, then other natural things will come.

Have you ever needed a word and went all over to look for it, and it never came. But then when you stopped and refocused on kingdom business, all of a sudden a season came and you were being called out here and there? We as believers must understand the timing and divine seasons that we walk in. I don't look for more prophecies; I fulfill the ones I have already received. Jesus was the primary model and example of walking in accordance to His Father's will and purpose in the earth.

ENCOUNTER THE PROPHETIC AS A YOUTH

The word of the Lord will find you at a place when you most need it. I can remember in my youth going to a church service at the age of fourteen. There was a woman of God who I did not know that people called a prophetess. She began to move in the Spirit of God and began to speak in tongues, and then she suddenly called me out before hundreds of people in front of the church and prophesied to me saying, "Young man, you have a unique call on your life, and God has called you from your mothers' womb and has anointed, appointed, and set you apart for His holy calling to become His prophet. You are called to be great. All this what I am saying to you might not make sense now, but later in life it will all make sense, and you will be His mouthpiece for His glory."

When this specific prophetic word came to me I was singing in a community choir. I did not have any clue what a prophet was and what nations I was called to. I can remember the woman of God laying her hands on me, and I fell down under the power of God and could not move because it felt like a huge hand was preventing me from moving. So, like Jeremiah and Isaiah, I encountered the same prophetic words that they received.

We must ask ourselves what we have been born to do and become for the Lord. In Isaiah 49:1 (NLT) it says, 'Listen to me, all you in distant lands! Pay attention, you who are far away! The LORD called me before my birth; from within the womb he called me by name." Paul the apostle said in Galatians 1:15 (ESV), "But when he who had set me apart before I was born, and who called me by his grace." But when it pleased God, Paul traced all his hopes of eternal life and all the good influences that had ever borne upon his mind to God. The question to ask is, Who separated Paul? That is, who destined him, or who purposed Paul from birth that he should be a preacher, teacher, and an apostle? Jesus, as well, was born on purpose and was born to fulfill what was written by the Law and prophesied by the Prophets of old.

God, who is the omniscient one, has total knowledge of everything concerning us, because He is the Creator and the Father of the universe. In Latin the word *omnis* means "all," and *sciens* means "knowing."[72] Omniscience is the capacity to know everything. With that in mind, God knew everything because everything started with Him.

Jesus Fulfilled His Father's Original Intent, Purpose, and Will

A person must first know without a shadow of a doubt why they were born and who created them. In understanding God's original intent,

---

72 Oxford English Dictionary, 3rd ed. (New York: Oxford University Press, 2005). See also http://en.wikipedia.org/wiki/Omniscience.

purpose, and plan for our lives, we need to seek the counsel of God for those imperative answers. Everything created in the universe came from a God-thought. That thought was a divine thought that brought into being that which was not there before in the natural. Whatever the Lord creates, He tests it out, and once it has passed His test, then He approves it by saying it is good to be used now.

For example, if I were created to be a one-passenger-seat racecar which had been designed for maximum speed and light cargo and then tried to function as an eight-passenger SUV, then I would be operating in a dysfunctional way, outside of the purpose that the manufacturer had engineered, modeled, and designed me to function as. Even though both are vehicles, a racecar is designed to be smaller, lighter, and drive with increased speed. On the other hand, an SUV is designed to seat more passengers with heavy cargo and is not created for racing purposes.

It's imperative to know why we are here, which can be found in the mind of God, the *man*-ufacturer. With any automobile company, the manufacturer of the model cars will test their product before they put it on the market for the consumers. So with the Lord, He has already test approved you before you were born.

FEARFULLY AND WONDERFULLY CREATED

We must understand that we are God-approved and can endure any task or test because He has already tested us out. There are not recalls when God creates you. King David in Psalm 139:14 (GW) said, "I will give thanks to you because I have been so amazingly and miraculously made. Your works are miraculous, and my soul is fully aware of this." David had a revelation that God's works were miraculous and amazing as he thought about God and creation. Understanding that you were born to fulfill a specific call and were made for His eternal purpose should make anyone praise the Lord as David did.

God created man in His image and according to His likeness, giving man divine legal rights to rule in the earth, and with that in mind, man can accomplish his God-given assignment and purpose knowing that he has been given dominion over the works of God's hands. When one comes into the full understanding and revelation that they were created by God on purpose and for His eternal plan, then His will in their lives can be accomplished successfully.

Many people ask these questions often: Why am I here? What should I be doing? Where am I to be going? and, Who am I called to be? These questions can be answered, as we know the nature of God and His intentions. God will never create anything that was not good.

Jeremiah was told by God what His plans were for him. He was on the mind of God. Our business is God's business. Likewise, Jesus was about His Father's business at a very young age, because that was on His mind and heart. He knew what He was destined to be, and you would find Jesus in the synagogues with the elders and Jewish teachers of His day. He was where He was supposed to have been in the temple, learning and growing in wisdom and stature of the Spirit.

God's Prophetic Blueprint for Your Life

You are God's business. In other words, God was minding His business concerning your destiny in life. Psalm 8:4 (NAS) says, "What is man that you are thoughtful of him, And the son of man that You care for him?" You are on the heart of God, and in His heart lies the blueprint of your life. He is the Master and Father of life. He has the overall master plan for your life.

Jeremiah like many of us today, needed to know that if the Lord knew him before the foundations of the world, then it was the Lord that also knew what he was able to accomplish in his prophetic journey. The Lord will not put too much on us so that we cannot handle the calling on our life. If the Lord has called you and made you to be what He desires, then He has already equipped you with the necessary tools to accomplish that task. We must understand that whatever God created, it is very good initially (Gen. 1:31).

Jeremiah needed reassurance and affirmation from God the Creator about the Father's identification that validated and confirmed the task and purpose of calling him. I believe that most people are trying to make sense out of life and are in search of their true identity, purpose, and destiny. The answer to their question is to be found in God, who is the originator of origination. In humans there is a quest to discover their true purpose for living and what they should be doing during their lifespan. Some may know at an early age why they were created while others can take a lifetime to finally discover their true assignment in the earth. Regardless, if it's early or late in one's life, the main thing that one must understand is who created them, why they were created and what they are created to do.

It is never too late to walk in your purpose when there is a sense of identity and affirmation from God Himself.

PROPHETIC TIMETABLE

God, being the Creator of life, had Jeremiah in mind before He decided to form and fashion him in the bowels of his mother. It all started in the mind of God. Psalm 31:14–15 (AMP) says, "But I trusted in, relied on, and was confident in You, O Lord; I said, You are my God. My times are in Your hands; deliver me from the hands of my foes and those who pursue me and persecute me." We must understand that we are in the timing of the Lord. What one does with their time ultimately will determine how fast one fulfills what God has called them to fulfill. It is imperative to know that regardless of age, time is an interruption of heaven's clock. Therefore, in eternity there is no time or space in God, but there is time in the earthly realm for man to fulfill their personal prophecy. Time is the measure of a person's life, and they must value their time by any means necessary.

We must move in the prophetic timetable of the Lord. We must understand by divine revelation in the above passage of Scripture that David submitted his time to the hands of the Lord. He said that his time was in the Lord's hands. God created time for man so they can measure their life and progress, but the Lord doesn't live by nor is He regulated by natural time or chorological seasons. Discovering God's original intent and eternal purposes is measured by the quality of usefulness of your time and knowing your identity in Christ. Time expires when you stop doing what you were born to do.

The main emphasis of this book and following chapters is discovering your prophetic voice, gift, nature, and identity in Christ Jesus. I believe everyone that was created by God was created to do something creative and unique for their generation. My desire and burden is to help a generation to fully embrace and know their God-given purpose, potential, calling, and to walk in prophetic fulfillment like so many examples of people throughout the Bible did.

The purpose of this book and why it was written with you in mind is to unlock the hidden gems, jewels, and spiritual treasures on the inside of you. I truly believe that you have been created with prophetic insight, abilities, gifts, talents, nature, and yes, your own voice. As I stated before, we've been birthed out by prophecies, and it is God's intention that we fulfill what He has spoken. Every believer who has the Holy Spirit dwelling on the inside of them has the prophetic nature of God and has a prophetic voice, meaning that you have something to say and that your voice shall be heard throughout the earth and unto your generation.

Speak Those Things into Being

The secret to finding your own prophetic voice and nature is hidden in God, who is a God of originality and creativity. The Bible says that the worlds were framed by the word of the Lord. You can create your own world and life by the words you speak. That is prophetic creativity. The Bible also tells us to call those things which be not as though they were (Rom. 4:17). That is the power of the spoken word. You are what you speak. In other words, you are what you prophesy. That is exactly what God did in Genesis.

Just imagine what you and I can accomplish and create in just one day when we access and discover our prophetic nature, ability, and culture. The prophetic or prophecy sets order, arranges, births, fashions, makes, frames, structures, establishes, affirms, confirms, validates, authenticates, mobilizes, releases, thrusts, shifts, imparts, stirs up, heals, delivers, changes, builds, exhorts, comforts, encourages, edifies, strengthens, constructs, supports, and accelerates. I know that not everyone is called to be a prophet, but everyone should learn and be trained, equipped, and activated to develop their voice in the prophetic, supernatural gift of the Holy Spirit.

Chapter Seventeen

STIRRING UP THE PROPHETIC GIFT

*Therefore I remind you to stir up the gift of God which
is in you through the laying on of my hands.*
—2 Timothy 1:6, NKJV

P ROPHECY IS SOMETHING that any believer can do. It's a spiritual gift. (The office of prophet is something rather different, even though some of the function is the same.)

The apostle Paul said he wished for all of us to prophesy. We may be weak or fragile as human beings, but we are conduits of the power of the Holy Spirit. God wants us to stir up the gifts of God on the inside of us. The prophetic gifts specifically can be stirred up or ignited. Second Corinthians 4:7 (NKJV) says, "But we have this treasure in earthen vessels, that the excellence of the power may be of God and not of us." There are treasures of God hidden in our earthly bodies, and those gifts are valuable and are to be discovered by you.

It is every believer's job to find their spiritual gifts, purposes, and callings. One of them should be the prophetic gift. I challenge you to search within by the Holy Spirit to discover your own prophetic voice, gift, nature, and identity in God. Below are just a few ways of developing a foundation to stir up, activate, and launching into the prophetic.

Training is necessary first to be able to really hear the voice of the Lord, to be able to paint the picture He's painting into words through people who see visions or perceive things. Often people have trouble with how to speak it, to be able to discern God's timing for speaking these things, and, for many of us, to simply have the courage to prophesy.

Some reading this book may question how this gift is different from a psychic, medium, ESP, clairvoyance, divination, and witch-craft. Let me be clear: there are two sources of power, God and Satan. God's power flows from Him; we're able to move in His power because of the Spirit of God within us. It's no power of our own, and it brings glory to Him. Satan's power is a counterfeit, a corruption of God's laws and His powers. Satan's power can be accurate in the same way that a con artist can tell the truth in order to advance a lie. His power is rather akin to cut glass, whereas God is diamonds.

The ministry gift of prophesying is simply God conveying His intention, will, plan, and eternal purpose to mankind. We have gone over many foundational scriptures on the gift of prophecy, the office of the prophet, and the gifts of the Holy Spirit as they relate to the Christian believer. The prophetic gift not only is beneficial for the building up of the church, but Spirit-filled believers can also benefit from being trained, activated, educated, and developed in the gift. The fivefold ascension ministry officers are called to equip and per-fect the saints to do the work of the ministry. We are told to fan the flames that are within us. We are to stir up the gift. Moreover, there are those who have come to be asking how they can active the gift. The simple answer to that question is to just do it!

In other words, when gifts are imparted into a person, they are imparted so that they can be activated and utilized. For example, I was out eating with my church and Dr. Bill Hamon prophesied over me, then he imparted the anointing to father and to reproduce myself to the next generation and laid his hands on me. Months later, I felt an unusual anointing and power in the prophetic. I found myself prophesying more than usual in one meeting because what he imparted was a grace to prophesy more and to start equipping, training, and raising up other prophets. God wanted me to go beyond the comfortable and be stretched. Bishop Hamon, a prophetic gen-eral, imparted into me the ability to prophesy with a greater measure, father others eagles, and reach nations. It was my responsibility to keep the gift stirred up and activated.

There are a lot of Spirit-filled believers in the local church sitting on their gift, call, and ministry. It is the Lord's idea that the church become a training center and spiritual hub for mature leaders to be developed, activated, and commissioned. We must be sharpened so that we are not dull. The Bible says iron sharpens iron. It would be wise to surround and build a working relationship with different types of iron in the body of Christ. Everyone has a specific edge and part that they can contribute. I have learned the best way to become stronger in your gift is to surround yourself with masters, strategists, experts, professionals, and leaders in their area of gifting; it causes me to be challenged to reach greater depths. I have provided six simple foundational ways to sharpen or stretch yourself in the gift of prophecy, but it is not limited to these below:

1. Personal Development of Your Prophetic Gift (Habakkuk 2:1–3)

As a beginner or one seasoned in the prophetic gift, one way I have learned to hear the voice of God was first through prayer. A consistent prayer life will fine-tune one's ability to hear what the Lord is saying. Before I ask for a word for someone, I pray in the spirit or in tongues. I have developed a good habit to get in the spirit. Praying in the spirit gives a believer access to God's throne room. While praying in the spirit, I would seek the counsel of the Lord in regards to an individual, city, group, leader, etc. Meanwhile, I am waiting on the Lord for a message, mental pictures, insight, and any expression on my five senses. God will use your five natural senses to get a word or message through. The Lord can also bring to your mind Bible verse, stories, or even situations that remind you of something that can speak specifically to a person.

For example, I remember ministering to this woman and she kept reminding me of my aunt, but she didn't look anything like her or sound like her. So I asked her, "Who is Lisa?" and she said that was her name. I was just as shocked as she was, because at eighteen years old that was my first time receiving a word of knowledge. My point is that God will give you symbols, colors, facts, information, and whatever He desires so that He can get His word across. We must pay attention to it.

In addition, we must maintain a consistent study habit in the Word so that we can articulate accurately what God is saying. A good habit to adopt is learning how to write down what you hear, see, feel, and sense in the spirit. I have also learned that writing down prophetic words is a good start. You can pray in the spirit and then wait on the Lord's prompting, then you can start out writing by saying, for example, "The word of the Lord came to me, saying, son or daughter, _____" This is an excellent start to prophesying. This is what I used when I started prophesying when I was very young, and this has helped beginners. What one will discover is that God will fill in the blank. Activation is just launching out and doing it and make it a habit to grow in it so that it will become second nature. Moreover, prophetic books, manuals, DVDs, CDs, the Internet, and other resources are great tools to educate and bring clarity to your gift. A person must know what they are operating in and be able to teach others.

2. Mentorship to Develop Prophetic Gift (1 Kings 19:19–21)

Another way to develop the prophetic gift is to find a mentor. Don't just find anyone, but someone that has many years in that specific area. Ask them to help you sharpen your prophetic gift. I've had many emerging prophetic minister request for me to mentor them in the prophetic gift. I enjoy helping people to grow, develop, and excel in the things of God. A mentor can give great feedback, challenge you to become better, protect you from burning, and give wisdom, insight, and support. Even if the person you want to mentor you is very busy and unable to give you the time, then you can glean from them by observing them. I always say that some things are "caught" then "taught." So that being said, you can watch how they operate in the gift and find out their study habits.

Paul said, imitate me as I imitate Christ. What the apostle was saying is that we should model, copy, or follow him as he become like Christ. There is nothing wrong with having mentors and even spiritual parents in the faith to love, nourish, protect, adjust, align, impart, and bless you. We all need someone in our lives that has more experience than we may because someone has taught us something. Make sure that your mentor is accountable to other leaders and plugged into a local church, whether they are the senior leader or a part of the leadership team. Moreover, God will send you different types of "irons," as I call them. Iron sharpens iron. Mentors will come and go depending on the season of maturation, but you still should have access to them when you need them. Never put all of your eggs in one basket. In other words, don't allow one person to be all or do it all in your life. Allow other people to speak into your life and help cultivate that prophetic work in you.

3. Prophetic Teams to Develop Prophetic Gift (1 Corinthians 14:29)

Being on a prophetic team is an excellent way to develop one's prophetic ministry. Even though many churches don't have prophetic teams, you can still find others to partner with as a team to minister with. If you have located a church that has a team of prophets leading them, I would recommend speaking to the leadership of that church to see if there is any way to be a part for training and development purposes. I have been a part of and have been privileged the opportunity to be a leader over one of the prophetic teams in my local church. In addition, we see that "team ministry" is a concept of God. Even in the Bible Jesus sent His apostles out two by two. My brother and I travel together as a prophetic team sometimes when we are ministering in churches. People love to see us prophesy together, which is unique itself being that we are twins.

Teams are not limited to the local church; there are home churches, cell groups, and others that develop prophetic ministers. One of the benefits of team ministry is that it will eliminate pride, selfishness, division, and haughtiness. Everyone in a team can contribute when ministering a prophetic word. If a person doesn't want to work with a team then I would check his or her motives for ministry. Team ministry is a safeguard against those who want authority and power and will not submit to others.

When prophesying on a team, a person can receive healthy feedback and will notice that they are not alone. Team ministry is also mutual accountability. Moreover, when a person is prophesying they are prophesying according to the measure of our faith. So in a team we can see the diversities of expressions of God's Word and gift being released toward someone. In a team, a person doesn't have to prove himself or compete, but is able to draw what others are receiving from the Lord and build from that place prophetically. Also, joining prayer intercessory teams and praise/worship teams is a great way for prophets and prophetic people to grow and hear from the Lord.

4. Local Churches to Develop Prophetic Gift (1 Corinthians 12–14)

The local assembly can become a wonderful environment for cultivating, training, equipping, and developing the prophetic gift. If your church or churches that you know of have prophetic teams, evangelistic teams, or prayer teams, it would be beneficial to consult with the leadership team of that church to see how you can join. If you have a prophetic word and would like to share, then it would be wise to ask the pastor of your local church the guidelines of releasing the word publicly. Guidelines are in place for the sole purpose of order and to protect the prophetic minister and the congregation (See 1 Corinthians 14:26–33).

Within the local church, if there is a prophetic team led by a prophet or pastor, I would suggest that you take notes and observe the flow of the team. Each team may function differently from other local churches depending on the leadership criteria. One good way of developing your prophetic gift is attending prophetic and apostolic conferences that will stir you up, where you can be imparted into by other ministry gifts, and relate with others who share the same passion, heartbeat, call, and DNA as yourself. I am affiliated with an apostolic company of IMPACT network under Apostle John Eckhardt and ICA (International Coalition of Apostles) under John P. Kelly, where I am a network leader. Being affiliated with other like-minded people will cause a person to be accountable, relational, and in covenant relationships with kingdom people.

5. Outside Prophetic Training Can Develop Your Gift

There are conferences, seminars, schools of ministry, prophetic and supernatural training that a prophetic minister can consider. I have been to several over the course of my prophetic career, which provided me the necessary impartation and training. I never limit myself in who can upgrade me and cause me to be cutting edge. As I stated before, everyone can enhance his or her prophetic abilities, and no one person has it all and knows it all. Receiving outside training is not walking in rebellion or being disobedient to your local leadership, as long as it doesn't conflict with what you are doing locally. One piece of advice would be to run your desire to get more training across your senior leader or leadership team. There is a saying that practice makes perfect, and I will go on to say that if you practice prophesying then you will be mature (perfect) in it. There is so much information out there on the prophetic—and anything, rather. Modern technology has given us the opportunity to enlarge ourselves and become effective in our gifts and call.

6. Wisdom Is Key in Developing Your Prophetic Gift (Proverbs 11:14)

The Bible says that there is safety in the multitude of counselors. When developing and operating in the prophetic gift, feedback must be welcome. It is imperative and necessary only for the purpose of being properly assessed by those whom you want to mentor or train you. Throughout my prophetic journey I had the opportunity of being around some great men and women in the kingdom. Spending time with them over lunch or dinner has literally revolutionized my life. Having someone willing to take you under their wings and help you is hard to come by these days. Much of what I had to learn, go and grow through in the prophetic gift and ministry was through trial and error. I had to learn a lot on my own; but I thank God that He sent spiritual fathers and mothers who believe in what God put in me.

Sometimes embracing a prophetic gift can be risky, but over time God will bring understanding of the relationship and each will value the other. There are those who think that constructive criticism is negative and even demonic, but actually it is to build you. There is criticism that is aimed to be negative, but constructive criticism is to build the area that needs work. It is good to ask others, even your peers, for feedback when you prophesy. When I was younger I would prophesy every chance I got. I would ask people if I could pray for them, and then I would give them a word and ask them what they thought about the word, or if they had anything to say. You want people to be honest with you so that you will know the areas that need a little work privately and personally. It doesn't matter how seasoned one may be in the prophetic ministry or gift; no one is exempt from needing to receive feedback. There has been a time where I had people ask me questions about a word that they were not clear about or wanted me to bring understanding. To reject wisdom and feedback from those you minister to or those you allow to mentor you will cause you to stunt your own development. Do not allow pride to keep you from walking in the prophetic ministry. Surround yourself with leaders that will love on you while at the same time correct you in love.

As you launch out in the prophetic gift, the most important principles of the prophetic are below:

- Prayers, praying in the spirit (tongues);

- Studying, reading, and speaking the Word of God;

- Meditation on the Word;

- Journaling what you hear, taste, sense, feel, and see in the Spirit from the Lord;

- Fasting and consecration;

- Worship, singing, dancing, and through anointed music;

- Connecting with other prophets and prophetic people;

- Finding a local church or ministry that embraces the prophetic;

- Impartation, activation, and receiving spiritual gifts from godly leadership;

- Humility, teachable, and meek;

- Faith, confidence and boldness;

- Love, unity and sobriety;

- Accountability, transparency and submission to local church;

- Writing down your dreams and visions and learning through the Word, symbols to interpret;

- Spiritual fathers and mothers, mentors and leaders who are experts in the prophetic field of interest.

PROPHETIC RESPONSE AND PRACTICE

Do not neglect your gift, which was given you through prophecy when the body of elders laid their hands on you. Be diligent in these matters; give yourself wholly to them, so that everyone may see your progress. Watch your life and doctrine closely. Persevere in them, because if you do, you will save both yourself and your hearers.

—1 TIMOTHY 4:14–16

The apostle Paul was admonishing his spiritual son, Timothy, not to neglect the gift that was within him. There were gifts that were imparted into him by the apostolic presbytery. Timothy was given charge to give himself to the calling and be diligent in the matter of it. In addition, he was told to watch his teaching and how he conducted his life. As the laying on of hands and prophecy following was a continual practice in the early church, it should be in the twenty-first century church. Prophecy and laying on hands by the leadership team of the local church was for the benefit and purpose of equipping of the saints, direction, edification, exhortation, comfort, confirmation, affirmation, learning, judgment, and setting and establishing people into their ministries. As we see the importance of prophecy partnering with the laying on hands allows ministries gifts to be identified, recognized, and released into ministry before the church. So Timothy was told, in other words, to put these things— such as the gift and call—into practice.

1. Prophetic record

At my local church we suggest that a person who wants to receive prophetic ministry use their phones or any recording device to record it. A person can review their prophecies with their spiritual covering or pastoral leadership team for spiritual maturation. We must understand that when we go back to listen to our personal prophecy, not everything outlined in the prophetic word will be applicable for that particular season. In 1 Thessalonians 5:19–21, the apostle Paul writes, "Do not quench the Spirit. In other words Paul was saying, "Do not despise the words of prophets, but test everything; hold fast to what is good."

One thing that we must put in consideration when we are reviewing the prophetic word is not to be judgmental or critical but receive the word with an open, loving heart. I had to learn that something will make sense later, or understanding will come later. When we are receiving prophetic words and going over them we are not to throw the baby out with the bath water unless the word is totally off. In addition, we should be very cautious calling a prophetic word false or a prophet false if the word doesn't apply to us. It may be the Lord trying to warn us or reveal an area of our lives that needs adjusting. I have been one who really didn't like words of correction, but as I have matured I realize that I would rather receive corrective words than good words all the time.

2. Prophetic warfare

I believe in warring over the prophetic word that has been spoken over your life. When the word of the Lord is spoken over you, the enemy doesn't know the mind of God toward you until He prophesies it. When the prophetic word is released over you, the enemy now declares war to hinder its fulfillment, just as he tried to assassinate the baby Jesus (Matt. 2). Moreover, in 1 Timothy 1:18 (NRSV) it says, "I am giving you these instructions, Timothy, my child, in accordance with the prophecies made earlier about you, so that by following them you may fight the good fight" I like this passage of Scripture because the apostle Paul is basically giving Timothy, his spiritual son, instruction and admonishment about warring over his prophecies. We are to fight the good fight of faith. When a prophetic word is released over our lives, we must take in account that we are now accountable of that word that we received from the Lord. I believe that when we receive a personal prophecy we should take those words seriously. We have to fight over and for our prophecy to come to pass. The greater the prophecy that has been declared over your life, the greater the warfare.

We should always war over our prophecies. How you war over your personal prophetic word is by praying it to pass. Things will not just happen in the earthly realm until it is spoken and released through prayer. We must pray God's eternal will to be done through us on earth as it is in heaven.

Consistently praying your prophecy through will accelerate the time of fulfillment. If a person does not pray their prophecy through, it may never come to full maturity. I liken it to a woman who is pregnant, and at the time of birthing the water breaks. Now it's time to push that baby out. The Bible says that the earth is in travail for the sons of God to manifest themselves in the earth. Speaking, declaring, and mediating on your personal prophetic word will release it. We must speak by faith what we want to see happen. The Bible says that faith is the substance of things hope for and the evidence of things not seen. We speak by faith what we already obtained in the spirit. We just have to pull what's in the spirit realm into our *now*, our present, and that's called "now faith."

3. Prophetic directives

When it comes to prophetic directives or instructions given to us by a prophet that regards to geographical relocation, opportunities, leaving or joining a ministry, marriage, or any decision, we must never make presumptuous or premature moves without inquiring of the Lord. The word of the Lord has to be confirmed several times and even with we must pray, fast and wait on the Lord to give us the specific. The Bible says in Proverbs 11:14 (NKJV), "Where there is no counsel, the people fall, But in the abundance of counselors there is safety." Through strategic prayer, counsel with godly leadership, and faith, God's eternal purposes can be established in a Christian believer's life. The Bible gives many examples of caution in the midst of a prophecy.

We see in 1 Samuel 16:13 that King David was watching sheep for many years after being told he would be king by the prophet Samuel. There were kings of the Old Testament who consulted prophets and were given detailed prophetic instructions and directives concerning their mandate and calling. Jehu and King Jehoshaphat both received divine words that they needed to follow through with.

4. Prophetic hindrance to fulfilling God's promise

When engaging our personal prophetic words, a believer should be willing to judge himself to make sure that he is able to hear the voice of the Lord. A person's attitude can delay or hinder their hearing from the Lord. Such an attitude can include having a negative mind-set or a low self-image, pride, self-justification, blame-shifting, self-reservation, people-pleasing, carnal and fleshly thinking, and sluggishness. Moreover, if there are unconfessed sins, unforgiveness, and bitterness in one's heart, that can also hinder his ability to incline their ears to hear the voice of the Lord. One biblical example of a leader needing to judge himself was King Saul. When the promises of God were presented to him, he rationalized God's instructions, and out of rebellion he chose to do what he thought was right in his own eyes. King Saul's rebellious action caused him to miss the promises of the Lord.

5. Prophetic patience

We are admonished in the Book of Isaiah 40:31 to wait patiently upon the Lord. The foundational biblical principle here that we must learn is waiting on the Lord, which can be found throughout Scripture. The biblical meaning for "wait" is to be actively waiting with expectant faith.

6. Prophetic character

When God is preparing and fashioning someone for ministry He first prepares their character through various methods and testing. It is through trying times, seasons of trials and tribulations that show what we are made of. Maturity, humility, obedience, and integrity are keys to longevity in anything that we do. Biblical patriarchs and matriarchs in the Bible such as Abraham, Moses, Jeremiah, Abel, Solomon, Job, Isaiah, Paul, Mary (Jesus' mother), Anna, Deborah,

Esther, Priscilla, Rachel, and many others had their character tested before they were ever given supernatural ministries by God. Through cultivation, maturation, and patience, these biblical leaders of the Old and New Testament had exceptional character and personalities that caused them to succeed in ministry and in their calling.

The foundation of a person's character will determine the height and depth of the person's ministry. I always say that a person's anointing can go as far their character can take them and keep them. God's prophetic timetable of ministry revolves around our ministry maturation and growth in Him, and our cooperation to permit Him to be Lord in every area of our lives. Our godly character and nature should always reflect the spiritual nature of Jesus. Typically, people tend to judge a person's ministry success as a determination of a person having good character, but there are ministries out there in the world today that may be successful but the leaders of those ministries may not possess godly character personally to sustain them in the long run. Anointing, gifting, and calling should not overshadow a person's character.

The Bible says we are living epistles read by men. So our lives should line up with the Word of God and strive to be more like Christ in word and deed. Prophets, Christian believers and leaders in the body of Christ should be a people of distinguished moral and ethical character. God always works on a person's character but He never changes their personality. A person's character is considered one's reputation and nature. What a person does with their character will ultimately determine how successful they will be. In Colossians 3:12–15 (ESV) it says, "Put on then, as God's chosen ones, holy and beloved, compassionate hearts, kindness, humility, meekness, and patience, bearing with one another and, if one has a complaint against another, forgiving each other; as the Lord has forgiven you, so you also must forgive. And above all these put on love, which binds everything together in perfect harmony. And let the peace of Christ rule in your hearts, to which indeed you were called in one body. And be thankful."

I love what Ephesians 4:24 says about godly character and nature in three translations below:

Put on the new self, created to be like God in true righteousness and holiness.

—Ephesians 4:24

Take on an entirely new way of life—a God-fashioned life, a life renewed from the inside and working itself into your conduct as God accurately reproduces his character in you.

—Ephesians 4:24, The Message

One way to test a person's character is test their willingness to submit to others, whether they are in leadership or not.

7. Prophetic faith exercised

Faith is the source and power of seeing prophetic words being fulfilled. Just as it takes faith to prophesy a word, it will require faith from the hearer to believe it and walk it out. The Bible says that faith comes by hearing and hearing by the Word of God. If you feel discouraged that a prophetic word that you have received has not come to pass as of yet, don't worry; God will see that you will fulfill it in His divine timing. I had to learn to continue to declare the promises of the Lord over my life and remind God of His Word. The Bible says that the promises of the Lord are yes and amen!

For example, if the Lord called you to train prophets and Christian believers in the prophetic, start that school of the prophets study course to prepare yourself for international travels or mission trips. Also start saving money so that you are prepared to fulfill the prophetic word. Be prepared for the Father to fulfill His promise toward you. The Bible says that the Lord's promises are yes and amen.

Finally, prophetic people must cooperate with the leaders that God has given them and team up with others prophetic people to exercise corporate faith, both for your personal prophecies and for corporate prophecies given to your local church. The prophet Joel prophesied that there will come a day that there will be an outpouring of God's Spirit, which was also declared by the apostle Peter in Acts 2:17. We are in the days of Elijah where we are seeing a great outpouring of God's Spirit around the world. God is releasing not only His Spirit, but His prophetic Spirit.

You were born to prophesy and declare His righteousness. The

Bible says that righteousness exalts a nation and sin brings reproach. God wants to release a prophetic generation that will turn nations and kingdoms to the Lord. The voice of the Lord will be heard through the church of Jesus Christ. The Lord will always reveal Himself to those who are open to hear Him. Are you ready to speak for Him? There is nothing to fear! God has given His Spirit and gifts to build, edify, encourage, exhort, and comfort His people. It is the Lord's burden for His people to eagerly desire to be used and equipped in the ministry of prophesying so that He can manifest Himself to unbelievers and the hurting through them. We are His prophetic ambassadors in the earth today.

The apostle Paul admonishes Timothy in 2 Timothy 1:6 to "fan into flame the gift of God, which is in you." Don't neglect it; rather, fan it into flame. Stir up the gift and let it burn within you! Cause it to blaze forth in its glory again in all its potential for good in the body of Christ. Practice makes perfect, but prophesying by faith makes a perfect (mature) prophetic believer.

CONCLUSION

Without prophetic vision people run wild, but
blessed are those who follow God's teachings.
—PROVERBS 29:18, GW

W HEN PEOPLE DO not have prophetic vision, the Bible says
that they run wild, but those who are followers of God's
Word, teaching, and prophetic message are blessed. The
prophetic is so vital in this hour. God doesn't want His people running around like chickens with their head cut off but like prophetic
eagles with great vision and foresight. Prophecy releases heaven's
view and purpose for your life. We must see through heaven's lenses
and perspective for our destiny. I believe that Daddy God is going
to give His people twenty–twenty vision in the realm of the spirit
and give them the prophetic edge to fulfill what they were born to
accomplish.

I am reminded of a passage of Scripture about having a "twenty–
twenty prophetic vision."

They rose early in the morning and went out to the wilderness
of Tekoa; and when they went out, Jehoshaphat stood and said,
"Listen to me, O Judah and inhabitants of Jerusalem, put your trust
in the LORD your God and you will be established. Put your trust
in His prophets and succeed.

—2 CHRONICLES 20:20, NAS

We can see that when we are God-focused and our trust is in the
Lord we are established, and if we trust His prophets or the prophetic
ministry it births success, prosperity, and favor. The prophetic ministry is the only ministry biblically that we see success connected to.

True prophetic ministry is not for merchandising but bringing godly success, fame, favor, and happiness.

The emphasis here on prophecy and prophetic ministry is that it is important to God. Let's take a look at several versions and translations of Proverbs 29:18 to see the heartbeat of the Lord in regard to the ministry gift of prophecy:

> Where there is no prophecy the people cast off restraint, but blessed is he who keeps the law.
>
> —PROVERBS 29:18, RSV

> Where there is no revelation, people cast off restraint; but blessed is the one who heeds wisdom's instruction.
>
> —PROVERBS 29:18, NIV

> When people do not accept divine guidance, they run wild. But whoever obeys the law is joyful.
>
> —PROVERBS 29:18, NLT

> When prophecy shall fail, the people shall be scattered abroad: but he that keepeth the law is blessed.
>
> —PROVERBS 29:18, DOUAY-RHEIMS

> Without a Vision is a people made naked, And whoso is keeping the law, O his happiness!
>
> —PROVERBS 29:18, YOUNG'S

> Where there is no vision, the people perish: but he that keepeth the law, happy is he.
>
> —PROVERBS 29:18, KJV

> Where there is no vision, the people are unrestrained, But happy is he who keeps the law.
>
> —PROVERBS 29:18, NAS

We can see by the passages of Scriptures provided above that without prophecy, vision, divine guidance, revelation, or the prophetic message of the Lord, people will become unrestrained, undisciplined, aimless, unconcerned, lost, confused, made naked, scattered, and perish. Prophecy is God's vehicle of bringing discipline, hope, life, structure, order, purpose, alignment, destiny, focus, determination, faith, and divine revelation. You were born to communicate with your Father and also to share what's on the Father's heart to others. The prophetic equips and activates the believer to become an overcomer and overachiever in Him.

First Samuel 3:1 says, "The boy Samuel ministered before the LORD under Eli. In those days the word of the LORD was rare; there were not many visions." One of the darkest moments in the history of Israel had been when there was no open vision, prophetic revelation, or word of the Lord revealed; at such a time the people "perish," are let loose, "are left to run wild."

Moreover, it is the devil's intention for you to miss your divine moment. One of the translations of Proverbs 29:18 states that without a vision "is a people made naked" (YOUNG's). In other words, they will live life exposed, ashamed, and vulnerable to what life brings their way. I am reminded of Adam when he disobeyed the commands of the Lord in the Garden of Eden; Adam and Eve were made naked and exposed. Both covered themselves and hid from the Lord's voice and presence (Gen. 3:1–13).

Prophecy releases the heartbeat and intent of the Lord for our lives. Without the voice of the Lord in our lives we can feel as though we are living life without His very presence and protection. God's desire is to use you to become His voice in the earth to bring justice, order, peace, hope, restoration, reconciliation, and His divine plans. You were born to fulfill His purposes. You are God's idea, and it was a very good idea.

In my conclusion, it is my passion and desire to encourage you that you were born from above, and it may not seem like it in your reality, but know that your life has already been mapped out for you. You don't have to live life aimlessly but can live life strategically. Your life is hid in Christ Jesus. Everything that needed to be fulfilled was accomplished in Him. Others may put their trust in money, cars, houses, spouses, and natural things, but fulfilling first your calling is primary.

Without God's prophetic word over our lives we can be running around like wild donkeys with no vision and direction. Prophecy empowers and enables the believer to see again and run their race precisely. In the Book of Exodus 32:25 it says, "Moses saw that the people were running wild and that Aaron had let them get out of control and so become a laughingstock to their enemies." When Moses, who represented the voice of the Lord to the people of Israel, spent forty days on the mountain, the people began to worship a golden calf and became unrestrained, wild, immoral, and a laughingstock. Likewise, we need the voice of the Lord in this hour when so many are falling away.

> "The time is surely coming," says the Sovereign Lord, "when I will send a famine on the land—not a famine of bread or water but of hearing the words of the Lord. People will stagger from sea to sea and wander from border to border searching for the word of the Lord, but they will not find it.
>
> —Amos 8:11–12, nlt

Could you imagine not hearing a prophetic message or prophecy from the Lord? The prophetic voice of the Lord was imperative then, and it is necessary today. Can you imagine life without the voice of the Lord and not hearing Him speak? Hearing the voice of God is just as essential as bread and water. There are religious churches today that are experiencing a prophetic famine or prophetic drought because they resist embracing the prophetic culture with modern-day prophets and prophetic believers prophesying. The Bible states, "Man shall not live on bread alone, but on every word that comes from the mouth of God" (Matt. 4:4). We need God's anointed mouthpiece (prophets) and prophetic people speaking today.

In the above passage of Scripture, the Lord stated that there would come a time that people would not hunger for bread to eat or thirst after water, but they would hunger and thirst after hearing the word of the Lord. The prophetic word, message, and voice of the Lord is life-sustaining and vital. Just as important as bread and water for our natural well-being and survival, so is the spiritual nourishment and refreshment that the word of the Lord brings to a believer. We need to hear the voice and word of the Lord in every facet of our lives, whether it's in our marriage, family, business, ministry, church, job, or personal life.

The Lord said in Amos 8:11 that the famine would not be an ordinary famine that the people were accustomed to in regard to natural resources of food and drink but hearing His voice; if you feel like you are in a prophetic personal famine and not hearing the voice of God, just repent and re-establish your covenant relationship with the Lord, and He will speak to you.

Finally, as we re-establish our relationship with the Lord, we will begin to experience and encounter the prophetic ministry like never before. You must know that the Father created you and birth *you* to change the world you live in. You were born to be God's spokesman or spokeswoman in the earth. There were times in history when the people of Israel wanted more for the Lord to speak through Moses than for God speak Himself. In the Book of Exodus 20:1–17, Moses was the mediator between God and the people of Israel. God spoke the Ten Commandments, and the people were terrified. They wanted God to speak to Moses only, rather than hear God directly. As a mediator, Moses would thereafter tell them the words of God, and they would not have to hear God's voice. The Holy Spirit is the Mediator through Christ, and God the Father still speaks and desires to speak to His children today as He did in the days of Moses. Today you can be God's prophetic mediator used by the Holy Spirit to prophesy. You can prophesy and were *born* to communicate, speak, and declare God's master plan to others to fulfill their God-given purpose and destiny so that present and future generations can benefit.

Prayer

Father, I come to You in the name that you have given that is above every name, which is Jesus Christ. Father, I pray that You will anoint and activate all born-again, Spirit-filled believers to come into present-day truth of the ministry of the prophets, prophecy, and the supernatural. Father, I pray that every believer that is reading this book will arise as a strong prophetic family, an army of the Lord. I pray that revelation knowledge will be their portion and that the seven-fold Spirit of God, the Spirit of the Lord, wisdom, understanding, counsel, might, knowledge, and the reverential fear of the Lord will be manifest in the reader's life. Father, I pray and break the spirit of unbelief, doubt, fear, intimidation, pride, low self-esteem, low confidence, and rejection. Father, I break every diabolical assignment and demonic resistance against the prophetic work. In Jesus' name I decree and declare that this reader has been called like Jeremiah from their mother's womb and was born to fulfill Your eternal purpose and plan in their generation.

Father, I release this prophetic leader, servant, son and daughter of the kingdom to advance in the things of the Lord, and Father, I break every charismatic witchcraft prayer and prophecy that has been spoken and released over your child. Father, in Jesus' name I speak that they are the head and not the tail, first and not last, and more than an overcomer in Christ Jesus. Father, You have called this reader to greatness and to leave a great legacy in the earth. Father, I imparted everything that you have given me to impart in this book, and Father God I pray that the reader will receive a great inheritance like Elisha, who received a double portion of the measure that was upon Elijah, his prophetic leader and spiritual father.

I say in Jesus' name, prophet and prophetic leader, arise and do what you have been born to do as God's mouthpiece in the earth. Amen!

ABOUT THE AUTHOR

Hakeem Collins is on the frontlines of what God is doing in the twenty-first century as an emerging vanguard leader with a dual apostolic and prophetic calling that releases signs, wonders, and the miraculous. His passion is to father and lead the next generation to initiate unprecedented moves of the Spirit while accurately communicating God's original plan, intent, and purpose for humanity. He is a sought-after conference, church, and ministry speaker who has traveled extensively throughout the United States preaching the message of the kingdom while equipping the next generation of world changers to discover God's eternal purpose and maximize their full potential in Christ.

Hakeem is founder/CEO of Champions International Ministries, an itinerant ministry located in Wilmington, Delaware, where he resides. He is an affiliated apostolic leader of the IMPACT Network under Apostle John Eckhardt of Chicago, an active member of the International Coalition of Apostles (ICA) under John P. Kelly and C. Peter Wagner, and an ordained prophet of the Eagle Fire Network under Apostles Dale and LuAnne Mast of Destiny Christian Church of Dover, Delaware.

CONTACT THE AUTHOR

E-mail:

championsinternational@gmail.com

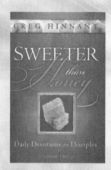